THE WORLD OF ELIA

Kennikat Press
National University Publications
Literary Criticism Series

General Editor
John E. Becker
Fairleigh Dickinson University

Fred V. Randel

THE WORLD OF ELIA

Charles Lamb's Essayistic Romanticism

National University Publications
KENNIKAT PRESS • 1975
Port Washington, N.Y. • London

Copyright © 1975 by Kennikat Press Corp. All rights reserved. No part of this publication may be reproduced, stored in a retrieval system, or transmitted, in any form or by any means, electronic, mechanical, photocopying, recording, or otherwise, without the prior written permission of the publisher.

Manufactured in the United States of America

Published by
Kennikat Press Corp.
Port Washington, N.Y./London

Library of Congress Cataloging in Publication Data

Randel, Fred V
    The world of Elia.

    (Kennikat Press national university publications)
(Literary criticism series)
    Includes bibliographical references and index.
    1. Lamb, Charles, 1775-1834. Essays of Elia.
2. English poetry—19th century—History and
criticism.   3. Romanticism—England. I. Title.
PR4861.R3   824'.7   75-31562
ISBN 0-8046-9118-5

CONTENTS

To my mother, Josephine, Amy, and Claire.

the modern critics
[refusing?] to recognize that
familiar essays, like
lyric poems + novels, can
[be works?] of art

PREFACE

Charles Lamb is probably the subtlest, liveliest, shrewdest, and most imaginative eighteenth- or nineteenth-century English writer to suffer nearly complete critical neglect for the past two generations. In late Victorian and
Edwardian England, when Pater and Swinburne wrote admiringly on Lamb
and A. C. Bradley called him "the best critic of the nineteenth century" and
prefaced a quotation by him on *King Lear* by saying "there is no higher
authority,"[1] Lamb's claim to be one of the principal English non-fictional
prose writers had strong support among leaders of critical opinion. But apart
from a few respectful allusions by Virginia Woolf, none of the major modern-
ists continued the applause, and by the centenary in 1934 of Lamb's death a
wide divergence between his traditional niche in literary history and his repu-
tation among advanced critics had become unmistakable.[2] In more recent
decades he has continued to figure in literary histories of the Romantic period,[3] but while critical interest in the Romantic poets has burgeoned, and
Hazlitt's thought, De Quincey's imaginative world, and Carlyle's art and ideas
have been scrutinized by recent commentators, little has been done to show
why Lamb is worth reading. He may once have suffered from the general
eclipse of Romanticism, but his contemporaries are out of that phase now,
while Lamb still is in the shadows.

Much that is irrelevant to the merit of what he wrote has contributed to
Lamb's fall from fashion: the modern critic's slowness to recognize that
familiar essays, like lyric poems and novels, can be works of art; the intellectual's exasperation with the triviality of Lamb's journalistic imitators; his
apologists' preoccupation with his personal charm or saintliness at the expense

[ix]

of the reasoned elucidation and evaluation of his best work; an age of anxiety's hankering for the dogmatic and authoritarian rather than the skeptical and self-deprecating; the modernist's tendency to slip from a principled disapproval of sentimentality to an uncritical rejection of sentiment; a certain post-modernist ennui in the face of whatever stops short of apocalypse; the political activist's impatience with apparent indifference to politics; the elitist's suspicion of writing that has delighted the unlearned; and perhaps even the snob's distaste or condescension for the lowly circumstances and subjects of an author whose father and maternal grandmother were servants, whose sister had been a dressmaker, and who himself spent over thirty years working as a clerk. Only one justification for reading and interpreting Lamb's essays is finally defensible: that they deserve such attention as works of art or thought. They eminently deserve it, and now that two hundred years have elapsed since Lamb's birth in 1775, the time is overdue for a full statement of the case for the greatness of his essays to be made in terms that are meaningful for the twentieth-century reader.[4] To meet this need is the purpose of the present book.

It is a pleasure to acknowledge my indebtedness to previous commentators on Lamb's life and works, particularly E. V. Lucas, Lamb's devoted editor and biographer. Among George L. Barnett's numerous contributions to Lamb scholarship is his article calling attention to the inaccuracies in Lucas's edition of the Lamb letters,[5] but until the new edition now being prepared by Edwin W. Marrs, Jr., appears, the Lucas edition remains the most complete version available to most readers. My policy in citing a Lamb letter has been to give in a footnote the appropriate reference to Lucas, followed by a reference to the manuscript if I have been able to check the original or a photocopy, as in most instances I have. In all such cases, wherever Lucas's text differs from the manuscript, I have adopted the latter both in quoting Lamb's letters and in verifying my own statements based upon them. I especially wish to thank Professor Marrs, who has graciously informed me of the locations of a number of Lamb letters and who has provided me with photocopies of some and transcriptions of several of them.

I am grateful to the following institutions and individuals for permission to quote manuscripts in their possession; abbreviations, as cited throughout the present book, are given in parentheses: the Henry E. Huntington Library (Hn.); the Henry W. and Albert A. Berg Collection of the New York Public Library, Astor, Lenox and Tilden Foundations (Br.); the Humanities Research Center, The University of Texas at Austin (Tx.); the Folger Shakespeare Library (F.); the Trustees of the British Museum (BM.); the Bodleian

Library, Oxford (Bd.); the Pierpont Morgan Library (M.); Dr. William's
Library, London (W.); the Lockwood Memorial Library, State University
of New York at Buffalo (L.); the Philip H. and A. S. W. Rosenbach Foundation, Philadelphia (R.); Mr. Raymond E. Hartz (Hartz) and Mr. W. Hugh
Peal (Peal). Grateful acknowledgment is also made to the editors of *ELH*
for permission to republish material that appeared in an article by me in
March 1970.[6]

I began to take Lamb's essays seriously in a graduate seminar conducted
at Yale University by A. Dwight Culler, who has been a generous source of
encouragement and criticism. For reading all or part of my manuscript and
offering useful suggestions, I am also indebted to Jeffrey Barnouw, Harold
Bloom, Cleanth Brooks, Michael Cooke, Robert Elliott, Edwin Fussell, Joan
Grenthot, Joseph Reed, and Andrew Wright. My students in English Romanticism and in the English Familiar Essay at the University of California, San
Diego, have helped me, by their questions, objections, and enthusiasms, to
see what to contract and what to expand. Research fellowships from the
National Endowment for the Humanities and the University of California
facilitated my work. I wish also to thank James Rolleston for assistance in
matters of German; Susie Munevar, Isabel Thurston, and my mother for
typing the various versions of this book; and my wife, Josephine McMahon
Randel, who counseled and listened.

NOTES

1. Walter Pater, *Appreciations* (1889; rpt. London: Macmillan, 1898).
pp. 107–126; Algernon Charles Swinburne, *Complete Works,* ed. Sir
Edmund Gosse and Thomas J. Wise (London: Heinemann, 1925–27),
XIV, 245–286; A. C. Bradley, *Oxford Lectures on Poetry* (1909; rpt.
Bloomington, Ind.: Indiana Univ. Press, 1961), p. 105, and *Shake-
spearean Tragedy* (1904; rpt. London: Macmillan, 1964), p. 253.
2. Amidst the spate of celebratory publications on Lamb in and about
1934, two essays that spoke for a critical vanguard were dismissive:
Graham Greene, "Lamb's Testimonials," *The Spectator,* 152 (March
30, 1934), 512–513; and Denys Thompson, "Our Debt to Lamb,"
Determinations (London: Chatto, 1934), pp. 199–217; F. R. Leavis
supplied an introduction for the latter volume. "I have formed a notion that he begins to be neglected," confessed one of Lamb's most
fervent twentieth-century admirers, Edmund Blunden, in *Charles Lamb*

and His Contemporaries (Cambridge, England: Cambridge Univ. Press, 1933), p. 3. But see Virginia Woolf, *The Common Reader,* 1st series (1925; rpt. New York: Harcourt, Brace & World, 1953), pp. 216-227.

3. See, for example, Samuel C. Chew and Richard D. Altick, "The Nineteenth Century and After," *A Literary History of England,* ed. Albert C. Baugh, 2nd ed. (New York: Appleton, 1967), pp. 1180-1184; Ernest Bernbaum, *Guide Through the Romantic Movement,* 2nd ed. (New York: Ronald, 1949), pp. 113-124; and Ian Jack, *English Literature 1815-1832* (Oxford: Clarendon Press, 1963), pp. 278-291.

4. Several illuminating analyses of narrower scope have appeared in recent years. The following studies will subsequently be cited simply by the last names of their authors: Richard Haven, "The Romantic Art of Charles Lamb," *ELH,* 30 (1963), 137-146; Daniel J. Mulcahy, "Charles Lamb: The Antithetical Manner and the Two Planes," *SEL,* 3 (1963), 517-542; Horst Weber, *Studien zur Form des Essays bei Charles Lamb* (Heidelberg: Carl Winter, Universitatsverlag, 1964); Donald H. Reiman, "Thematic Unity in Lamb's Familiar Essays," *JEGP,* 64 (1965), 470-478; John R. Nabholtz, "Drama and Rhetoric in Lamb's Essays of the Imagination," *SEL,* 12 (1972), 683-703; and James Scoggins, "Images of Eden in the Essays of Elia," *JEGP,* 71 (1972), 198-210. Geoffrey Tillotson, "The Historical Importance of Certain *Essays of Elia,*" *Some British Romantics,* ed. James V. Logan et. al. (Columbus, Ohio: Ohio State Univ. Press, 1966), pp. 89-116, is a suggestive analysis of Lamb's relation to Victorian writers, especially the novelists and Robert Browning. Stuart M. Tave's contribution to *The English Romantic Poets and Essayists: A Review of Research and Criticism,* ed. C. W. and L. H. Houtchens, rev. ed. (New York: New York Univ. Press, 1966), pp. 58-74, is a judicious account of the mass of criticism that had been done on Lamb up to 1964.

5. "A Critical Analysis of the Lucas Edition of Lamb's Letters," *MLQ,* 9 (1948), 303-314.

6 "Eating and Drinking in Lamb's Elia Essays," *ELH,* 37 (1970), 57-76, (c) The Johns Hopkins University Press.

THE WORLD OF ELIA

Chapter One

IMITATION, ORIGINALITY, AND IDENTITY

Lamb's essential artistic achievement was to merge some of the characteristic impulses and schemas of English Romantic poetry with some of the attitudes and techniques of the familiar essay tradition and to effect this combination in a way that asserted his individuality as a maker. At the same time that he resisted, but assimilated, the domineering thrust of the spirit of his age and the history of his genre, he also grappled with more private threats to his identity. He converted personal and familial pressures and fears into a form that speaks to us of inescapable defeats and equivocal triumphs with a distinctive, troubled, and often humorous voice. Because his artistic achievement was also an historical and psychological feat, we will need to invoke perspectives of literary history and psychology to recognize the influences and forces that he engaged. But to comprehend the order which he composed, we will need to use a criticism that attends at once to the structure of individual essays and to the structure of consciousness that is Lamb's own.

He had some knowledge of the works of every one of the major English Romantic poets. Blake, Shelley, and Byron receive comment in his letters, and he reviewed Keats's 1820 volume, but his connection with Coleridge and Wordsworth was longer and more profound. When his Elia essays began to appear in the *London Magazine* in 1820, he had known Coleridge for over thirty years—since both were schoolboys at Christ's Hospital—and Wordsworth for over twenty—at least since their summer excursion together from Nether Stowey in 1797, which Coleridge celebrated in "This Lime-Tree Bower My Prison." Coleridge introduced Lamb to literary society, published poetry jointly with him, wrote encouraging words when calamity threatened

[3]

to overwhelm him, and received from him abundant recompense in some remarkable letters of 1796 and 1797. In this correspondence Lamb pecked away at the turgidity of Coleridge's early verse and prodded him in the direction of Cowperesque simplicity and also of a "Sublime" that might encompass such subjects as "the Origin of Evil" or "the description (from a vision or dream, suppose) of an Utopia in one of the planets (the Moon for instance)."[1] Later, Wordsworth and Southey belittled *The Rime of the Ancient Mariner*, but Lamb anticipated the modern estimate of its worth. He dedicated one of the volumes of his *Works* (1818) to Coleridge, and in 1834 when the latter died, Lamb acknowledged his influence fulsomely: "I cannot think a thought, I cannot make a criticism on men or books, without an ineffectual turning and reference to him. He was the proof and touchstone of all my cogitations."[2]

His letters also record his interest in Wordsworth as a person and his selective admiration for him as a writer from May 1796 (his first reference to Wordsworth's poetry) to 1834, the last year of Lamb's life. He visited the Lake District, including Dove Cottage, and escorted Wordsworth to Bartholomew Fair before the poet dealt with that subject in Book VII of *The Prelude*. After the sinking of the *Earl of Abergavenny* in 1805, Lamb, making use of his position at the East India Company, gathered information about the circumstances of Captain John Wordsworth's death, and apparently misled Wordsworth to ease the poet's mind. At Wordsworth's request Lamb reviewed *The Excursion* for *The Quarterly Review*, but the resulting essay seemed "very imperfect" to Lamb and "spurious" by the time the editor finished tampering with it.[3] For Lamb as a writer the principal product of the long-lasting relationship with Wordsworth was an opportunity to know himself better and to express that knowledge, at first in letters that are among his best, and eventually, less overtly, in the Elia essays.

Writing in a period when, as W. Jackson Bate and Harold Bloom have recently emphasized,[4] poets carried the heavy psychological burden of wanting to be different from their great predecessors, Lamb bore witness in his own special circumstances to a prose writer's vulnerability, also, to the anxieties of influence and, increasingly, to his power to emulate, and yet differentiate himself from, those he admired. Lamb's immensely rewarding link with Coleridge and Wordsworth depended for its value partly on his perception that they were for him a threat. He admitted as much to Wordsworth in a letter in 1816:

Coleridge is absent but 4 miles, & the neighborhood of such a man is as

exciting as the presence of 50 ordinary Persons. Tis enough to be within the whiff & wind of his genius, for us not to possess our souls in quiet. If I lived with him or the *author of the Excursion,* I should in a very little time lose my own identity, & be dragged along in the current of other peoples thoughts, hampered in a net. How cool I sit in this office, with no possible interruption further than what I may term *material.* . . .
N. B. Nothing said above to the contrary but that I hold the personal presence of the two mentioned potent spirits at a rate as high as any, but I pay dearer, what amuses others robs me of my self, my mind is positively discharged into their greater currents, but flows with a willing violence.[5]

The passage strains to defend Lamb's individuality while staying friendly toward the two poets. At first a balance is struck between mere proximity (four miles), which is acceptable, and living together, which is not. But this compromise, seeming to hint that four miles are close enough, appears frigid a moment later, and an afterthought proposes an alternative solution: a willing surrender to dominance, accompanied by an insistence that such amiable self-bestowal amounts to getting robbed. The danger to the self is a rush of water in both cases: to be "dragged along in the current of other peoples thoughts" seems intolerable; yet, soon afterwards, "my mind is positively discharged into their greater currents, but flows with a willing violence." In either case the candid, tactful tone lends an air of achieved synthesis which the sense of the passage does not support. But there is considerable self-awareness in this confession: the recognition that what most imperils him is what he most admires and the nonplussed amiability of his address to one who puts him in jeopardy.

Part of the price that Lamb paid for this self-knowledge was his earlier quarrels with Coleridge and Wordsworth as he sought, not always diplomatically, to define his identity in contrast with theirs. In late 1796, for example, he mounted a theological and moral critique upon Coleridge's egoism. When the latter suggested that God has granted men "a portion as it were of His Omnipresence!" Lamb replied with an accusation of "blasphemy." In 1798 he sent Coleridge a list of sarcastic gibes set in the form of theological theses for disputation. A major thrust of his attack was that Coleridge, while claiming powers more than human, had failed to measure up to "merely human virtue."[6] Lamb soon dropped his reliance on theological criticism, and he learned to employ an irony no longer crude and vituperative, but skepticism toward grandiose or superhuman claims stayed with him into the period of his major essays.

In January 1801 Lamb wrote Wordsworth an exceptionally perceptive and energetic letter, which contained a defense of *The Rime of the Ancient Mariner* and some reservations about the second edition of *Lyrical Ballads*. Wordsworth responded "almost instantaneously" with "a long letter of four sweating pages," as Lamb recounted the episode in an amusing letter to Thomas Manning on February 15. The poet lamented that Lamb's "range of Sensibility" was not "more extended," and claimed for his own poems a "Union of Tenderness & Imagination, which in the sense he used Imag. was not the characteristic of Shakesp. but which Milton possessed in a degree far exceeding other Poets"; and that such a union was nothing less than "the highest species of Poetry." Lamb found it possible to value Wordsworth's poems, while observing the ludicrousness of having "a fellow start up, and prate about some unknown quality, which Shakspere possess'd in a degree inferior to Milton and somebody else! !" Coleridge also made himself a target for Lamb's humor on the same occasion by getting up "from his bed of sickness, to reprove me for my hardy presumption" in a letter of "four long pages, equally sweaty, and more tedious." "What am I to do with such people?" Lamb wondered. He decided immediately: "I certainly shall write them a very merry Letter."[7] The author of Elia shows himself to be as allergic to the presumptuousness of the poets here as he was in his earlier remonstrances to Coleridge. But religious and moral exhortation has been supplanted now by an irony which mocks their pretensions even while it remains open to their worth.

The second component of Lamb's distinctive manner to emerge from his disagreement with Wordsworth was the choice of an urban, specifically London, subject matter, in contrast to Wordsworth's preference for mountains and rustics. "Low and rustic life was generally chosen," wrote Wordsworth in the sometimes clogged prose of the 1800 "Preface" to *Lyrical Ballads* that Lamb had just read,

because in that situation the essential passions of the heart find a better soil in which they can attain their maturity, are less under restraint, and speak a plainer and more emphatic language; because in that situation our elementary feelings exist in a state of greater simplicity and consequently may be more accurately contemplated and more forcibly communicated; because the manners of rural life germinate from those elementary feelings; and from the necessary character of rural occupations are more easily comprehended; and are more durable; and lastly, because in that situation the passions of men are incorporated with the beautiful and permanent forms of nature.[8]

One superb passage from Lamb's letter to Wordsworth which provoked the poet's sweating and haughty reply was an eloquent demonstration that urban feelings too can be accurately contemplated and forcibly communicated:

Separate from the pleasure of your company, I dont much care if I never see a mountain in my life.—I have passed all my days in London, until I have formed as many and intense local attachments, as any of you Mountaineers can have done with dead nature. The Lighted shops of the Strand and Fleet Street, the innumerable trades, tradesmen and customers, coaches, waggons, playhouses, all the bustle and wickedness round about Covent Garden, the very women of the Town, the Watchmen, drunken scenes, rattles;—life awake, if you awake, at all hours of the night, the impossibility of being dull in Fleet Street, the crowds, the very dirt & mud, the Sun shining upon houses and pavements, the print shops, the old Book stalls, parsons cheap'ning books, coffee houses, steams of soups from kitchens, the pantomimes, London itself a pantomime and a masquerade, all these things work themselves into my mind and feed me without a power of satiating me. The wonder of these sights impells me into night-walks about her crowded streets, and I often shed tears in the motley Strand from fullness of joy.at so much Life.—All these emotions must be strange to you. So are your rural emotions to me.—But consider, what must I have been doing all my life, not to have lent great portions of my heart with usury to such scenes?—[9]

Wordsworth interpreted his preference for the countryside as owing to the superior worth of rural settings, but Lamb reinterpreted it as owing to nothing more than habituation. Since Lamb himself was accustomed to London, its scenes could be as meaningful to him as Cumberland's or Westmoreland's were to Wordsworth. Insofar as he claimed equal worth for urban experience, he was attacking the hierarchy of values stated in Wordsworth's "Preface." But insofar as Lamb's comments allowed for the validity of Wordsworth's celebration of his native region and seconded the poet's leveling muse by glorifying "low" life even to "the very dirt & mud," he was merely building upon and extending the example of Wordsworth. There is a kind of influence observable in this relationship, but it works by combat and produces valuable echoes only when the recipient of the influence insists on recognizing and guarding his distinctiveness.

When we turn from the vivifying personal jousts of the early letters to the subtle artistry of the Elia essays, we can still see an ironical deprecation of pretentiousness and a zest for autobiographical, mainly urban, experience; yet these continuities by themselves tell us little about the complexity of form and meaning that distinguishes the Elia essays. The more illuminating relevance to Elia of the encounters with the poets is that Lamb's principal essays convert a relationship between personalities into a relationship between structures. Moreover, structures visible in the poetry of Coleridge and Wordsworth are often present in other Romantic poets as well. So, as the essays begin to implicate such patterns, their critique is no longer limited to two poets; rather, it extends to a period style, or at least to some of the features that recur in English Romanticism. Yet the indebtedness to Coleridge, which Lamb often declared, the strand of agreement with and extension of Wordsworth's example in the exchange of 1801, and the passage embracing domination by the two poets in the letter of 1816 also find an analogue in the structure of the Elia essays. Lamb employs some common Romantic patterns partly to subvert them but partly too to show his commitment to them. They exist for him as more than allusions or notions to be discarded; they are so central to his best essays that we are right to say he is in them, in some degree, as well as they in him. We will need to look hard at the concreteness of his essays to see both his criticism and his creative use of Romantic patterns and to see also the unity that he built in the midst of such ambivalence.

Some presuppositions about Romanticism are unavoidable for this undertaking, though the stereotypes of literary history could ruin it. The single most wide-ranging and judicious compendium of English Romantic principles of organization is M. H. Abrams's *Natural Supernaturalism,* which enlists capacious knowledge of Romantic writers, as well as their commentators, antecedents, and successors. Abrams stresses the Romantic positives—"life, love, liberty, hope, and joy"—and demonstrates the presence in the major Romantics of patterns that affirm these values. One such pattern observed by Abrams is the three-stage developmental series, leading in a progressive spiral from a naive unity through a painful experience of division to an arduously won and alertly apprehended higher unity. In this pattern dejection and suffering are understood as a stage through which man passes from the Eden he has lost to the fulfillment within his reach. That such patterns are present in English Romantic poetry is less problematic than whether the patterns are equivalent to the meaning of the poems. On the latter issue Abrams's book is less satisfactory. *Natural Supernaturalism* is, among other things, a massive commentary on Wordsworth's "Prospectus" to *The Recluse,* showing the similarities of that eloquent manifesto to other writings of the period.[10] But because Romantic works vary in the degree of credence with which they use such patterns, a study of Romanticism centering on Wordsworth's Lucy poems or Keats's odes would stress a more skeptical, less confident attitude than Abrams mainly emphasizes. Within Romanticism itself the Romantic schemas are sometimes exuberantly endorsed, sometimes painfully doubted; they are sometimes the objects of attainment, sometimes only of aspiration, sometimes of regretful loss. A study which catalogued all the observable stances toward the schemas during the Romantic period would be more complicated and heterogeneous than Abrams's admirable book, which is more interested in the schemas themselves. For our purposes, *Natural Supernaturalism,* like some of Georges Poulet's criticism, will be useful as a description of a variety of patterns that Romantic poets exploit. Because the poets sometimes creatively subvert these configurations (as Lamb in his Elia essays nearly always does), there is less distance between his essays and their poetry than between his essays and the schemas which he and they employ.

Nevertheless, the recognition of differentiation from the poets is not merely a biographical episode and a stage in the genesis of Elia. A contrast between "the lean and meagre figure of your insignificant Essayist,"[11] as Elia once calls himself, and more pretentious and conceivably profound personages, who express their visions in verse, is usually latent and occasionally manifest in the Elia essays. This contrast suggests why, in a period and circle of acquaintances dominated by poets, Lamb chose to write familiar essays. The conclusion of "Witches, and Other Night-Fears" points to a contrast between the urban subjects of Elia's dreams and two categories of dream subject matter that are unavailable to him—mountains, specifically Wordsworth's beloved "Westmoreland fells," which Elia mentions having visited; and a more exotic type of sublimity: "There is Coleridge, at his will can conjure up icy domes, and pleasure-houses for Kubla Khan, and Abyssinian maids, and songs of Abara, and caverns,

Where Alph, the sacred river, runs,

to solace his night solitudes—when I cannot muster a fiddle" (p. 69).

The self-disparagement of these contrasts with Wordsworth and Coleridge is qualified by the enumerative energy of Elia's description of the cities of his own dreams and by the progressive aspect, apparent from the essay as a whole, of his developing beyond the terrifying nightmares of childhood. The passage that best expresses the imaginative vitality, as well as the ludicrousness, of Elia's adult dreams treats a realm that Coleridge in *The Rime of the Ancient Mariner* and several conversation poems and Wordsworth in the "Intimations Ode" and *The Prelude* had associated with the profoundest human experience—the sea:

Methought I was upon the ocean billows at some sea nuptials, riding and mounted high, with the customary train sounding their conchs before me, (I myself, you may be sure, the *leading god,*) and jollily we went careering over the main, till just where Ino Leucothea should have greeted me (I think it was Ino) with a white embrace, the billows gradually subsiding, fell from a sea-roughness to a sea-calm, and thence to a river-motion, and that river (as happens in the familiarization of dreams) was no other than the gentle Thames, which landed me, in the wafture of a placid wave or two, alone, safe and inglorious, somewhere at the foot of Lambeth palace. (p. 69)

The journey seaward, the culminating marriage, the apotheosis of the self— all this Romantic paraphernalia is set in a context of self-deprecation and amused contemplation, and the irony spares neither Elia nor the ambitious tropes that he alludes to and incorporates. The urbanized banks of the Thames must be a somewhat pleasing destination after all: so much assurance (beneath the modesty) and so much merriment could not consist with a conviction that one has been excluded from all that is most valuable. The mixture of attitudes in this remarkable sentence works subtly and implicitly to defend the validity of the perspective which Elia is contrasting with that of the Romantic poets. The issue of genre becomes explicit in the succeeding passage, the essay's conclusion:

The degree of the soul's creativeness in sleep might furnish no whimsical criterion of the quantum of poetical faculty resident in the same soul waking. An old gentleman, a friend of mine, and a humorist, used to carry this notion so far, that when he saw any stripling of his acquaintance ambitious of becoming a poet, his first question would be,—"Young man, what sort of dreams have you?" I have so much faith in my old friend's theory, that when I feel that idle vein returning upon me, I presently subside into my proper element of prose, remembering those eluding nereids, and that inauspicious inland landing. (pp. 69–70)

Prose seems the mark of one who lacks what it takes to be a poet, but in the context of the preceding sentences, such failure is a kind of strength. Prose emerges as the suitable medium of a skeptical fellow-traveler toward any Romantic faith.

The familiar essay genre had long nourished attitudes that have much in common with those which the Elia essays identify as prosaic or essayistic. In the tradition that began with Montaigne the essay's principal declared allegiance is to the experience of the essayistic voice (who need not wholly coincide with the real author, as the *Spectator* papers of Goldsmith's *Citizen of the World* make evident) rather than to any theory or plot. This "experience" which fascinates may be personal or social. It may be found by looking largely inward, as in Montaigne, or mainly outward, as in Bacon. It may

[10]

inhere in the concreteness of anecdote or, as in Johnson, in the weightiness of disillusioned but responsible generalization. But in any case it is avowedly anti-schematic, even if a coherent world-view implicitly emerges and even if the essayistic voice tries his hand at theorizing from time to time. Often the familiar essay alludes ironically to stoic or scholastic philosophers or pedants, who, the essayist confides, sought system at the expense of openness to homely, grubby, squirming events. Its brevity suits its refusal to bind itself, as systematic philosophy or literary genres that stress plot or character development must do, to an architecture that appears separable from the speaker's experience. On the other hand, the familiar essay, whether or not it moralizes, posits a minimal distance between speaker and common reader. By its tone of candor, its overt recognition of the reader's presence, its avoidance of specialization in subject, its shunning of heroic, mystical, superhuman, exceptionally virtuous, or other grandiose claims, and even by its dependence upon prose, often of an informal type, the essayistic voice stresses its affinities with the lives of its generality of readers. Northrop Frye has classified the familiar essay as the "short form" of the confession,[12] but much autobiographical writing, unlike the familiar essay, emphasizes access to extraordinary experience, conversions, moments of transcendence, success in acquiring exceptional wealth or power. On the other hand, familiar essays like the *Spectator* papers stay away from confessionalism. The autobiographical familiar essay is not just short autobiography, because it has a distinctive scope which can be described in terms that also apply to familiar essays that are not autobiographical, and it is the inclusive genre—the medium of Montaigne and Addison and Steele and Johnson—that Lamb appropriated for the Elia essays.

That he expected these essays to be read in relation to the capabilities of their genre is evidenced by his own critical procedure in reviewing the first volume of William Hazlitt's *Table-Talk* during the period of the Elia essays. Lamb's central concern in this still unpublished manuscript was Hazlitt neither "as a controversial writer" nor "even as a critic," but "as an Essayist."[13] The review therefore compares Hazlitt with earlier essayists. The "fathers of Essay writing," according to Lamb, were "Plutarch in a measure, and Montaigne without mercy or measure." But Lamb's most detailed remarks concern Steele, Addison, and Samuel Johnson among authors earlier than Hazlitt himself. (Goldsmith is the only other essayist mentioned.) Lamb emphasizes the value of imparting a "pervading character" to an essay series in order to "give a unity" or "identity" to it. Some essayists, he notes, achieve this end by lending "their own personal peculiarities to their themes," and the "Author of the Rambler" is unexpectedly placed together with Montaigne and Hazlitt in this category. Johnson "deals out opinion, which he would have you take for argument; and is perpetually obtruding his own particular views of life for universal truths." Even *The Rambler*'s "ponderous levities . . . and unwieldy efforts at being sprightly . . . may detract less from the general effect, than if something better in kind, but less in keeping, had been substituted in place of them." According to Lamb a second division of essayists, with Steele's creation of Isaac Bickerstaff for *The Tatler* as the most notable instance, invented a persona or *"ideal character;* which left them a still fuller licence in the delivery of their peculiar humours and opinions, under the masqued battery of a fictitious appellation." (Nestor Ironside in *The Guardian* showed "a few feeble sparks" of the same procedure.) In contrast with this type and responsible for extinguishing it is the Addisonian essay series, "little more than bundles of Essays (valuable indeed, and elegant reading above our praise) but hanging together with very slender principles of bond or union." However impressive *The Spectator*'s reasonings, suggests Lamb, they cannot suffice to provide an adequate unity because they are not presented as the characteristic utterances of a distinctive personality: "In fact we use the word Spectator, and mean a Book. At mention of the Tatler we sigh, and think of Isaac Bickerstaff." Lamb's complaint is a variant of the essayist's generic opposition to bookishness which has become divorced from experience. If he is unfair to *The Spectator,* the reason is that his Romantic commitment to self-revelation disables him from recognizing that experience can be rendered by a Bacon and an Addison at their best without depending upon the expression of the writer's personality.

Lamb's innovations in the familiar essay are usually discussed in terms of an infusion of personality, an extension of subject matter, and a decrease in formality of style and organization—in short, as an enterprise parallel to that of Wordsworth, Coleridge, and others in verse.[14] Such an analysis points to real differences between the Elia essays and the *Spectator* variety, but it confuses Lamb's position in literary history in four respects: (1) by minimizing the similarities between Addison or Johnson and Lamb, it loses contact with the continuity of the essay tradition; (2) it fails to distinguish Lamb from Montaigne, whose late essays were also personal, varied, and *apparently* meandering; (3) it overlooks the structural coherence—at least as rigorous, in many cases, as anything achieved by Addison or Johnson—of the best Elia essays; and (4) it oversimplifies the problematic relation between the Elia essays and Romantic poetry, especially that of Wordsworth and Coleridge. I suggest that Lamb's essays differ from their predecessors—within the shared framework of the genre already described—by presenting themselves as an experience-drenched alternative, no longer primarily to stoic or scholastic philosophers, pedants, irresponsible wits, or even dull sermonizers, but to contemporary (we would say *Romantic*) poets. But the Elia essays do not simply negate the contrary mode of discourse that they ironically implicate. (Neither did earlier familiar essayists simply negate their contraries.) Lamb's essays are indeed parallel to much Romantic verse: in their emphasis upon the speaker's personal experiences, often presented in process and sometimes located at particular times and places; and less expectedly, in their inclusion of an impulse toward transcending limitations of time, space, and finitude itself. For these skeptical, ironical essays not only share characteristics of the poetry of experience, which Robert Langbaum has persuasively identified,[15] but also engage in a sympathetic experimentation with Romantic Prometheanism, an aspiration toward an infinitude which is of this world, not some other.

If "Witches, and Other Night-Fears" marks the distance between Elia and the Romantic poets, "The Two Races of Men" exhibits his differentiation from his predecessors among the essayists. The opening sentences, celebrating monetary indebtedness and improvidence, overturn the counsels of prudence which had traditionally received an English essayist's allegiance. Lamb chooses as the object of more specific reversals an essayist whose preachments and life sometimes conflicted. Sir Richard Steele, named in Lamb's second paragraph as one of "the greatest borrowers of all ages," had written this in *The Tatler* (No. 180): "The greatest of all distinctions in civil life is that of debtor and creditor, and there needs no great progress in logic to know which, in that case, is the advantageous side."[16] Steele wished to commend frugality to the middle classes and to ridicule those elegant gentlemen who bring tradesmen into financial difficulties by running up bills which they cannot meet. So he argued that the debtor, whatever his social station, places himself beneath his creditor, whatever his station. Lamb begins his essay with a similar distinction but an opposite valuation:

The human species, according to the best theory I can form of it, is composed of two distinct races, *the men who borrow,* and *the men who lend.* . . . The infinite superiority of the former, which I choose to designate as the *great race,* is discernible in their figure, port, and a certain instinctive sovereignty. The latter are born degraded. (p. 22)

Yet Elia's panegyric on the habitual borrower takes note of its own excess, for instance in the parenthesis within this exclamation: "What contempt for

[13]

money,—accounting it (yours and mine especially) no better than dross!" (p. 23). The reader who observes such an irony may conclude that we are not far from *The Tatler* after all, and in fact one other passage by Steele from that essay series bears a striking resemblance to the opening paragraphs in the Elia essay:

In every party there are two sorts of men, the rigid and the supple. The rigid are an intractable race of mortals, who act upon principle, and will not, forsooth, fall into any measures that are not consistent with their received notions of honour. These are persons of a stubborn, unpliant morality, that sullenly adhere to their friends when they are disgraced, and to their princi- ples, though they are exploded. I shall therefore give up this stiff-necked generation to their own obstinacy, and turn my thoughts to the advantage of the supple, who pay their homage to places, and not persons. . . . (No. 214)

But Steele's irony consists in his declaring a value judgment opposite to what he means, damning by fulsome praise, while Elia means what he says and the opposite too. His irony issues in nothing so simple as a separation of sheep from goats. Lamb's Ralph Bigod, for instance, is the subject of a mock hero- ic character sketch ("In his periegesis, or triumphant progress throughout this island, it has been calculated that he laid a tythe part of the inhabitants under contribution") (p. 24), which never quite becomes satirical because traits suggestive of moral irresponsibility are inseparable in Bigod from traits like "his fiery glow of heart" and "his swell of feeling" (p. 25). Opposite evaluations of his vivid presence remain poised in conflict, without simplify- ing to a moral decision, and the result is more than incoherence or meaning- lessness because Lamb's underlying theme is not really whether it is better to take or make a loan. Stuck in unobtrusively among the Elian exclamations about borrowers is a sentence that not only partakes of mock heroic praise but also points to this essay's central concern:

What a liberal confounding of those pedantic distinctions of *meum* and *tuum!* or rather, what a noble simplification of language (beyond Tooke), resolving these supposed opposites into one clear, intelligible pronoun ad- jective! (p. 23)

While Steele's essays, like those of his eighteenth-century successors, assume or defend moral and intellectual dichotomies, Elia is fascinated by blendings or reconciliations of opposites. Hence Steele kept the improvidence of his life out of his essays, while Elia can assimilate Steele's very contradictoriness within *his* essay. The climactic embodiment of such a procedure in "The

Two Races of Men" is Comberbatch, or S. T. C., the alias and initials of the principal English Romantic theoretician of the reconciliation of opposites, Coleridge himself. Although he is at first introduced as one of the *"borrowers of books,"* the essay quickly casts doubt on whether he is a borrower at all. He has a theory, which Elia cannot refute, that "the title to property in a book (my Bonaventure, for instance), is in exact ratio to the claimant's powers of understanding and appreciating the same" (p. 25). Unable any longer to remember who owns some of the books which he possesses, Coleridge leaves them in Elia's library, and he enriches his borrowings "with annotations, tripling their value" (p. 26). Bigod could not be placed within the polar categories of good and bad, while Coleridge escapes in the end from the simple alternatives of borrower and lender. When he is said to be "matchless in his depredations!" (p. 25), moral censure is absent because his depredations are too matchless to be depredations in the ordinary sense. The language of moral classification and judgment appears too clumsy to touch Bigod's or Coleridge's living particularity, so that in retrospect even the division asserted in the essay's opening sentence gets discredited. "The Two Races of Men" ends by appealing for blendings in place of barriers: "I counsel thee, shut not thy heart, nor thy library, against S. T. C." (p. 27).

The central interpretative task for understanding the Elia essays is, from the point of view of content, to describe the precise mixture of aspirations, typically Romantic, and reservations, typically essayistic, that Elia expresses. But if these pieces add up to only a hodge-podge of diversities, their claim to artistic distinction is dashed. The case for the fineness of the Elia essays, as well as for Lamb's triumphant assertion of personal identity, rests on the essays' achievement of forms that cohere in the midst of intellectual and emotional ambivalence. Walter Pater said of Lamb, "In the making of prose he realises the principle of art for its own sake, as completely as Keats in the making of verse."[17] Pater's remark, like Swinburne's panegyric, was unfortunate insofar as it made Lamb seem the special preserve of initiates in the mysteries of art, and thus helped drive between Lamb and the general reader a wedge that was incompatible with the affinity required by the familiar essay genre. (It is ironic that the prophet of Victorian aestheticism embraced a writer whose fascination with London characters and places is likely to remind us of Dickens.) But Pater was right to the extent that, while such writers as Montaigne and Bacon can be valued for their ideas even when their artistry is neglected, Lamb's artistry and his intellectual stature are inseparable. His verbal and structural whimsicalities or subtleties are in the Elia essays usually nothing less than expressive forms, and they become intelligible as forms only by reference to what they express. Therefore the present study will try to seek out the meeting-places between the artistic structure of the Elia essays and their world-view.

The artist's necessary "dominion" over his materials, involving "active" imagination and hence "shaping and consistency," was Lamb's subject in an essay, "The Sanity of True Genius," that points to pressures more menacing than those of literary influence: "So far from the position holding true, that great wit (or genius, in our modern way of speaking), has a necessary alliance with insanity, the greatest wits, on the contrary, will ever be found to be the sanest writers" (p. 187). Lamb quickly makes clear that he is not proposing that literature stick to sensible characters inhabiting a commonplace world. What especially fascinates him is the literary portrayal of insanity or of creatures and environments unavailable to the five senses: the "mad" King Lear, Timon—for "to hate mankind," says Lamb, is "a sort of madness"—, Caliban, the Witches in *Macbeth*, "the fairy grounds of Spenser" (pp. 187-188). The essay argues that the great wit can incorporate such subjects, while subordinating them to the artist's "dominion" and to "the law of . . . [Nature's] consistency." Not so much the sanity which ignores hallucination, but the sanity which knows it and subdues it receives Lamb's homage.

Although this essay was published as one of the largely autobiographical Elia essays, it makes no explicit reference to Lamb's or Elia's personal history. But Lamb was no detached commentator on insanity. His earliest extant letter informs Coleridge of his confinement "in a mad house at Hoxton" for six weeks in the winter of 1795-1796. On September 22, 1796, Lamb's sister Mary, as he wrote Coleridge, "in a fit of insanity has been the death of her own mother. I was at hand only time enough to snatch the knife out of her grasp. She is at present in a mad house . . . ." A coroner's inquest considered the case the next day, and as the *Morning Chronicle* reported on September 26, "brought in their Verdict, *Lunacy*." "I must be serious, circumspect, & deeply religious thro' life; by such means may *both* of us escape madness in future, if it so please the Almighty," declared Lamb a week later. Mary and Charles Lamb lived together for the rest of his life, except for her periodic returns to mental institutions. When in 1819 he proposed marriage to the actress Fanny Kelly, she declined on the grounds that she loved someone else, but ten days later, she let her sister know the real motive: "I was indeed sorry to refuse him, for he shows the most tender and loyal affections. But even at the peril of my decision causing him great despondency, which I rather feared, I could have no other course than to say the truth that I could not accept his offer. I could not give my assent to a proposal which would bring me into that atmosphere of sad mental uncertainty which surrounds his domestic life." Just after his retirement from the East India Company in 1825, Lamb's letters refer to a "nervous attack" or "nervous Fever" which then afflicted him.[18] His essay "The Convalescent" arose out of this ailment, and "The Superannuated Man" speaks of a nervous condition that preceded, and helped to cause, his retirement. These biographical circumstances raise the likelihood of a continuing struggle against psychic fragility in Lamb's life, and they are grounds for wondering whether such a stance is observable in his art. The present study will argue that some recurrent motifs in Lamb's writings are intelligible in just such a context, but that in the Elia essays he brought his neurotic preoccupations under his dominion as an artist. Even while, in his best writings, he betrays psychic vulnerability, he exemplifies what he praised, the sanity of true genius.

The pressures of literary influence and those of private life prompted in Lamb's Elia essays the same response: a reliance upon artistic "shaping and consistency" less as an escape than as an assimilator. But Romantic poets and madness had an even closer link for Lamb, as he already intimated a few months after his own confinement but before his sister's fateful derangement: "Dream not Coleridge, of having tasted all the grandeur & wildness of Fancy, till you have gone mad." In January 1798 he bore witness to a similar, though now more frightening, connection between poets and madness in responding to Coleridge's invitation to his sister and himself: " . . . your invitation went to my very heart—but you have a power of exciting interest, of leading all hearts captive, too forcible to admit of Mary's being with you—I consider her as perpetually on the brink of madness—I think, you would almost make her dance within an inch of the precipice—she must be with duller fancies, & cooler intellects. . . . I know a young man of this description, who has suited her these twenty years, & may live to do so still—if we are one day restor'd to each other." Acting from a sense of "duty" after his mother's death, Lamb burned one of Coleridge's poems, as he admitted to Coleridge in a letter of December 10, 1796. He burned much besides—his own verses, his journal, his "book of extracts from Beaumont and Fletcher and a thousand sources." And he got rid of Coleridge's letters, at first planning to burn them too, then deciding to lend them out to a friend, and later discovering that they could no longer be retrieved. In short, at the traumatic time of the family catastrophe Lamb associated versifying, belles lettres, Coleridge, and lunacy. By the time he writes this remarkable letter, however, he wishes to distance himself from such philistinism—partly by suggesting that his judgment earlier was not reliable, and partly by distinguishing even his past perspective from that of his brother John. He spirited away Coleridge's letters, he claims, to keep them from arousing John's fury against their author. But this attempt at opposing Lamb's present viewpoint to any distrust for imagination is unconvincing: his "highly agitated . . . state of mind" a few months before was only *"perhaps* distorted"; his dutiful motive for burning vestiges of imagination was more likely to preserve his sanity and practicality and therefore his ability to care for Mary than to prevent John from seeing them; and the summary of John's attitude toward Coleridge elides the connectives that would clearly indicate indirect discourse, leaving us with a passage that announces an accusation that the John in Charles Lamb evidently believes: "it has been his fashion ever since to depreciate and cry you down,—you were the cause of my madness—you and your damned foolish sensibility and melancholy." In Lamb's first surviving letter (May 27, 1796) he masks a similar accusation—perhaps even from himself—in a genial expression of friendship: "Coleridge it may convince you of my regards for you when I tell you my head ran on you in my Madness as much almost as on another Person, who I am inclined to think was the more immediate cause of my temporary frenzy."[19] The prosaic dreams described near the end of "Witches, and Other Night-Fears" save him from mental instability, as well as from the poetical heights or depths available to Wordsworth and Coleridge.

The psychological difficulties of Charles Lamb have sometimes been related to his writings by the theory that he increasingly screened out the distressing until in the Elia essays he had excluded whatever disturbed him.[20] I suggest by contrast that the Elia essays raise the most disturbing encounters in Lamb's life to a level of universality and verbal power that he never equaled earlier or later. Like the Tennyson of *In Memoriam,* he converted a painful and idiosyncratic personal situation into a cultural paradigm. The resulting confluence of psychic energy and meaningful form made him a worthy interlocutor of the other major familiar essayists and of the Romantic poets.

The following chapters examine a series of patterns that, first of all, are central to the imaginative world—the identity—of the Elia essays and that, secondly, display points of contact with Romantic poetry, the familiar essay tradition, and in some cases Lamb's psychic burdens. Lamb's muse is a daughter of memory but is not the less imaginative for that fact; hence, two chapters on time stress the various ways in which memory functions imaginatively in the Elia essays. The fourth chapter ponders the Elian experience of space. The spatial metaphor of narrowness has been applied to Lamb,[21] but no one has observed that his essays themselves manipulate a spatial model in which constriction is balanced against complementary tendencies. The fifth and sixth chapters confront the suspicion that Lamb's essays are trivial by analyzing two exceptionally prominent but apparently inconsequential leitmotifs: eating or drinking and playing. The book as a whole argues that a consistent perspective of impressive intelligence underlies the Elian treatments of time, space, ingestion, and play; that this perspective is the intellectual order that Lamb composed out of the literary and biographical situation sketched in the present chapter; and that if the Elia essays are read in relation to this perspective, their formal complexity and coherence become evident, and we may be readier to open ourselves to their spell.

NOTES

1. *The Letters of Charles Lamb,* ed. E. V. Lucas (New Haven: Yale Univ. Press, 1935), I, 94–95 (MS. Hn.); George Whalley, "Coleridge's Debt to Charles Lamb," *Essays and Studies,* NS 11 (1958), 68–85.
2. *The Works of Charles and Mary Lamb,* ed. E. V. Lucas (London: Methuen, 1903), V, 1–2; I, 351.
3. *Letters* I, 315 (MS. Hn.) and II, 148 (MS. Tx.); Mary Moorman, *William Wordsworth: A Biography,* I and II (1957 and 1965; rpt. London: Oxford Univ. Press, 1968); E. L. McAdam, Jr., "Wordsworth's Shipwreck," *PMLA,* 77 (1962), 240–247.
4. Bate, *The Burden of the Past and the English Poet* (Cambridge, Mass.: Harvard Univ. Press, 1970); Bloom, "Coleridge: The Anxiety of Influence," *Diacritics,* 2 (1972), 36–41, and *The Anxiety of Influence* (New York: Oxford Univ. Press, 1973).
5. *Letters,* II, 191 (MS. Tx.).
6. I, 48–49; 126–127 (MS. M.).
7. I, 245–247 (MS. F.).
8. *Literary Criticism of William Wordsworth,* ed. Paul M. Zall (Lincoln, Neb.: Univ. of Nebraska Press, 1966), p. 18.
9. *Letters,* I, 241 (MS. Tx.).
10. (New York: Norton, 1971), p. 431 and passim.
11. *Works,* II, 187. All references to the Elia essays will be to this edition, and page citations will be included in the text.
12. *Anatomy of Criticism* (1957; rpt. New York: Atheneum, 1966), p. 307.
13. My quotations in this paragraph are from pp. 1, 2, and 20 of the MS., which is now at the Berg Collection. The volume under review was published in 1821.
14. William Frank Bryan and R. S. Crane, *The English Familiar Essay* (Boston: Ginn, 1916), pp. xli–xlix; Marie Hamilton Law, *The English Familiar Essay in the Early Nineteenth Century* (1934; rpt. New York: Russell & Russell, 1965); Melvin R. Watson, "The *Spectator* Tradition

and the Development of the Familiar Essay," *ELH*, 13 (1946), 189–215, and *Magazine Serials and the Essay Tradition 1746-1820* (Baton Rouge: Louisiana State Univ. Press, 1956); George L. Barnett, *Charles Lamb: The Evolution of Elia* (Bloomington: Indiana Univ. Press, 1964), pp. 9-47.

15. *The Poetry of Experience* (1957; rpt. New York: Norton, 1963). On some relationships between genres and countergenres see Claudio Guillén, *Literature as System* (Princeton: Princeton University Press, 1971).

16. For *The Tatler* I have used the edition by G. A. Aitken, 4 vols. (London: Duckworth, 1898-99) and profited from Richmond P. Bond, *The Tatler; The Making of a Literary Journal* (Cambridge: Harvard Univ. Press, 1971). Further citations to *The Tatler* will omit footnotes but include issue numbers in the text.

17. *Appreciations*, pp. 111-112.

18. *Letters*, I, 2 (MS. Hn.); 39; 46 (MS. Hn.); II, 256; III, 7-10 (MSS. BM.); E. V. Lucas, *The Life of Charles Lamb*, 5th ed. (London: Methuen, 1921). The most detailed account of Mary Lamb's life is Ernest Ross, *The Ordeal of Bridget Elia* (Norman: Univ. of Oklahoma Press, 1940). Lionel Trilling, *The Liberal Imagination* (1950; rpt. Garden City, N. Y.: Doubleday, 1957), pp. 42-43, 155, honors the wisdom Lamb distills in "The Sanity of True Genius" from an intimate knowledge of both art and madness.

19. I, 17, 119 (MSS. Hn.); 72-73 (the italics are mine); 2 (MS. Hn.).

20. The fullest defense of this thesis is F. V. Morley, *Lamb Before Elia* (London: Jonathan Cape, 1932).

21. Mario Praz, *The Hero in Eclipse in Victorian Fiction*, trans. Angus Davidson (1956; rpt. London: Oxford Univ. Press, 1969), pp. 65-74; John Gross, *The Rise and Fall of the Man of Letters* (1969; rpt. Harmondsworth: Penguin, 1973), p. 25.

Chapter Two

THE DISCONTINUITY
OF DURATION

When Thomas De Quincey used the word "discontinuity" to describe Lamb's essays, he referred to the absence of the sustained and the pompous in Lamb's prose style. "The least observing reader of *Elia*," De Quincey remarks, "cannot have failed to notice that the most felicitous passages always accomplish their circuit in a few sentences. The gyration within which his sentiment wheels, no matter of what kind it may be, is always the shortest possible. It does not prolong itself—it does not repeat itself—it does not propagate itself."[1] *Continuity*, as J. Hillis Miller has demonstrated, was central to De Quincey's own imaginative world.[2] It is not surprising, therefore, that De Quincey accounts for Lamb's *discontinuity* by reference to sub-literary and sub-philosophical causes, namely, Lamb's refusal of his greatest potentialities and his susceptibility to interruption by friends and business. I propose to adopt De Quincey's word and his descriptive insight, but to argue that the inner necessities of Lamb's imaginative world make a discontinuous manner an expressive form. At the root of discontinuity in Lamb's greatest work is his understanding of human time.

"New Year's Eve" is the bluntest of the Elia essays that grapple with the problem of fleeting time. Therefore it makes an excellent preparative for other essays that more obliquely treat the same issue. In "New Year's Eve" Elia is obviously voicing what he calls his "intolerable disinclination to dying" (p. 30); yet it may not be obvious to every reader what he has against it. He does not fear being cut off before his time; a guaranteed longevity would not stop his anxiety. His central fear is not that death will be the end of everything or that it will consign him to hell; a guaranteed afterlife in heaven would still leave him troubled. His eloquent enumeration of the irreplaceable pleasures of earth makes clear that in a different world, as in no world at all, Elia would no longer be Elia. The source of his lamentation in "New Year's Eve" is that what he is differs utterly from what he was and, worse yet, from what he will be.

Retrospection is no escape from the experience of discontinuity in this essay. Instead, Elia distinguishes three stages of his existence and stresses the breaks between them. The dividing line between the first and second stages is not assigned to a specific moment, but Elia indicates that he feels a lack of identity with himself in his childhood and even some aspects of his young manhood. His present self can love his past self "without the imputation of self-love" (p. 28). Lamb introduces the idea of the changeling, used in "The Praise of Chimney-Sweepers" to blur the distinctions between the classes, in order to point up the distinction between what Elia is and what he was: "I must take leave to cherish the remembrance of that young master—with as little reference, I protest, to this stupid changeling of five-and-forty, as if it had been a child of some other house, and not of my parents" (p. 28). Now in the stage of adulthood Elia looks back not upon the gradual unfolding of his present self out of his past experiences; instead, he recalls, as though from across an abyss, that "other me" (p. 28). Some connection exists between past and present, for his past self is a norm against which he measures his present character. But the norm has so little relation to his adult condition that he wonders whether his memory carries a fraudulent image of his childhood, and he thus tears away the continuity which would seem to be implied in the very possibility of memory: "From what have I not fallen, if the child I remember was indeed myself,—and not some dissembling guardian, presenting a false identity, to give the rule to my unpractised steps, and regulate the tone of my moral being!" (p. 28). In this passage the emphasis is placed upon the superiority of his earlier self. On the other hand, the child is presented in several passages as having a less complete awareness of the conditions of mortality than the adult's. Measured by the standard of knowledge of these conditions, as well as by the richness of remembered experiences, the adult has an advantage over the child. Lamb's relative valuation of past and present is, therefore, somewhat ambiguous. But this much is clear: the essay rises through memory to question seriously the truth of perceiving identity in Elia's past and present selves. Montaigne had voiced a remarkably similar conception with an air of untroubled self-sufficiency that could not be Elia's: "My selfe now, and my selfe anon, are indeed two; but when better, in good sooth I cannot tell."[3] Elia looks back upon an interval of unfilled space between his present and his past.

When he looks forward, he experiences a similar, though more horrifying, chasm. The future stretches out, perhaps familiar enough for a while, but then abruptly altered by the coming of death. Many men try to span this discontinuity by thinking of death in terms drawn from life; they want to domesticate the specter. Throughout the essay Elia dissociates himself from such escapists, and professes his unwillingness to find consolation in the conventional narcotic comparisons: "I am not content to pass away 'like a weaver's shuttle.' Those metaphors solace me not, nor sweeten the unpalatable draught of mortality. I care not to be carried with the tide, that smoothly bears human life to eternity; and reluct at the inevitable course of destiny. . . . I do not want to be weaned by age; or drop, like mellow fruit, as they say, into the grave" (p. 29). In these two passages Elia moves from imagery of mechanical or inorganic processes to imagery of animal or vegetable life. He continues, a few paragraphs later, in a passage that stresses a comparison with human sexual fulfillment: "I have heard some profess an indifference to life. Such hail the end of their existence as a port of refuge; and speak of the grave as of some soft arms, in which they may slumber as on a pillow. Some have wooed death—but out upon thee, I say, thou foul, ugly phantom!" (p. 30). Death is associated a few lines later with another aspect of human life, society more than sexuality: "For what satisfaction hath a man, that he shall 'lie down with kings and emperors in death,' who in his life-time never greatly coveted the society of such bed-fellows?—or, forsooth, that 'so shall the fairest face appear?'—Why, to comfort me, must Alice W—n be a goblin?" (p. 30). The sequence in which Elia considers these consolations is not always strictly logical; for instance, the "port of refuge" disrupts the ascending pattern, though it is dominated by the sexual image of the passage. Lamb gives enough logic to the sequence to suggest a survey of possible solutions to his problem, but he avoids strict continuity so as not to disrupt his style of informality and random reflection. It is, we may conclude, not very convincing to say that death is like some aspect of life.

But what alternative have we? The dualists claim that death brings an existence not only different from earthly life but better than it. Such a theory tends to place the soul in a dominant position within the self. The other world accommodates the main facet of the self, and the radical dichotomy between present and future is lessened. The soul steps intact across the hiatus between this world and the next. But Elia finds in the physical world of his present experience indispensable conditions for maintaining his humanity, individuality, and fulfillment:

Sun, and sky, and breeze, and solitary walks, and summer holidays, and the greenness of fields, and the delicious juices of meats and fishes, and society, and the cheerful glass, and candle-light, and fire-side conversations, and innocent vanities, and jests, and *irony itself*—do these things go out with life?

Can a ghost laugh, or shake his gaunt sides, when you are pleasant with him? (pp. 29–30)

Just as the inventory of metaphorical consolations approximates a hierarchical sequence, this present passage is more than a casual list of particulars. The enumeration moves from the pleasures of nature to those of civilization, from "sun" to "society." All these trivia, when taken together, form a fairly representative portrait of human existence as we know it. Elia goes on to mock the study habits of pure spirits in a passage which, like the references to irony and laughter, suggests that Elia would no longer be Elia when he enters upon a "new state of being" (p. 29): "And you, my midnight darlings, my Folios! must I part with the intense delight of having you (huge armfuls) in my embraces? Must knowledge come to me, if it come at all, by some awkward experiment of intuition, and no longer by this familiar process of reading?" (p. 30). The humor keeps the emotion from getting out of control, but the seriousness of Elia's abhorrence of the discontinuity between his present and future conditions remains evident. Although he is far from certain about what to expect after death—a lapse into non-being or a new state of being—he is sure that he will lose what most nourishes his present self: "In no way can I be brought to digest thee, thou thin, melancholy *Privation*, or more frightful and confounding *Positive!*" (p. 30). He wants a duration that would encompass past, present, and future, but he has only the "mortal duration" referred to in the opening sentence, and he is not sure that the same "I" has persisted even through this.

Lamb's conception of personal duration in the Elia papers resembles many of Johnson's essays insofar as Johnson stressed man's knack for turning his thoughts from the present to engage in memory, hope, or fear. "The greatest part of our ideas arises . . . ," according to *The Rambler*, "from the view before or behind us, and we are happy or miserable, according as we are affected by the survey of our life, or our prospect of future existence." Johnson's use of this idea, unlike Lamb's, was fundamentally otherworldly and moral. Man's retrospection and anticipation are, for Johnson, evidence of his "celestial nature"; no present earthly object can fill his mind since his home is elsewhere than on earth. Further, his success in eternity depends on his morality now, and his conduct relies on his ability to use memory, hope, and fear in the present as supporters of virtuous action, rather than as inducements to passivity or irresponsibility. "The great consideration which ought to influence us in the use of the present moment," he declares, "is to arise from the effect, which, as well or ill applied, it must have upon the time to come; for though its actual existence be inconceivably short, yet its effects are unlimited, and there is not the smallest point of time but may extend its consequences, either to our hurt or our advantage, through all eternity, and give us reason to remember it for ever, with anguish or exultation."[4] Johnson's perception of human duration issues in a call to moral activity, while Lamb's leads to an attempt within his essays at an imaginative coalescence of separate segments of time.

The joining together through imagination of what reason has put asunder is one of the principal impulses of Romantic poetry. It sometimes works specifically on human time, transmuting change into continuity or even simultaneity. Wordsworth's "Tintern Abbey," for instance, which Lamb in 1801 had classified among his favorite poems in the two volumes of *Lyrical Ballads*, begins with a verse paragraph describing a scene in terms that stress a contrast between the speaker's sense of change ("the length/ Of five long winters") and the landscape's permanence. Hence he keeps repeating—"Five years," "five summers," "five long winters," "Once again/ Do I behold," "Once again I see"—as he marvels that the place is still the same, and still available to him, though so much has happened since his last visit. At the same time, however, the opening passage dwells upon spatial continuity. There are no sharp boundaries in this scene. The natural and the artificial, the domesticated and the wild, one sector of land and another, merge gradually. The cliffs connect the landscape and the sky. Stylistic sleight-of-hand (for instance, one natural object is said to "impress thoughts" on another natural object) links the human and the natural. In the meditation which occupies the rest of the poem, the model of continuity is transferred from the spatial realm to the temporal, thus mediating between the opposites of change and permanence that initiated the lyric. Two developmental conceptions of mind are sketched, one concerning the hierarchy of effects which a perception has in memory (11. 22-57), the other concerning a person's changing modes of perception as he grows up (11. 58-111). The poem seeks to achieve the certitude that nothing is wholly lost as time passes—

> These beauteous forms,
> Through a long absence, have not been to me
> As is a landscape to a blind man's eye:

—or, if "That time is past,/ And all its aching joys are now no more," at least

"other gifts/ Have followed; for such loss, I would believe,/ Abundant recompense." Finally, the last verse paragraph turns to his "dearest Friend"
(in life, his sister), whom he sees as repeating in the present his prior self
("what I was once") and as capable of carrying into the future his present
self, both by maturing to his present stage and by remembering the present
moment. Temporal discontinuity is never wholly suppressed in Wordsworth's
major poetry. It lurks beneath the euphemism of "If I should be where I no
more can hear/ Thy voice" in "Tintern Abbey," and it becomes more explicit in such contexts as the conclusion to "She Dwelt Among the Untrodden
Ways,"

> But she is in her grave, and, oh,
> The difference to me!

and the specter that rises in the second book of *The Prelude:*

>   so wide appears
> The vacancy between me and those days
> Which yet have such self-presence in my mind,
> That, musing on them, often do I seem
> Two consciousnesses, conscious of myself
> And of some other Being. (11. 28-33)[5]

But "Tintern Abbey" subordinates even the ultimate temporal discontinuity
to its system of linkages and duplications among past, present, and future,
and *The Prelude* discovers, beneath the traumas of its protagonist's life, that
he is still essentially the country boy who skated on Esthwaite and Winder-
mere, though he has gradually become much besides.

    Georges Poulet has discussed Coleridge in some detail in the course of call-
ing attention to the tendency, among the Romantics, to elude the successiveness of time through simultaneous possession of past, present, and future:
"They took hold of the idea of eternity; but they removed it from its empy-
rean world into their own. In brief, paradoxically, they brought Eternity
into Time." "Many Romantic writers," notes M. H. Abrams in *Natural
Supernaturalism,* "testified to a deeply significant experience in which an instant of consciousness, or else an ordinary object or event, suddenly blazes
into revelation; the unsustainable moment seems to arrest what is passing,
and is often described as an intersection of eternity with time." Poulet's
analysis of a certain kind of memory as one of the mechanisms for reaching
this state is especially relevant to Lamb, whom Poulet never mentions. The

memory which Poulet discusses is not the ordinary kind, which dims with the passing of time. He refers rather to a recollection so intense that it "has the vividness of the present." "It is then," he continues, "not only as if the images of the past were suddenly brought to our inner eye with a singular force, but as if our own feelings, habits, ideas of long ago were instantaneously repossessing themselves of our soul, and substituting our past self for our present one."[6] Lamb made use, as we shall see, of the idea of such an experience, but he portrayed Elia's memory as significantly less potent than the memory which Poulet analyzes. In addition, Lamb employed a strategy of foresight (unstressed in this essay by Poulet) by which he sought to bridge the gap between present and future.

The latter method is exemplified by "The Child Angel," not one of Lamb's best essays but one that assumes a significant place in his canon when it is viewed as an attempt to repair the discontinuity of duration. "The Child Angel" is a dream vision which Elia experiences after reading the "Loves of the Angels." He had gone to bed wondering "what could come of it" (p. 244), and this thought introduces the problem of the hidden nature of futurity. The dream itself relates to this problem by overcoming for a while the discontinuity between present and future modes of existence.

In the dream the male angel Nadir has a child by the female mortal Adah. Nadir transports the child, or a mirror image of it, to heaven, where it combines qualities of its two parents: "And it could not taste of death, by reason of its adoption into immortal palaces: but it was to know weakness, and reliance, and the shadow of human imbecility; and it went with a lame gait; but in its goings it exceeded all mortal children in grace and swiftness" (p. 245). This hybrid—named Ge-Urania—helps fill up the space between mortals and pure spirits, and the angels themselves perform a similar service (for Elia, as well as for Ge-Urania) by becoming humanized. They pretend to be aged female attendants; they diminish the volume of the angelic harps; and they adapt their intuitive mental powers to the slower comprehension of the newcomer. The child is not the only one to gain by the process, for the angels, in becoming humanized, become better: "Then pity first sprang up in angelic bosoms; and yearnings (like the human) touched them at the sight of the immortal lame one" (p. 245). Lamb combines the idea of transcending time with the idea of the child angel's weakness as compared with the capacities of ordinary angels, and the result is that the child angel remains always a child, "for ever to put forth shoots, and to fall fluttering, because its birth was not of the unmixed vigour of heaven" (p. 245). Time flows, even in heaven, but for the child angel it brings no change and hence it can be said to have no real existence: "And myriads of years rolled round (in dreams Time is nothing), and still it kept, and is to keep, perpetual childhood, and is the Tutelar Genius of Childhood upon earth, and still goes lame and lovely" (p. 245). In an essay that is primarily concerned with the hiatus between life and afterlife, this is the one concession to the method of transcending time by overcoming the irrevocable loss of childhood. Elia is fully aware that his attempt to establish continuity between this world and the next is only a wish fulfillment, but at least it answers his needs more completely than the more venerable accounts of the afterlife: "I was suddenly transported, how or whither I could scarcely make out—but to some celestial region. It was not the real heavens neither—not the downright Bible heaven— but a kind of fairyland heaven, about which a poor human fancy may have leave to sport and air itself, I will hope, without presumption" (p. 244). In bridging one gap, however, the essay reveals another—that between fact and value. Elia knows that he has not really solved his problem of mortality, and the essay closes on a reminder that the child's mother remains dead: "but Adah sleepeth by the river Pison" (p. 246).

"To the Shade of Elliston," which first appeared after the death of the famous actor, also employs a contrast between traditional accounts of the afterlife and Elia's account of what an afterlife should be. In a series of images of buildings Elia considers the venerable notion of an escape from earthly imprisonment: the "vain Platonist dreams of this *body* to be no better than a county gaol, forsooth, or some house of durance vile, whereof the five senses are the fetters" (p. 166). Elliston thought of his body as a different sort of building: "It was thy Pleasure House, thy Palace of Dainty Devices; thy Louvre, or thy White Hall" (p. 166). But the Platonist afterlife is a third kind of building, in Elia's view, and it contrasts forbiddingly with the delightful structure just described: "What new mysterious lodgings dost thou tenant now? or when may we expect thy aerial house-warming?" (p. 166). Warmth is, by implication, unlikely there, and neither Elliston nor Elia would feel at home. Elia then turns to a second traditional conception, that of the passage over the river Styx, and this section of the essay is dominated by imagery of denudation: "It irks me to think, that, stript of thy regalities, thou shouldst ferry over, a poor forked shade, in crazy Stygian wherry" (pp. 166-167). The stripping suggests a loss of physicality, as well as the opportunity to exhibit the professional skills and idiosyncrasies that gave Elliston a kind of kingliness. When the process is finished, nothing is left but a pure spirit:

Aye, now 'tis done. You are just boat
weight; *pura et puta anima.*
But bless me, how *little* you look!
So shall we all look—kings, and
keysars—stript for the last voyage. (p. 167)

Elia soothes his sorrow by falling back upon one of the old saws that he had
discarded in "New Year's Eve," that all classes will come to a similar end.
But despite this consolation, the main effect of the passage is a lament for
the loss of that familiar, fleshy context within which men find pleasure and
grandeur.

Each time that Elia considers one of the traditional notions of the afterlife, he reacts against it by conjuring up his own variation on tradition. After
the section on the "vain Platonist," he thinks of Milton's Limbo of Vanities,
and conjectures that perhaps there exists a Limbo for Players. Unlike Milton,
Elia stresses the value of the trivia which are associated with it. He rewrites
a passage from *Paradise Lost* (Book III, ll. 445–459), and makes clear that
his kind of Limbo would be adequate insofar as it allowed Elliston to do the
things he had done on earth: "There, by the neighbouring moon (by some
not improperly supposed thy Regent Planet upon earth) mayst thou not still
be acting thy managerial pranks, great disembodied Lessee? but Lessee still,
and still a Manager" (p. 166). Similarly, after watching Elliston get stripped
and then push off across the River Styx, Elia fancifully wishes that Rhada-
manthus, "who tries the lighter causes below," may allow the actor to live
much as he has lived: ". . . after a lenient castigation, with rods lighter than
of those Medusean ringlets, but just enough to 'whip the offending Adam
out of thee'—[Rhadamanthus] shall courteously dismiss thee at the right
hand gate—the O. P. side of Hades—that conducts to masques, and merry-
makings, in the Theatre Royal of Proserpine" (p. 167). Elia's mind invents
the Limbo for Players and the Theatre Royal of Proserpine as half-serious,
half-joking descriptions of what a life after death should be. The two places
are seriously introduced in the sense that they embody the life-affirming
values which Elia espouses, but the places are not presented as facts or even
as serious possibilities. To imagine such places is to heal the schism between
present and future, but only momentarily. There is an underlying sadness
in this essay, and it derives from the premise that no afterlife different from
our present world could be satisfying, but no afterlife like our present world
is possible.

Sadness is not a part of Addison's response to anticipations of what happens to a person after death. One of his recurrent devices, supplying a pre-

cedent for Elia's essays of anticipation, is a visit to the place of the afterlife by some representative of a non-Christian culture. Three pieces in *The Tatler* treat journeys to the underworld in *The Odyssey, The Aeneid,* and Fénelon's *Télémaque* (Nos. 152, 154, 156); and *The Spectator* includes essays which claim to recount American Indian and Oriental stories of someone's encounter with a pastoral region reserved for the virtuous dead (Nos. 56, 159).[7] Addison's rationale for this preoccupation displays a confidence which Elia cannot muster: "I must confess, I take a particular delight in these prospects of futurity, whether grounded upon the probable suggestions of a fine imagination, or the more severe conclusions of philosophy; as a man loves to hear all the discoveries or conjectures relating to a foreign country which he is, at some time, to inhabit" (*Tatler,* No. 156). For Addison the future holds no frightening discontinuity, and there is no hesitation in preferring a forward to a backward look: "For my own part, I love to range through that half of eternity which is still to come, rather than look on that which is already run out ..." (*Tatler,* No. 152). Lamb rarely wrote essays of anticipation, not only because the invisible world presented itself as too lacking in specificity for varied literary treatment, but also because his thisworldly premises made essays of memory more expressive of his deepest response to time. To link the past with the present had the advantage of focusing upon two earthly, physical, and assuredly real modes of existence—childhood and adulthood. So Lamb most often came to grips with the discontinuity of existence by looking backward. He allowed Elia two principal methods for attempting to attain timelessness by fusing past and present, and the rest of this chapter will explore these methods and Lamb's skeptical testing of them. Sometimes Elia seeks through memory an identification between past and present, but he finds that memory works better for others than for himself. Sometimes Elia strives to duplicate in his adulthood the mental processes of his childhood, but he runs into difficulties.

Perhaps the clearest instance of the first method is "Captain Jackson," which owes much, but not this, to Oliver Goldsmith's portrayal of a character whom Lamb's essay names in its closing paragraph—Beau Tibbs from the *Citizen of the World* essay series. Tibbs and Jackson share a habit of talking as if they are elevated in fortune although really they are poor. Each boasts of the prospect from his tenement's window, and each speaks as if the paltry meal he can offer a guest is a gourmet's feast. But Tibbs is the creature of social forms, the pursuer and ape of aristocrats, the dropper of titled names. His parasitism is unmistakable in his habitual pleas for a hand-out and in his (and his wife's) ruination of the pawnbroker's widow's evening at Vauxhall by disparaging present amusements as beneath the relish of the genteel. Like the fashionable fops who are his models, Tibbs expresses the wish that women had no souls, so that they would let him treat them as the animals which he likes to think them.[8] Captain Jackson, however, is never said to imitate or prey upon anyone else, and he makes the most (and more) of available pleasures for himself and everyone around him. It is typical of his possession of something which deserves to be called an inner life that this impecunious retired soldier not only transcends the drabness of his home by thinking it fine, but also escapes the limitations of the present moment by recalling an incident of his youth. When Captain Jackson married, he rode through Glasgow in a chaise and four:

I suppose it was the only occasion, upon which his own actual splendour at all corresponded with the world's notions on that subject. In homely cart, or travelling caravan, by whatever humble vehicle they chanced to be transported in less prosperous days, the ride through Glasgow came back upon his fancy, not as a humiliating contrast, but as a fair occasion for reverting to that one day's state. It seemed an "equipage etern" from which no power of fate or fortune, once mounted, had power thereafter to dislodge him. (p. 192)

Since Captain Jackson is retired, the straitened current circumstances of the family are themselves the product of time, but memory so completely brings the one glorious moment of youth back into his mind that the disjunction between past and present disappears. In closing the space between past and present the Captain is elevated above the limitations of time, just as his imagination frees him from poverty by convincing him that his wealth and importance are considerable. Elia, however, is never deluded by the Captain's pretensions. He contrasts the real boundaries of Jackson's life with the centrifugal movement of Jackson's imagination, and he rests his admiration for the man's delusion on the premise that it is a delusion: "He had a stock of wealth in his mind; not that which is properly termed *Content*, for in truth he was not to be *contained* at all, but overflowed all bounds by the force of a magnificent self-delusion" (p. 192).

Memory, like imagination, does not work so well for Elia. He had practically forgotten Captain Jackson until he came across his name in an obituary: "Alack, how good men, and the good turns they do us, slide out of memory, and are recalled but by the surprise of some such sad memento as that which now lies before us!" (pp. 189-190). In thinking of the Captain's wedding, which Jackson could perpetuate in recollection all his life, Elia finds that the intervening years defeat his memory's attempts to revert to that one day's state: "It is long since, and my memory waxes dim on some subjects, or I should wish to convey some notion of the manner in which the pleasant creature described the circumstances of his own wedding-day. I faintly remember something of a chaise and four, in which he made his entry into Glasgow on that morning to fetch the bride home, or carry her thither, I forget which" (p. 192). Elia and Captain Jackson are both responding to the hiatus between past and present. Jackson overcomes it and makes a timeless paradise out of retirement in a shabby tenement, while Elia is too powerless, because Lamb is too tough-minded, to escape the successiveness of duration.

The contrast between Captain Jackson and Elia reveals Lamb's intuition of the power of time, but Elia's sympathy for Jackson demonstrates the author's yearning to transcend time. The judicious phrasing of the essay's last sentences, their sadness, and firmness of tone, are expressive of a mind which is as free from delusion as it is full of sympathy. Memory may not succeed, for Elia, in totally fusing past and present, but it nevertheless has its uses. Even a relatively weak memory, like Elia's, can perceive a person or event since doomed by time, and it can preserve an awareness of human possibilities other than one's self. Most importantly, by juxtaposing Elia's memory with Captain Jackson's, Lamb employs a powerful technique for dramatizing the tension in his own sense of man's involvement in time.

Another essay in which Elia is linked by sympathy with a person who has a more effective memory than his own is "Mackery End, in Hertfordshire." Not until the second half of the essay does Elia come to describe his vacation trip to the residence of his deceased great-aunt. The first half concerns his relationship with his cousin Bridget Elia, who is based upon Lamb's sister Mary. The emphasis here is upon a concord of opposites: "We agree pretty well in our tastes and habits—yet so, as 'with a difference.' We are generally in harmony, with occasional bickerings—as it should be among near relations" (p. 75). Several of their differences spring from their differing relationships to time. The first anecdote in her character sketch touches upon this issue: "once, upon my dissembling a tone in my voice more kind than ordinary, my cousin burst into tears, and complained that I was altered" (p. 75). Bridget likes novels, while Elia is uninterested in that continuity of event with event which makes up a plot; he prefers the non-fictional prose writers who reveal their idiosyncrasy without depending upon "the progress of events" (p. 75). The association of Bridget with temporal constancy or continuity is carried over into the discussion of her moral solidity: "That which was good and venerable to her, when a child, retains its authority over her mind still. She never juggles or plays tricks with her understanding" (p. 76). For this reason, Elia finds her to be more dependable than himself "upon moral points," that is, "upon something proper to be done, or let alone" (p. 76). He is generally right about units isolated from a continuum—"in matters of fact, dates, and circumstances" (p. 76)—but she is more reliable when deciding upon involvement in the network of action and result.

In the second half of the essay Elia, his cousin Bridget, and his friend B. F. leave the boundaries of their ordinary adult lives and take a vacation trip to Mackery End in the country. B. F., who has no previous connection with the area, is rather surprised by all the hospitality he sees and receives. Elia had spent some of his childhood there more than forty years before, but his connection with the place is less direct than might be expected. He had always talked with Bridget about Mackery End, and he accounted it the oldest thing that he remembered. When he sees the spot, however, it differs from the image in his memory. He is compelled to recognize that he has confused his personal memory with the memory that he possesses vicariously through Bridget. For she, unlike Elia, has kept an accurate image inscribed in her mind all these years. Except for a few inevitable alterations, the people and the landscape which she now looks upon match her recollections:

Bridget's was more a waking bliss than mine, for she easily remembered her old acquaintance again—some altered features, of course, a little grudged at. At first, indeed, she was ready to disbelieve for joy; but the scene soon reconfirmed itself in her affections—and she traversed every out-post of the old mansion, to the wood-house, the orchard, the place where the pigeon-house had stood (house and birds were alike flown)—with a breathless impatience of recognition, which was more pardonable perhaps than decorous at the age of fifty odd. But Bridget in some things is behind her years. (pp. 77-78)

Her pardonable enthusiasm, as well as her memory, allies her present self with her childhood, though suggestions of the flow of time are retained as a subordinate motif. Elia, despite his awakening to the fallibility of his memory, enjoys the sight of Mackery End because he can share so fully in Bridget's experience.

Just as she unifies past and present, she also closes another dichotomy for Elia in the last paragraph of the essay. Elia concedes that he is "terribly shy in making myself known to strangers and out-of-date kinsfolk" (p. 78). If the situation had been left to him, the visitors would never have gained entrance to the house or spoken with its present inhabitants. The difficulty would have been, for Elia, "insurmountable" (p. 78), like a high wall separating himself and his party from the people inside. But Bridget seems gifted with a more than natural power that whisks her over the obstacle: "Love, stronger than scruple, winged my cousin in without me; but she soon returned with a creature that might have sat to a sculptor for the image of Welcome" (p. 78). Reconciliations of opposites and the closing of gaps occur on all sides. The hearty hostess had become mistress of the mansion by marriage, "But this adopted Bruton, in my mind, was better than they all—more comely" (p. 78). Her memory, like Bridget's, bridges the distance between past and present: "She just recollected in early life to have had her cousin Bridget once pointed out to her, climbing a style" (p. 78). Although she "was born too late to have remembered" Elia, she welcomes him because of the "name of kindred, and of cousinship": "Those slender ties, that prove slight as gossamer in the rending atmosphere of a metropolis, bind faster, as we found it, in hearty, homely, loving Hertfordshire" (p. 78). In this atmosphere of perfect correspondence between all things, life seems to measure up to the wishes of mind, just as does the appearance of the hostess: "There was a grace and dignity, an amplitude of form and stature, answering to her mind, in this farmer's wife, which would have shined in a palace—or so we thought it" (p. 78). The characters in this essay form a hierarchy in their relation to continuity and reconciliation—from the outsider B. F. through Elia and Bridget (who is sufficiently idiosyncratic to be impatient at times with a visitor's questioning her while she is reading) to Mrs. Bruton, whose hospitality is so unqualified that she might be a model for an allegorical statue of Welcome. Bridget makes it possible for Elia and B. F.—and the reader—to leave the world of separation and discontinuity and to enter "those pretty pastoral walks" (p. 79) in Hertfordshire, where the Brutons and Gladmans abide.

Elia remains partly, however, outside Mrs. Bruton's pastoral dominion. It is significant that she cannot remember him. Nor is he altogether united with his cousin Bridget, "who, as I have said, is older than myself by some ten years. I wish that I could throw into a heap the remainder of our joint existences, that we might share them in equal division. But that is impossible" (p. 77). He cannot relinquish his awareness that they are separate and mortal. In the long last sentence of the essay, he recalls again the effectiveness of Bridget's memory and, by implication, the dubiousness of his own, and he equalizes them momentarily by imagining a kind of contract: let his "country cousins" and Bridget herself forget him "when" he forgets this day's events. It is no accident that his word is "when" rather than "if." He supplies no guarantee that he will make their part of the bargain superfluous.

Elia's memory is tested by these comparisons with the effective memories of Captain Jackson and Bridget Elia, and it does not pass the test. Jackson and Bridget are able to vanquish time; Elia is left with a sense of his own weakness in the struggle with mutability. On the other hand, in several Elian essays the speaker's awareness of his weakness is derived not from a comparison with the powers of other persons but from a comparison between his own adult and childhood capabilities. In these essays Elia the child has a dual function: he is at once the object of memory and the representative of successful transcendence of the temporal world's discontinuity. The drama and complexity of these essays resides in the adult Elia's attempt to go beyond memory and to duplicate his childhood mental processes.

Elia returns, in "Blakesmoor in H——shire," to another of his childhood scenes. In "Mackery End, in Hertfordshire" his anticipated uniting of past and present was qualified by his inability to recognize the place because his memory had failed to preserve a true image. In the Blakesmoor essay his similar expectations are disappointed by the completeness with which the mansion has been leveled. At first, his mind is foiled in its wish to experience again the imaginative wanderings of his childhood, and this frustration is associated with the problem of human mortality: "Death does not shrink up his human victim at this rate. The burnt ashes of a man weigh more in their proportion" (p. 154). There is bitter irony in the limited respect in which the human victim fares better than the house—a mere matter of proportional weight. The individuality, the firm boundaries, of man and mansion are eventually reduced to nothing but the "indistinction" (p. 154) of ashes and ruins. The hiatus between the past mansion and the present ruins is matched by a second hiatus between man's present life and his future condition after death. Elia's memory, however, comes to his aid in overcoming the loss of Blakesmoor, even if it is too late to stop the wreckers: "I should have cried out to them to spare a plank at least out of the cheerful store-room, in whose hot window-seat I used to sit and read Cowley, with the grass-plat before, and the hum and flappings of that one solitary wasp that ever haunted it about me—it is in mine ears now, as oft as summer returns; or a pannel of the yellow room" (p. 154). This passage reveals the possibility of healing the dichotomy between past and present through memory. The main thrust of Elia's efforts in the rest of the essay is to duplicate a mental process of Elia's childhood. At that time another kind of discontinuity stood between Elia and Blakesmoor, the gap between his modest economic and social class and the aristocratic mansion which he visited. But Elia overcame the gap, and perhaps the recollection of how he managed such a feat will help him in his present situation.

He recalls three stages of his childhood reaction to Blakesmoor: exploration, acceptance of limits, and appropriation. At first he thinks of when he began to discover the world through what the old mansion had to offer. He read Cowley in the window-seat, peeked at Ovidian tapestries, and crept into the room where Mrs. Battle died. The result of his explorations was that he knew every detail of the house's space: "But I was a lonely child, and had the range at will of every apartment, knew every nook and corner, wondered and worshipped everywhere" (p. 155). Knowledge bred acceptance. He never wanted to go beyond the boundaries of the place, even to see a nearby lake half hidden by trees. In the completeness of his rapport with Blakesmoor he seemed to escape the separateness of living in a fallen world: "Variegated views, extensive prospects—and those at no great distance from the house—I was told of such—what were they to me, being out of the boundaries of my Eden?" (p. 155). The major obstacle to the child's complete appropriation of Blakesmoor was the fact that it is one thing to be just a plebeian visitor and another to be the owner of the mansion. Yet this was no obstacle for the child Elia. He stood looking intently upon the noble family's escutcheon "till, every dreg of peasantry purging off, I received into myself Very Gentility" (p. 156). The intensity of his contemplation of the house and its contents was the key to his entrance into nobility. On the other hand, the heirs by blood had forfeited their rights to the place by indifference. Although Elia's ancestor was some poor anonymous shepherd and not the founder of Blakesmoor, "I was the true descendant of those old W——s; and not the present family of that name, who had fled the old waste places" (p. 156). Therefore, "Mine was that gallery of good old family portraits . . . ," "Mine too, BLAKESMOOR, was thy noble Marble Hall . . . ," "Mine too, thy lofty Justice Hall . . . ," and "Mine too—whose else?—thy costly fruit-garden" (pp. 156–157). The power of contemplation and desire shattered the separateness of the lower-class visitor from the home of aristocracy.

At the same time the young Elia gained communication with the past. Even when he visited it as a child, Blakesmoor had stopped bustling with present life; it had been deserted by its heirs, and its interest lay largely in its traditions. The process by which Elia overcame the disjunction between his origins and the mansion also led him to bring the traditions of the place alive once again. His explorations were directed toward legacies, such as Cowley and Ovid, of other ages, but these legacies had all the fascination of life. His motive for entering the room where Mrs. Battle died extended to all the details of the old dwelling: "a sneaking curiosity, terror-tainted, to hold communication with the past" (p. 155). Elia's youthful appropriation of Blakesmoor is compared to an antiquarian's relation to antiquity: "The pride of ancestry may be had on cheaper terms than to be obliged to an importunate race of ancestors; and the coatless antiquary in his unemblazoned cell, revolving the long line of a Mowbray's or DeClifford's pedigree, at those sounding names may warm himself into as gay a vanity as those who do inherit them" (p. 156). When the act of gazing at the family's escutcheon caused Elia to take on "Very Gentility," he also saw this old relic as having a present potency. Its motto was "Resurgam," and it did rise to live again in his fierce contemplation. The "good old family portraits" which he appropriated for his own became not merely articles stashed away in his mind, but breathing, communicating beings: "Mine was that gallery of good old family portraits, which as I have gone over, giving them in fancy my own family name, one—and then another—would seem to smile, reaching forward from the canvas, to recognise the new relationship; while the rest looked grave, as it seemed, at the vacancy in their dwelling, and thoughts of fled posterity" (pp. 156-157). The other things which he thought of as his own took on a similar vitality, and the ancient sacred object in the center of the old garden got his worship, as though it was more to him than an archaeological curiosity: "child of Athens or old Rome paid never a sincerer worship to Pan or to Sylvanus in their native groves, than I to that fragmental mystery" (p. 157). In Elia's childhood, closing the interval between classes was indissolubly linked with closing that between periods of time. When in *The Spectator* (No. 109) Sir Roger de Coverley conducted Steele's persona through the gallery of de Coverley family portraits, he betrayed that delightful preoccupation with the past which discredited him and his class for present or future leadership in society. But the child Elia's rapport with such a gallery and with the past bears witness to a potential imaginative strength which the adult Elia wants to recover.

If Elia's present self could duplicate the mental processes of his childhood, the gap between the present ruins and the past mansion would be bridged, and so, by analogy, would that between his present self and his future condition. The duplication is successful in several ways. Elia recalls in considerable detail the house and his experiences there; he at no time mentions a lapse in memory. Moreover, the grammar of the essay is expressive of a process of increasing rapport between the adult Elia and the aristocratic dwelling. In the first two paragraphs Elia is distanced from Blakesmoor by his manner of alluding to it: he discusses the general category of old buildings, whether mansions or churches, and then cites, but does not name "an old great house with which I had been impressed in this way in infancy" (p. 154). Blakesmoor is present not as a particular which is mentally confronted, but as an unspecified instance of a general proposition. At the same time, Elia engages in direct grammatical confrontation with the reader, whom he addresses in the second person singular and in the imperative mood: "But would'st thou know the beauty of holiness?—go alone on some week-day, borrowing the keys of good Master Sexton, traverse the cool aisles of some country church . . ." (p. 154). The sight of Blakesmoor's ruins jolts Elia out of this grammatical intimacy with the reader, but he continues to speak of the mansion in the third person, and without naming it. Then two pivotal events happen simultaneously: Elia recalls how as a child he attained "Very Gentility" and communication with tradition, and he alters his way of relating to the mansion in the present:

Or wherefore, else, O tattered and diminished 'Scutcheon that hung upon the time-worn walls of thy princely stairs, BLAKESMOOR! have I in childhood so oft stood poring upon thy mystic characters—thy emblematic supporters, with their prophetic "Resurgam"—till, every dreg of peasantry purging off, I received into myself Very Gentility? Thou wert first in my morning eyes; and of nights, hast detained my steps from bedward, till it was but a step from gazing at thee to dreaming on thee. (p. 156)

For the first time in the essay Elia names the place and addresses it directly. In the last paragraphs, as he repeats the parallel phrases of how "Mine was" this and that element of Blakesmoor, he twice more cites its proper name, and he continues the apostrophe. Now the audience of which he is aware is not the reader, but Blakesmoor itself. The shift from indirect to direct grammatical confrontation suggests that, just as the child Elia appropriated Blakesmoor in the past, the adult Elia is able to speak to it in the present.

Several elements, however, indicate that the parallel between the mental processes of Elia the child and those of Elia the adult is less than complete. The adult can easily duplicate the first stage of the child's response to Blakesmoor: he can vicariously explore the old place through remembrance of himself as a child. But he can not so readily repeat the other two stages of his youthful experience.[9] The mature Elia is too aware of diverse possibilities to commit himself as totally as he once did to the limits of the mansion; hence his childhood acceptance of those limits seems odd to him:

So strange a passion for the place possessed me in those years, that, though there lay—I shame to say how few roods distant from the mansion—half hid by trees, what I judged some romantic lake, such was the spell which bound me to the house, and such my carefulness not to pass its strict and proper precincts, that the idle waters lay unexplored for me; and not till late in life, curiosity prevailing over elder devotion, I found, to my astonishment, a pretty brawling brook had been the Lacus Incognitus of my infancy. (p. 155)

The adult speaker is a little embarrassed by his former naivete, and he suggests the constriction of his earlier attitude by choosing to blame it on a "spell." His present criticism of his earlier unrealism is emphasized further by his calling the place "my chosen prison" a few lines later. Since in adulthood he wanted to see beyond this prison, he took a walk over to the supposedly "idle waters" and found instead a "pretty brawling brook," which reveals by its vivacity the inadequacy of his childhood understanding. The adult Elia feels compelled to justify his childhood activities. He had been used to "Snug firesides—the low-built roof—parlours ten feet by ten—frugal boards": "Yet, without impeachment to their tenderest lessons, I am not sorry to have had glances of something beyond; and to have taken, if but a peep, in childhood, at the contrasting accidents of a great fortune" (pp. 155-156). This justification in terms of a transcendence of narrow boundaries contrasts with the child Elia's high valuation of being "hemmed in" (p. 155). As an adult Elia is too aware of multiple possibilities to rest easily in one possibility. Mature awareness breeds detachment and makes more difficult a repetition of complete immersion in Blakesmoor. In this same passage the adult Elia shows by his choice of words ("glances," "if but a peep") that he now conceives the link between himself and the house to have been more tenuous than it once seemed.

A further contrast is evident between the nature of the child's appropriation of Blakesmoor and the adult's recollection of it. In the earlier period the process was non-intellectualized. As Elia commented previously, "The solitude of childhood is not so much the mother of thought, as it is the feeder of love, and silence, and admiration" (p. 155). Elia had gazed intently upon the escutcheon, until the interaction of two particulars, the thing and himself, had generated "Very Gentility." As an adult, Elia has to go through a process of analysis to reach a sympathetic understanding of his previous intensity. The central element of the analysis is the following passage: "The claims of birth are ideal merely, and what herald shall go about to strip me of an idea?" (p. 156). Although the analytic process culminates in the apostrophe by which Elia, in the present, confronts Blakesmoor as a unique entity, the process qualifies the extent of the speaker's possession of the mansion. The terms of the analysis suggest that all Elia succeeded in obtaining was the idea of gentility. In place of a confrontation between mind and thing, there is a confrontation between mind and idea. Elia possessed the house and its traditions, but only in a sense. Such a qualification would have been foreign to his childhood sensibility, and the qualification has an important bearing upon the essay's resolution of the problem of mortality.

If Elia simply fails to recapture his youthful mental processes, the space between life and death, between present and future, remains a void. But in fact Elia partially succeeds. There is a real link between Elia now and Elia then; hence he can recall earlier events, and he can reconstitute his youthful attainment of gentility at least to the extent of imagining the attainment of the idea of gentility. On the other hand, there are, as we have seen, important differences between his childhood and his adult mental processes. In the last paragraph he adverts to the ploughing under of the mansion and thus dissolves the revivification of the past. This balance is reflected in the essay's final position toward the hiatus between life and death: "I sometimes think that as men, when they die, do not die all, so of their extinguished habitations there may be a hope—a germ to be revivified" (p. 157). The ambiguity in this sentence centers upon the connection between "I sometimes think" and "as men, when they die, do not die all." Does the tentativeness of the opening phrase refer to men, as well as to houses? Insofar as the answer is affirmative, the essay introduces human resurrection, or meaningful immortality, as no more than an idea which one gets at times. Insofar as the answer is negative, there is genuine bridging of life and death, but only to the extent that "there may be a hope—a germ to be revivified." Just as the adult Elia conceives his earlier achievement as the attainment of the *idea* of gentility, he now limits the bridging of life and death to an idea and a hope. The logic of the essay suggests that there may be no more likelihood that the hope will become fact than that Elia will be made a peer.

Nevertheless, "Blakesmoor in H——shire" takes a more optimistic view of the possibilities of spanning discontinuities than does the essay "Dream-Children; A Reverie." On a superficial level, this essay might be regarded as the wish-fulfillment of Charles Lamb, a middle-aged bachelor who had proposed marriage unsuccessfully once or twice in his life. The trouble with this interpretation is that "Dream-Children" makes rather grim escapist fare: two of its main characters die, both after considerable suffering, another is unattainable, two dissolve into "less than nothing" (p. 103), and the reality of Elia's bachelor's existence is forcefully present in the closing lines. The essay is more inclusive and complex than a wish-fulfillment, and it contains considerable detail that is unconnected with the relative merits of marriage and bachelorhood.

The latter issue had been a central concern of essays by Steele and Addison, who wanted to restore the social prestige of marriage after a period of fashionable sexual license. Steele's *Tatler*, No. 95, not only expressed a depth of sentiment which, as in a number of Steele's essays, anticipated Elia,[10] but also explicitly contrasted Isaac Bickerstaff's narrow bachelor's life with the superior satisfactions of matrimony. After visiting a married friend and his family, "I went home, considering the different conditions of a married life and that of a bachelor," writes Bickerstaff as the essay ends, "and I must confess, it struck me with a secret concern, to reflect, that whenever I go off, I shall leave no traces behind me. In this pensive mood I returned to my family; that is to say, to my maid, my dog and my cat, who only can be the better or worse for what happens to me." The conclusion of "Dream-Children" is probably indebted to this passage, but as in Lamb's earlier and simpler essay, "A Bachelor's Complaint of the Behaviour of Married People," where he inverted many of the value judgments in *Tatler*, No. 95, while retaining Steele's basic situation, Lamb builds on precedent for his own distinctive purposes. The complexity of "Dream-Children" becomes intelligible if we avoid reading it as mere wish-fulfillment or as a belated installment of an Augustan essay series and view it instead as Lamb's most concentrated attempt to give form to his quest to overcome the discontinuity of duration.

The separation between past and present is emphasized in "Dream-Children" by the recurrent motif of death and loss: the house where Grandmother Field lives has been largely torn down, she and James Elia have died, and Alice W——n is divided forever from the speaker. Such separations carry within them the implication of a further break, between present and future, as is made most explicit in Elia's comment on his brother's death: "when he died, though he had not been dead an hour, it seemed as if he had died a great while ago, such a distance there is betwixt life and death" (p. 103). The continual ticking away of life's finite moments—dramatized syntactically by the repetition of "Then" and "Here" in Elia's narration to us of his reverie[11]—is converted at death into a compression of a prolonged series into little more than an instant. An hour becomes a great while, as death mocks, by parody, man's way of trying to defeat mutability by encompassing in one moment many segments of time. Although Elia speaks at this point of the death of his brother, an event from the past, he shifts to the present tense, as we all do, when he comes to generalize: "such a distance there is betwixt life and death" (p. 103). The threat posed by this geography inhabits his future, as well as his past. Now is not the first time he has felt disturbed at the space between his own life and the condition after death, for even as a child he was frightened by the "apparition of two infants" which some saw "gliding up and down the great staircase" (p. 101). The two infants fuse with the two murdered children from the ballad, "The Children in the Wood," mentioned in the opening lines, and they step back from the invisible world to haunt the residence of the living. (This fusion is made possible in part by Lamb's alteration of the geographical basis for this essay. The house of the Plumers, which Lamb had visited during his grandmother's employment there as a housekeeper, was in Hertfordshire, not Norfolk, but by locating the mansion in Norfolk in this essay he puts it in the same county as the setting of "The Children in the Wood").[12] The apparitions go up and down a stairway, as though between two worlds, but they provide no consoling linkage of present and future because, as their "gliding" indicates, they are too unearthly. They are another ghastly parody of man's efforts to span the void between this life and the next.

Nevertheless, in Elia's childhood, three characters, including himself, achieved distinctive ways to live in a world of time. For Grandmother Field it was still possible to find in traditional conceptions of servant and master a pattern sufficient to give order to one's life. Times were changing; the wealthy owner of the house of which she had charge "preferred living in a newer and more fashionable mansion which he had purchased somewhere in the adjoining county" (p. 101). But she stayed in the old place, not only taking care of it for him, but maintaining to some extent the way of life that it represented: "still she lived in it in a manner as if it had been her own, and kept up the dignity of the great house in a sort while she lived . . ." (p. 101). Her role as loyal servant of the family was paralleled by her understanding of her relation with God. Lamb's early poem "The Grandame" introduced an explicit parallel between his grandmother's service to "her master's house" and her service to "her *heavenly master.*" "You may think," he wrote to Coleridge in June 1796, "that I have not kept enough apart the ideas of her heavenly and her earthly master but recollect I have designedly given in to her own way of feeling—and if she had a failing, 'twas that she respected her master's family too much, not reverenced her Maker too little."[13] In "Dream-Children" Elia three times calls her "good" and "religious," and he notes her devotion to the Scriptures: "she knew all the Psaltery by heart, ay, and a great part of the Testament besides" (p. 101). She flourished within the limits of the house, which took on significance for her as her "charge" before her earthly and heavenly masters. Her adherence to traditional religious conceptions made her feel in contact with the life after death. She "believed" in the "apparition of two infants," and was confident that "those innocents would do her no harm" (p. 101). Time was real in her experience: once the county's best dancer she contracted a cancer that "bowed her down with pain" (p. 101). But her religious premises enabled her to keep her spirits "still upright" (p. 101). Thus, although Grandmother Field witnessed social change and experienced physical deterioration, her pattern of life enabled her to triumph over time. Tradition was preserved, the self experienced a real rapport with the boundaries of life in the present, and the future held no terrors. When she died, however, the old house declined: it "afterwards came to decay, and was nearly pulled down, and all its old ornaments stripped and carried away to the owner's other house, where they were set up, and looked as awkward as if some one were to carry away the old tombs they had seen lately at the Abbey, and stick them up in Lady C.'s tawdry gilt drawing-room" (p. 101). The decline of the mansion symbolizes not only her death, but also the passing of the way of life which she represents. The movement of the articles to another location involves a degeneration into vulgarity, and the transition from Abbey to drawing-room suggests a change from sacred to secular. The servant-master relationship plays no part in the lives of her grandsons, either in its social or in its religious meaning.

John L. and Elia exemplify, respectively, the possibilities of action and contemplation. John liked to "mount the most mettlesome horse he could get" (p. 102) and go out riding and hunting. The mansion was fine in his estimate, but his distinctive relation to it was to override its limits: "and yet he loved the old great house and gardens too, but had too much spirit to be always pent up within their boundaries..." (p. 102). His imagination converted temporal into spatial limitation, and he fought time by centrifugal movement. Since Elia was lame-footed, his older brother would carry him on his back about the country. John was so complete a masculine figure— "brave," "handsome," and venturesome—that he was loved in a special way by Grandmother Field. Everyone admired him when he grew up. It is bitterly ironic that his later physical deterioration took the form of a painful lame foot which eventually caused his leg to be amputated. He was thereby deprived of the physical foundation for his aggressiveness, and in his later years he grew impatient at his plight. Unlike his grandmother, he had no pattern by which to endure physical decay. His approach to life made him a "king" for a while (p. 102), but its vulnerability to time was apparent to anyone who, like Elia, lived to see his "crossness" and his death.

The child Elia, forced by his bad leg into a life of relative tameness, over-comes the limitations of his existence by a contemplative achievement of identity with things outside himself. Inside the house he likes to look upon some statues of ancient men: "I in particular used to spend many hours by myself, in gazing upon the old busts of the Twelve Caesars, that had been Emperors of Rome, till the old marble heads would seem to live again, or I to be turned into marble with them" (p. 102). The differences between pres-ent and past, life and death, contemplation and action, are overcome as Elia and the statues take on the same order of reality. A similar process occurs in Elia's childhood relation with the garden. As in many Elia essays the gar-den is associated with Eden because the problems of a fallen world were transcended in childhood. The only limitations upon Elia were the occasion-al presence of another person and the prohibition on eating the fruit: "some-times in the spacious old-fashioned gardens, which I had almost to myself, unless when now and then a solitary gardening man would cross me—and how the nectarines and peaches hung upon the walls, without my ever offer-ing to pluck them, because they were forbidden fruit, unless now and then . . ." (p. 102). The two "unless" clauses relegate the limitations to subordinate status. The first suggests that the gardener was not an important problem; the second lets us know that Elia violated the taboo on the fruit with no very dire results. So far Elia's achievements in the garden have been negative, but in the subsequent lines he moves on to a more positive approach:

and because I had more pleasure in strolling about among the old melancholy-looking yew trees, or the firs, and picking up the red berries, and the fir apples, which were good for nothing but to look at—or in lying about upon the fresh grass, with all the fine garden smells around me—or basking in the orangery, till I could almost fancy myself ripening too along with the oranges and the limes in that grateful warmth—or in watching the dace that darted to and fro in the fish-pond, at the bottom of the garden, with here and there a great sulky pike hanging midway down the water in silent state, as if it mocked at their impertinent friskings,—I had more pleasure in these busy-idle diversions than in all the sweet flavours of peaches, nectarines, oranges, and such like common baits of children. (p. 102)

In a sequence of parallel gerunds, he experiences an increasingly close rela-tion with the garden. At first he is merely strolling, picking up, and looking. The style has a detachment which fits the coolness of the childhood attitude: "which were good for nothing but to look at." Then his posture changes, and a new sense is invoked: he lies in the garden and is aware of its smells. The changes reflect a decreasing detachment, an increasing intimacy with the place. "Basking" adds to "lying" more intensity and involvement. To lie upon something is to be closely juxtaposed with it, but to bask is to be acted upon by environment and to share the experience of nearby things, in this case fruits. The latter suggestion is strengthened when Elia notes that he seemed to be "ripening too along with the oranges and the limes." The last member of the syntactical parallelism seems to revert to the earlier, more detached stage: Elia is merely watching. But now for the first time the object of his contemplation becomes, as he watches it, symbolic of his own contemplative process.[14] While the dace dart to and fro, "a great sulky pike" joins Elia in both observing them and mocking their "impertinent friskings." The mockery is the contemplative mind's triumph over the stir of activists, while the contemplation includes the dace too and thereby somehow encompasses activity. Because Elia's observation includes the dace and the pike, it can be called a "busy-idle" diversion. Yet the pike fuses with Elia in a more complete way than any of the previous inhabitants of the garden. Through intense contemplation of the particulars within that garden, the child Elia overcomes the separation of subject and object, as well as that between contemplation and action, just as his contemplation of the twelve Caesars' busts overcame the divisions between past and present, between life and death.

Elia's reverie "the other evening" is his attempt in adulthood to recapture the unfallen condition of childhood. Much of it is an exercise in memory. Children are said to like "to stretch their imagination to the conception of a traditionary great-uncle, or grandame, whom they never saw" (p. 100). Similarly, Elia wants to escape from his present segment of time by stretching his memory back to the people and scenes that he once saw. The device of the imagined children, Alice and John, prompts memory to be exceptionally precise, for Elia fancies himself as telling a story to persons who were not even alive in the time that he describes. An audience of dream-children also affects Elia's style. The simplicity of the diction and the infantilism of some phrases ("a hundred times bigger than that in which they and papa lived") are a response to an imagined childish audience, and this use of language has the thematically relevant function of bringing to stylistic life some childish ways of thinking.[15] For the central aspiration of "Dream-Children," like that of "Blakesmoor in H——shire," is not merely to remember but to duplicate the contemplative potency that Elia can remember.

The two limitations in the garden of childhood were the presence of the gardener and the prohibition on plucking fruit. In place of a superfluous other person there is now a scarcity of desired persons. Instead of the taboo there is Alice's refusal of Elia's marriage proposal. He reacts by inventing imaginative mirror images of the two persons whom he misses most—his brother and his beloved. The two dream-children not only perpetuate the names of the two missing persons, but also duplicate their idiosyncrasies. Moreover, when "Alice's little right foot played an involuntary movement" (p. 101) at the moment that Elia mentions Grandmother's dancing, Grandmother herself is revealed in the little girl. The children repair what makes Elia's world seem inadequate to him, and thus come to mirror his own feelings. They want to stretch their imagination back to his past, just as he wants to stretch his memory. The look "put out" by little Alice at one point expresses disapproval of an alteration in the chimney-piece; Elia himself clearly disapproves the alteration. A few lines later John shares Elia's critical view of other modern changes: "Here John smiled, as much as to say, 'that would be foolish indeed' " (p. 101). There is an apparent exception to this pattern when the two children conspire to eat some grapes while Elia is announcing that he used to enjoy contemplating fruit more than tasting it. But Elia as a child violated the taboo "now and then," and he might have eaten the fruit more often if there had been no adult prohibition such as the one he now gently imposes upon his imaginary offspring. The climax of the dream-children's function as mirrors of other persons comes when Elia begins to talk about Alice W——n: "suddenly, turning to Alice, the soul of the first Alice looked out at her eyes with such a reality of re-presentment, that I became in doubt which of them stood there before me, or whose that bright hair was . . ." (p. 103). The two Alices, past and present, seem fused in simultaneity, but immediately the "reality" of the dream-children fades to "nothing; less than nothing, and dreams" (p. 103). They are themselves empty spaces which can do nothing to fill up the voids between moments of time and between the self and the world. The mirrors are broken.

The suddenness of this reversal causes the reader to experience for himself the shock of turning from a world of mirrors to a world of irreducibly separate beings. Yet the pressure of time has been growing through the essay in several respects. The transition from Grandmother to himself as a child involves a heightened sense of loss. This process continues when the recently dead John is introduced "in somewhat a more heightened tone" (p. 102). The mention of Alice W——n strikes even closer to home since she separated herself from Elia before allowing their relation to come to fruition. Also, Elia for the first time is in danger of having to lie to the dream-children, for he cannot admit that Alice W——n's progressive "coyness, and difficulty, and denial" (p. 103) were final. Elia is thus divided from himself, and he cannot sustain his reverie. A similar process occurs in Charles Lamb's relation to the essay. In the fictional world of Elia, the speaker's nearest male relative (modeled on Lamb's brother) is a cousin named James Elia, as in "My Relations." In the real world of Charles Lamb, the author's brother was John Lamb, who died in 1821, the year before this essay appeared in the *London Magazine.* Since "Dream-Children" pretends to represent Elia's reverie, we expect to hear of a cousin, James Elia. Instead we are told that Grandmother Field especially loved "their uncle, John L——" (p. 102), and the male dream-child, named after his uncle, is not James but John. As the essay moves from Grandmother Field and Elia's childhood to the character of "John L——" it partially breaks out of its fictional mold to introduce the personal problems of its author. Finally, when at the end Elia is divided from himself and reverie is separated from reality, the essay first makes explicit the problem surrounding the identity of the brother: "but John L. (or James Elia) was gone for ever" (p. 103). The pressure of reality has punctured the reverie and left the speaker aware of the distinction between two orders of representation, that of John Lamb and that of James Elia. The sudden recession of the dream-children near the end of this essay is the most dramatic element in an overall pattern of increasing threats to the imaginative attempt to overcome the disjunctions of a temporal world.

It is easy to conclude that Elia failed to solve his problem because he relied upon imagination rather than real participation in life. If he had married and become a father, he would not be vulnerable to the conversion of his offspring to "less than nothing, and dreams." Lamb, however, has suggested the inadequacy of this interpretation by alluding to the old ballad, "The Children in the Wood." The story was "carved out in wood upon the chimney-piece of the great hall, the whole story down to the Robin Redbreasts, till a foolish rich person pulled it down to set up a marble one of modern invention in its stead, with no story upon it" (p. 101). In the ballad the dying parents of the little boy and girl are foiled in their attempt to leave duplicates of themselves behind in the world to inherit their riches. The children die as a result of the uncle's murderous plot, and the uncle takes, but quickly loses, the inheritance. Elia fails to sustain through contemplation a world that is a projection of himself as the parents in the ballad fail to achieve through activity a similar end. The parallel failures suggest that all man's striving to gain timelessness, or to establish lasting continuity, is bound to miss its desired results. Even the artistic record of the quest is vulnerable to time, as the "foolish rich person" unwittingly demonstrates by discarding the chimney-piece on which the story was carved. In place of Steele's propagandistic celebration of the superiority of marriage over bachelorhood, Lamb portrays a human condition in which the married and the single, like the contemplative and the active, suffer the same fundamental limitations and frustrations.

In a sense, then, "Dream-Children" is a failure. Like the other essays we have considered in this chapter, it records Elia's failure to move beyond discontinuous duration despite his energetic and ingenious efforts to do so. But to record failure is to be a failure only in a specialized sense. The record may have an intelligibility, a form, which, whether or not it is remembered, lifts it out of the implacable march of mere events. In the present case, it exhibits Lamb's skepticism toward the comforting beliefs of an enviable but now obsolete cultural moment represented by his grandmother and his skeptical resistance also toward the more exalted claims made by his contemporaries for the power of the human mind. Further, the record of a failure can succeed in making a world of discontinuity itself comprehensible by locating it on a scale of hypothetical possibilities. When Elia and the reader look at reality with this scale in mind, they do not surrender to time; they evaluate time by human standards. They end by seeing how far reality falls short of paradise, but they also see that the realm of time offers genuine, though limited, satisfactions. To awake from sleep in an arm-chair "with the faithful Bridget unchanged by my side" (p. 103) is not to experience Eden, but it is to encounter a valued person who lives only in the real world. Bridget is absent from Elia's dreams.

NOTES

1. *The Collected Writings of Thomas De Quincey,* ed. David Masson (1889–90; rpt. London: A. & C. Black, 1897), V, 231–236; III, 88.
2. *The Disappearance of God* (1963; rpt. New York: Schocken, 1965), pp. 37–39. Miller's chapter on De Quincey is a major contribution to the criticism of English non-fictional prose as imaginative literature. It has been a methodological stimulus to the present work.
3. *Essays,* trans. John Florio (1603; rpt. London: Dent, 1965), III, 206. Donald M. Frame's recent translation of Montaigne's *Complete Essays* (Stanford, Calif.: Stanford Univ. Press, 1958), p. 736, substitutes "a while ago" for Florio's "anon," thus making the parallel with Lamb's "New Year's Eve" still more exact.
4. *The Yale Edition of the Works of Samuel Johnson,* III, ed. W. J. Bate and A. B. Strauss (New Haven: Yale Univ. Press, 1969), pp. 221–226.

All my citations to Johnson's essays are to this edition, and hence-forth essay numbers will be given in the text.

5. Lamb, *Letters*, I, 240 (MS. Tx.); *The Poetical Works of William Wordsworth*, ed. E. de Selincourt, II, 2nd ed. (Oxford: Clarendon Press, 1952), pp. 259–263, 30; *The Prelude*, ed. E. de Selincourt, 2nd ed. rev. by Helen Darbishire (Oxford: Clarendon Press, 1959), pp. 43–45. Writing to Manning, Lamb copied the whole of "She Dwelt Among the Untrodden Ways" and called it "choice and genuine" (*Letters*, I, 247) (MS. F.).

6. Poulet, "Timelessness and Romanticism," *JHI*, 15 (1954), 3–22, 7, 4; Abrams, p. 385.

7. For *The Spectator* I have relied upon Donald F. Bond's edition, 5 vols. (Oxford: Clarendon Press, 1965), further citations to which will omit footnotes but include issue numbers in the text.

8. *Collected Works of Oliver Goldsmith*, ed. Arthur Friedman (Oxford: Clarendon Press, 1966), II, Letters LIV, LV, LXXI, XCIX, CV, CXXIII. Future references to this edition will be confined to letter numbers in the text.

9. Cf. Mulcahy, especially pp. 524–528. Mulcahy sees the imaginative rebuilding of the house as foreshadowing man's resurrection after death. But because he does not distinguish the three stages of the child Elia's response to the place, he makes the reconstitution of the past, and the solution to the problem of mortality, more complete than I believe is warranted.

10. The other chief example is *The Tatler*, No. 181. Lamb's unpublished review of Hazlitt's *Table-Talk* refers to "the better (because the more pathetic) parts of the Tatler" (MS. Br., p. 8).

11. Cf. Weber, p. 76.

12. On Blakesware, the house where Mrs. Field lived and worked, see E. V. Lucas, *The Life of Charles Lamb*, I, 24–45, and Reginald L. Hine, *Charles Lamb and his Hertfordshire* (London: Dent, 1949).

13. *Works*, V, 5–6; *Letters*, I, 27.

14. Cf. W. K. Wimsatt, Jr., "The Structure of Romantic Nature Imagery," *The Verbal Icon* (1954; rpt. New York: Noonday, 1958), pp. 103–116.

15. Weber, p. 75.

Chapter Three

THE SHAPE OF TIME

Unable to escape from time, Lamb seeks to discover its meaning. In this effort he tries to transcend the otherness of temporality, its separation from mind or pattern, rather than to transcend temporality itself. He starts with two severe limitations—a diffidence about exploring large stretches of history and a habit of viewing change as discontinuous. Because he can give assent only to what he has tested in his own experience, he stresses that segment of history that he and his contemporaries can remember. Sometimes his concern with change is limited to what an individual was by comparison to what he is. Sometimes he deals with how newspapers or comic drama or a piece of architecture have fared from the time of Elia's childhood or a little earlier. Occasionally—as in "The Old and the New Schoolmaster"—he views his own age in relation to a more distant period with which, by long reading, he has become familiar. Because his perception of change includes a strong sense of discontinuity, he neglects to dwell on the linkage of event with event by which one stage in an individual's or a society's history is replaced by the next. We will not find him illuminating on the causes of individual or social change. Instead, he sets side by side different stages of time, and often without entering upon the problem of how the first evolved into the second, he will try to discover, by comparing and contrasting the two stages, whether time has a meaningful shape.

He is keeping up the familiar essay genre's preoccupation with mirroring process—a preoccupation already conspicuous in the opening sentences of Montaigne's "Of Repenting," with its announcement, "I describe not the essence, but the passage,"[1] and continued through Bacon's "Of Innovations" and preference, even in style, for whatever will promote growth, Addison's and Steele's acclaim for the increasing power of merchants, and such tough-minded meditations on temporality from Johnson's *Rambler* as Nos. 2 and 17. Among the major essays that predate Lamb's, probably the nearest to the Elia essays in this respect are the skeptical passages on the theory of progress—not to be confused with the passages that support the dogmatism of ancient superiority—in Sir William Temple's "An Essay upon the Ancient and Modern Learning," to which Elia refers with approval in "The Genteel Style in Writing" (pp. 201-202).

Lamb's way of carrying on such an enterprise reveals that he is a part, though a skeptical part, of Romantic culture. Two conceptual models, the fall and progress, dominate his ruminations, and his sense of discontinuity is apparent in their relation with each other. Nineteenth-century English writers as various as Blake and Tennyson envisioned the two models as complementary: the past was idyllic, the present is difficult, and the future holds unbounded possibilities. We "fall" from the first to the second stage but advance from the second to the third, and we come to recognize that the fall was fortunate since what will be is better than what was. The spiral journey, beginning as a painful fall into division and ending in a return to the lost paradise of unity while also including a more highly developed consciousness, is one of the principal themes of M. H. Abrams's *Natural Supernaturalism,* which demonstrates its presence in the major English Romantic poets and the German philosophers of approximately the same period. Only once, however, do the Elia essays link the two models chronologically, and in this instance ("The Superannuated Man") the idea of the fall enters merely through a passing reference to "the abundant play-time" (p. 193) which Elia abandoned at fourteen for a job in a counting-house. "A Dissertation upon Roast Pig" entertains both theories in one essay, but not as successive steps in the unfolding of time. Elia usually treats the two conceptions as alternatives, separately, rather than as segments in a single continuum. His characteristic approach is to meditate upon the shape of time by using a relatively simple model as a point of departure, and then by introducing complications which bridge the gap between the austerity of his schema and the density of life. In short, he is not a philosopher of history, but he is an artist who portrays the process of seeking a pattern in the historical dimension of human life.

The model most readily available to Lamb was the fall from paradise.[2] It dominates his first works, especially *Rosamund Gray* and the early poems, where completed falls are evident, as tainted adulthood looks back nostalgically upon lost innocence, vanished ideal maidens, and departed familiar faces. Sometimes in his later writings the idea of the fall is alluded to in a non-serious context, as in "On the Melancholy of Tailors," where Lamb's mouthpiece, "Burton, Junior," announces a new explanation for the solemnity of tailors: "And first, may it not be, that the custom of wearing apparel being derived to us from the fall, and one of the most mortifying products of that unhappy event, a certain *seriousness* (to say no more of it) may in the order of things have been intended to be impressed upon the minds of that race of men to whom in all ages the care of contriving the human apparel has been entrusted . . . ." In one of Lamb's non-Elian essays published during the Elian period, "Suspensurus" writes to the editor of the *London Magazine* confessing a fear that he will steal money from the banking house in which he works. Such a crime would merely complete a fall initiated in his childhood when he violated an adult prohibition by plucking a peach from a nobleman's garden. His villainy then was halted before he finished the act by eating the fruit:

Some few rain drops just then fell; the sky (from a bright day) became overcast; and I was a type of our first parents, after the eating of that fatal fruit. I felt myself naked and ashamed; stripped of my virtue, spiritless. The downy fruit, whose sight rather than savour had tempted me, dropt from my hand, never to be tasted. All the commentators in the world cannot persuade me but that the Hebrew word in the second chapter of Genesis, translated apple, should be rendered peach. Only this way can I reconcile that mysterious story.[3]

Although the speaker's exegetical proposal is fatuous, it reveals that the story of the fall becomes meaningful to him only insofar as it corresponds with a pattern in his own life. The myth of the fall organizes his perception of his present weakness. Whether or not it is true as the history of Adam and Eve, it is validated by its relevance to his own personal history. "The Last Peach" is typical of Lamb's meditations in its method of seeking the shape of history not through recording the activities of mankind from the birth of the species, but through examining a limited segment of time, often within an individual life, for a typological pattern. The bizarre aspect of the essay, however, introduces a qualifying irony: the model of the fall accounts for the experience of "Suspensurus," but he seems a ludicrous figure, too obsessed and therefore too narrow to provide a sufficiently inclusive image of life.

Two of the Elian essays already considered contain overt references to the Biblical account of the fall. In "Blakesmoor in H——shire" the child Elia has no wish to roam outside of "the boundaries of my Eden" (p. 155), but as an adult he wonders what sin of his separated him from that paradise: "Was it for this, that I kissed my childish hands too fervently in your idol worship, walks and windings of BLAKESMOOR! for this, or what sin of mine, has the plough passed over your pleasant places?" (p. 157). The first question can be answered only negatively, for the fervor with which the child Elia involved himself in Blakesmoor is presented not as sin but as the life-giving source of whatever memories remain. In "Dream-Children," also, the scene of childhood is associated with Eden: it is a garden, where the young Elia may wander freely on condition that he abstain from snatching the fruit. The adult Elia finds himself somewhere outside of paradise in both essays, and he would like to get back his earlier powers to transcend the limitations of time. The superiority of the childhood state is not unequivocal, however, for the adult Elia has grown in his awareness of what it means to live in time.

Several other Elian essays introduce more explicit qualifications of the paradigm of the fall without entirely abandoning that basic framework. Recalling the buildings and gardens of Elia's childhood, "The Old Benchers of the Inner Temple" comments upon a now "almost effaced" sundial: "It was the primitive clock, the horologe of the first world. Adam could scarce have missed it in Paradise" (p. 83). Richard Haven, in his perceptive essay, "The Romantic Art of Charles Lamb," has noted the relation between the sundial and Elia's childhood: "Like the 'first world,' the Garden of Eden, to which the sun dial, the 'primitive clock,' seems to belong, the world of childhood is a world of magic and a world of myth, a world filled with objects that mean more than their mere physical appearance."[4] The old benchers themselves were seen by Elia as "the mythology of the Temple" (p. 90). Haven continues:

From Coventry, "whose person was quadrate, his step massy . . . his gait . . . indivertible from his way as a moving column," and in whom there is something of both the sun dial and the statue, to Loval [sic], that man "of an incorrigible and losing honesty," and to the more briefly mentioned Mingay whose iron hand Lamb "reconciled to my ideas as an emblem of power— somewhat like the horns of Michael Angelo's Moses," these are in their dramatic setting not items of history but figures of enchantment.

Elia finds satisfaction in his present life by trying to recapture his past through memory. The attempt is not wholly successful because "reason" comes in now "to tear away the preternatural mist" (p. 90) that surrounded the old benchers in his childhood. Yet, though memory reduces or diminishes the imaginings of childhood, it also, at least in part, reduces or leads back the vitality of the past: "While childhood, and while dreams, reducing childhood, shall be left, imagination shall not have spread her holy wings totally to fly the earth" (p. 90). But the notion of a fall is not adequate to describe the passage between childhood and adulthood, as Elia makes clear in a postscript.[5] The unimaginative R. N. has let Elia know that the latter's childhood understanding of Samuel Salt's character is erroneous, and Elia is forced to make a concession to adulthood: "I have done injustice to the soft shade of Samuel Salt. See what it is to trust to imperfect memory, and the erring notices of childhood!" (p. 90). Moreover, even the earlier part of the essay contains a suggestion that reason's action in tearing away "the preternatural mist" is hardly ruinous. Most of the character sketches of the old benchers are written in a more level-headed style than the passages which Haven quotes. For instance, when we are told that Samuel Salt's knowledge of the law was overrated and that Coventry was rather miserly, we are indebted to Elia's reason, rather than to his mythologizing, for vivid analysis of character. We are not at all sure that we would prefer the "inexplicable, half-understood appearances" (p. 90) that Elia's childhood perception could provide. The passage from awe-struck imagination to detached reason is not merely a fall.

A more surprising aspect of this essay's treatment of the fall is the prominence of sexual overtones. Folded in the maternal security of the Inner Temple, with its enclosing walls and its familiar scenes, Elia felt that everything ministered to his own needs, just as the great Thames seemed "but a stream that watered our pleasant places" (p. 82). He was perfectly at home amidst the vitality of those fountains and gardens, and his precociousness surpassed the expectations of his contemporaries: "What a collegiate aspect has that fine Elizabethan hall, where the fountain plays, which I have made to rise and fall, how many times! to the astoundment of the young urchins, my contemporaries, who, not being able to guess at its recondite machinery, were almost tempted to hail the wondrous work as magic!" (p. 83). Elia's childhood, spent in the vicinity of the "place of my kindly engendure" (p. 83), is associated with an entirely fulfilling, guilt-free sexuality, much like that of some statues which have since been destroyed: "Four little winged marble boys used to play their virgin fancies, spouting out ever fresh streams from their innocent-wanton lips, in the square of Lincoln's-inn, when I was no bigger than they were figured" (p. 84). Maturity has failed to bring an increase in fulfillment. Instead the fountains of the metropolis are now mostly "dried up, or bricked over" (p. 84). In the wasteland of adulthood, as presented in the body of this essay, there are no satisfactory man-woman relationships. Thomas Coventry is a miser who has the odd habit of standing by the window in his "gloomy house opposite the pump in Serjeant's-inn, Fleet Street ... to watch, as he said, 'the maids drawing water all day long' " (p. 87). There is ambiguity in Elia's choice of a verb when he asks, "But what insolent familiar durst have mated Thomas Coventry?" (p. 85). Samuel Salt refused to respond to Susan P.'s forty years of "hopeless passion" (p. 86), and the other benchers are usually described in terms that suggest the negation of life. Peter Pierson's "cheeks were colourless, even to whiteness" (p. 88). During his year as treasurer, Daines Barrington was responsible for the following expenditure, which was later "unanimously disallowed by the bench": " 'Item, disbursed Mr. Allen, the gardener, twenty shillings, for stuff to poison the sparrows, by my orders' " (p. 89). Old Barton was "a jolly negation" (p. 89). Twopenny was less than well filled out, but "If T. was thin, Wharry was attenuated and fleeting" (p. 89). Yet the child Elia saw all these men as figures of power, just as he saw Mingay:

I had almost forgotten Mingay with the iron hand—but he was somewhat later. He had lost his right hand by some accident, and supplied it with a grappling hook, which he wielded with a tolerable adroitness. I detected the substitute, before I was old enough to reason whether it were artificial or not. I remember the astonishment it raised in me. He was a blustering, loud-talking person; and I reconciled the phenomenon to my ideas as an emblem of power .... (pp. 89–90)

The adult Elia can detect behind the facade of each of these benchers enough to "make ye so sorry a figure in my relation" (p. 90). The artificial limb was for the child an emblem of power; it is made for us into an emblem of the artificial, even the unnatural, supplanting what is most alive.

Perhaps the most interesting character sketch in the essay is that of Samuel Salt's servant, Lovel, who is based upon Lamb's father.[6] The sketch closes with this passage:

At intervals, too, he would speak of his former life, and how he came up a little boy from Lincoln to go to service, and how his mother cried at parting with him, and how he returned, after some few years' absence, in his smart new livery to see her, and she blessed herself at the change, and could hardly be brought to believe that it was 'her own bairn.' And then, the excitement subsiding, he would weep, till I have wished that sad second-childhood might have a mother still to lay its head upon her lap. But the common mother of us all in no long time after received him gently into hers. (p. 88)

At this point the essay's fictional status begins to break down, as it did in the references to John L. in "Dream-Children." Although Elia's father is alluded to directly in "Poor Relations," the only indication within the Elia essays that Lovel is identical with him is the rather general circumstance of their common origin in Lincoln. On the level of fictional reality, Elia seems to have no relation to Lovel. Yet the warmth of "I knew this Lovel" (p. 87) and much of the subsequent portrait suggests that Lamb's fiction is not an entirely adequate objective correlative for the importance of this portrait. In this instance, Lamb introduces a reference not to Elia's father, but to his own. The striking omission from the sketch of Lovel is any mention of his wife, Lamb's mother. Instead, Lovel's most important relationship in the character sketch is with *his* mother. Lamb is projecting upon his main competitor his own tendency to find his most satisfying relationship in the maternal past. The result is to echo Elia's own attitudes and to prevent any explicit competition between Lovel and Elia from emerging in the essay.

The postscript, however, disrupts the consistency with which the sexual aspects of life are portrayed as declining with the coming of adulthood. Elia learns that Samuel Salt was once married and that his wife died in childbirth. Salt's later rejection of Susan P. is not, as Elia and we suspected, the result of a refusal to become involved in a mature relationship. It is, rather, the consequence of his devotion to his deceased wife. The closing lines, addressed to the "New Benchers of the Inner Temple," reverse the life-negating emphasis of much of the essay. The poisoned sparrows are symbolically resuscitated, an infant's presence crowns the renewal of mature sexuality, and the benchers enjoy the sight of a pretty nursery maid. Lamb echoes his previous phraseology in "reductive of juvenescent emotion" (p. 91). Now the vitality of the present is a sufficient restorative; it is no longer necessary to resort to one's own childhood and dreams "reducing childhood" to make contact with the sources of life. The importance of childhood is retained, but the stress now is upon adulthood's power to introduce "younkers of this generation" so that the interaction of old and young may continue into the future, as it has existed in the past. (When Lamb crossed out "that lived before ye!" in his manuscript and substituted "that solemnized the Parade before ye!" as the essay's last clause, he removed an emphasis upon the vitality of the Old Worthies of the past that would have blurred the postscript's concentration upon the vitality of the present.)[7] The postscript as it stands not only declares that mature reason compares favorably with youthful imagination; it also criticizes the paradigm of the fall by revealing that the adult present is as full of vigor as the childish past.

"The Old Benchers of the Inner Temple" is the expression of a divided mind. In the body of the essay, except for a few undertones, Lamb portrays life as a fall and memory as a cushion. In the postscript he attempts to correct an imbalance which he would not have perceived if he were wholly committed to the belief that things keep getting worse. Lamb's ambivalence during the Elian period is made particularly apparent if we compare two essays describing his first attendance at a play. The earlier version appeared anonymously in Leigh Hunt's *Examiner,* December 19, 1813. Lucas first collected it with Lamb's writings and entitled it "Play-house Memoranda." Like the Elian "My First Play" it deals with a performance of *Artaxerxes,* and it uses some of the same wording, as the following passage indicates:

It was all enchantment and a dream. No such pleasure has since visited me but in dreams. I was in Persia for the time, and the burning idol of their devotion in the Temple almost converted me into a worshipper. I was awestruck, and believed those significations to be something more than elemental fires.[8]

In this version the preference for an unsophisticated response, such as childhood provided, is almost unequivocal. The passage on *Artaxerxes* is one of three sections which espouse similar values. We are told that a blind man wept at a scene in *Richard III,* while those who could see the inappropriate appearance of some of the performers, as well as the sightless listener's intensity, merely watched and tittered. The blind man's vantage point is associated with freedom from sophistication: "Having no drawback of sight to impair his sensibilities, he simply attended to the scene, and received its unsophisticated impression." Lamb contrasts those who criticize and those who simply admire, entirely to the advantage of the latter: "Still now and then, a *genuine spectator* is to be found among them, a shopkeeper and his family, whose honest titillations of mirth, and generous chucklings of applause, cannot wait or be at leisure to take the cue from the sour judging faces about them." The only qualification of the essay's predominant anti-intellectualism is a mocking section concerning some rustics who mistook an obscure actor for a famous one of the same name. But here the main criticism is directed against their inattention to the play, rather than against their lack of critical power. On the whole, the essay expresses an attitude of clear affirmation: "We crush the faculty of delight and wonder in children, by explaining every thing." The essay omits all suggestion that adulthood or the development of reason brings anything of value.

In "My First Play" the equation between growing up and falling down is preserved as a motif. The essay opens with an emblematic architectural change. A portal that used to lead to the Old Drury of Garrick now marks the entrance to a printer's office: it has been "reduced to humble use" (p. 97). The deterioration in the imaginative interest of the portal's function is mirrored in the change that overtakes Elia's response to theater. He repeats almost exactly the above-quoted passage on *Artaxerxes,* even to the following declaration: "No such pleasure has since visited me but in dreams" (p. 99). So immersed was he in the play that he viewed it not as a play and the actors not as actors, but he thought he witnessed history as it was being made. Some other plays seen soon after aroused a similar intensity of response. When Elia returned to the theater as an adolescent, however, he discovered that he had changed. Never again would he experience the breathless anticipation, the religious awe, and the total immersion that characterized his childhood response to the theater.

In "My First Play," however, Lamb does not allow the contrast between childhood and adulthood to remain entirely in the former's favor. In the 1813 version he had recalled only *Artaxerxes* from his early play-going, but in the Elian version several comedies and pantomimes are remembered also. In watching these, Elia as a child failed to notice anything funny. The following passage is typical of his recollection of how insensitive he once was to comedy:

My third play followed in quick succession. It was the Way of the World. I think I must have sat at it as grave as a judge; for, I remember, the hysteric affectations of good Lady Wishfort affected me like some solemn tragic passion. Robinson Crusoe followed: in which Crusoe, man Friday, and the parrot, were as good and authentic as in the story.—The clownery and pantaloonery of these pantomimes have clean passed out of my head. I believe, I no more laughed at them, than at the same age I should have been disposed to laugh at the grotesque Gothic heads (seeming to me then replete with devout meaning) that gape, and grin, in stone around the inside of the old Round Church (my church) of the Templars. (p. 99)

The verve of such phrases as "clownery and pantaloonery" and "gape, and grin" suggests that the comic perception of adulthood is pleasurable and vital. It bites into chunks of life from which awe withdrew. On the other hand, the inability of the adult Elia to see more than comedy in Gothic sculpture suggests that, even in this passage, the child has some genuine powers of perception which the adult lacks.

Elia's appreciation of acting, like his appreciation of comedy, increased with the passing of childhood. When he first watched plays, "I knew not players" (p. 99)—not only in the sense of not knowing the names of players but also in the deeper sense of not fully realizing that he was looking at an actor playing a role. Therefore, it is fitting that the first mention in the essay of a particular performer occurs at the end, when Elia is describing his present way of responding to a play. He can distinguish between mediocre and great acting only after he has learned to see and accept "men and women painted" (p. 100). He concedes that after his adolescent disillusionment he had to get rid of "some unreasonable expectations, which might have interfered with the genuine emotions with which I was soon after enabled to enter upon the first appearance to me of Mrs. Siddons in Isabella" (p. 100). The movement from childhood to adulthood causes not a loss of imagination, but a replacement of one kind of imagination by another. Hence, even after discovering that the actors wear paint and the stage is full of props, Elia avoids hastening away to his ledgers or his folios. He finds in the theater the comedy and "genuine emotions" which his newly developed faculties enable him to appreciate: "Comparison and retrospection soon yielded to the present attraction of the scene; and the theatre became to me, upon a new stock, the most delightful of recreations" (p. 100). "My First Play" contrasts sharply with the earlier version by balancing the motif of the fall with an affirmation of the value of growing up.

Any man of the early nineteenth century had an obvious alternative to conceiving history as a fall: man's involvement in time could be understood as a growth from the less valuable to the more valuable. Perhaps history was the story of man's progress, and perhaps the individual's history repeats that process on a smaller scale. Lamb's stand on this possibility is as ambiguous as his speculations on history as a fall. But the idea of progress, like the idea of the fall, became an important structural element in several of the Elian essays. Two related conceptions of progress enter prominently into Lamb's ruminations. On one hand, history may be considered as man's emergence from barbarity into civilization. Progress, in this view, consists in the achievement of stable forms, the erection of firm boundaries to keep out the disagreeable. On the other hand, history may be a movement from mental and social rigidities to a greater openness. Progress, from this perspective, would be the process by which restrictive forms are exchanged for liberating ones. Lamb wrote several essays which examine history in relation to one or the other of these patterns.

A relatively simple critique of the first conception of progress is "Modern Gallantry," which displays the stridency to which Lamb sometimes succumbed when he adopted a righteous stance. The essay opens with a reminder that refinement of manners is often regarded as an instance of modernity's supremacy to the past. Out of coarseness and surliness man has progressed to gallantry, which subdues his rudeness and organizes his responses within bounds of propriety: "In comparing modern with ancient manners, we are pleased to compliment ourselves upon the point of gallantry; a certain obsequiousness, or deferential respect, which we are supposed to pay to females, as females" (p. 79). While not denying that English society is often brightened by the gloss of politeness, Lamb argues that this high polish is obtained by being applied only to the choicest specimens. He objects not to the banishment of rudeness from the circle of the civilized, but to the exclusion of the unfortunate from the civilities of the gallant. Many women, he observes, are still treated contemptuously. Female criminals are whipped publicly and sometimes hanged; actresses get hissed; and the homely, poor and aged learn that their femininity is no refuge from abuse. When he concludes that modern gallantry seems to be no more than "a conventional fiction" or "a pageant" (p. 80), he implies that such a form has been achieved by a withdrawal from the most intractable materials. It is not enough to establish order; in Lamb's view, a civilized form would result from a process of inclusion and transformation. Courtesy would be extended to all women simply because they are women, and even the most mundane relationships between the sexes would be permeated by the power of gallantry. Because society has not yet achieved such manners, modern gallantry is no proof of progress.

Although progress in this area is not yet a fact, the case of one of the directors of the South-Sea Company suggests that it is a possibility. Joseph Paice had once been like most men in being civil to some women and not to others. One day Susan Winstanley, the young lady whom he was courting, reprimanded him for his rudeness to a girl who had failed to deliver his cravats on time. She concluded that if chance had made her a milliner, she would have received similar abuse from Paice. Hence she gave him an ultimatum: "and I was determined not to accept any fine speeches, to the compromise of that sex, the belonging to which was after all my strongest claim and title to them" (p. 81). Although she died before she and Paice could be married, her rebuke changed his life, and afterwards he was a model of true gallantry. Lamb is not so blinded by his feminism as to overlook women's share of responsibility for the contemporary situation: "I wish the whole female world would entertain the same notion of these things that Miss Winstanley showed. Then we should see something of the spirit of consistent gallantry ..." (p. 82). The power to change society must come largely from the most privileged elements, those who profit by the system of exclusion. Once such persons are enlisted in the cause of civilization, it is possible to effect a progress to a system of inclusive forms. Joseph Paice and especially Susan Winstanley exemplify the possibility of improvement and point the way toward the revitalization of the social order. (Joseph Paice's lifelong bachelorhood suggests a further explanation for his gallantry: the fervor which finds no release in marriage is channeled into elaborate civility toward women. Lamb's parallel situation perhaps contributed toward his stress upon reverence for women not as persons, but as something finer, as women.)

In "Modern Gallantry" the individual's unqualified growth becomes an ideal which society may perhaps some day attain. Lamb did not often take so unequivocal a stand on the possibilities of progress. More characteristic of his mental habits and much more complex is an essay which considers a different aspect of civilization, the extent to which forms have been evolved to control the superstitious fears of the citizens. "Witches, and Other Night-Fears" addresses an audience that has learned to abolish superstition, or so it believes. The opening paragraph assumes that "we" enlightened moderns pride ourselves upon our consistent rationalism and our superiority to the witch hunters of the benighted past. Elia begins his argument by questioning this claim to superiority: "We are too hasty when we set down our ancestors in the gross for fools, for the monstrous inconsistencies (as they seem to us) involved in their creed of witchcraft" (p. 65). This is not to say that Elia is ready to endorse witch-hunting. But he suggests that his ancestors cannot reasonably be criticized for thinking that anything is possible from an evil spirit: "when once the invisible world was supposed to be opened, and the lawless agency of bad spirits assumed, what measures of probability, of decency, of fitness, or proportion—of that which distinguishes the likely from the palpable absurd—could they have to guide them in the rejection or admission of any particular testimony?" (p. 65). No allegation—even, for instance, that devils would pass by "the flower and pomp of the earth" in order to "lay preposterous siege to the weak fantasy of indigent eld" (p. 65) —can be dismissed as unlikely, once the reality of an invisible world and its contact with our world are admitted. But if the invisible world is so chaotic, at least by our standards, how can civilization bring it under control?

Our ancestors tried the procedures of the civil courts. If they spotted a witch, they prosecuted her. Elia's criticism of the days of witch-hunting is directed not against the credulity of his forebears, but against their confidence: "Amidst the universal belief that these wretches were in league with the author of all evil, holding hell tributary to their muttering, no simple Justice of the Peace seems to have scrupled issuing, or silly Headborough serving, a warrant upon them—as if they should subpoena Satan!" (p. 65). Likewise, Spenser arranges matters so that the Fiend can tear up Guyon only if he lapses from virtue: "What stops the Fiend in Spenser from tearing Guyon to pieces—or who had made it a condition of his prey, that Guyon must take assay of the glorious bait—we have no guess. We do not know the laws of that country" (pp. 65–66). In both instances, the inhabitants of the invisible world are physically constrained by the artifices of men. The disproportion between the laws and the culprits reduces this method of civilization to absurdity.

A subtler method was employed in Elia's childhood. If a person's contact with the invisible world were limited to a carefully organized system of religious belief, the unfortunate intrusions of evil spirits might be eliminated. Instead of trying to lock up devils, Stackhouse's history of the Bible attempted to direct the imaginations of men. Elia considers its effectiveness in the next section of the essay. The book "consisted of Old Testament stories, orderly set down, with the *objection* appended to each story, and the *solution* of the objection regularly tacked to that" (p. 66). The neatness of this arrangement was contrived to exclude the possibility of unorthodox meditations on the part of the reader: "To doubts so put, and so quashed, there seemed to be an end for ever" (p. 66). But the system failed to work for Elia; instead the book almost made him an infidel: "The habit of expecting objections to every passage, set me upon starting more objections, for the glory of finding a solution of my own for them. I became staggered and perplexed, a sceptic in long coats" (p. 66). Just as men in earlier ages underestimated the strangeness of evil spirits, Stackhouse operated on the basis of a ludicrously oversimplified psychology. His illustrations, because they could be carried more easily in memory than his analyses, had more serious effects. Even after Elia was deprived of the book, he was haunted days and especially nights by one of the pictures: "Be old Stackhouse then acquitted in part, if I say, that to his picture of the Witch raising up Samuel —(O that old man covered with a mantle!) I owe—not my midnight terrors, the hell of my infancy—but the shape and manner of their visitation" (p. 67). Stackhouse's book is representative of all attempts to bring irrational fears under control by a precisely stated system of beliefs and a literal rendering of visual symbols. Such a method, despite its relative sophistication, shares with the subpoenas of our ancestors an unrealistic confidence that the creatures of the invisible world, once admitted into our imaginations, may be subjected to rational control.

A third possible method for dealing with superstitious terrors is to prevent such matters from even entering our minds. If all contact with devils and other denizens of the realm of invisibility is excluded, superstition will give way to enlightenment. This distinctively modern strategy had already been employed in the raising of T. H. (based upon Leigh Hunt's son, Thornton). Did the method work?

Dear little T. H. who of all children has been brought up with the most scrupulous exclusion of every taint of superstition—who was never allowed to hear of goblin or apparition, or scarcely to be told of bad men, or to read or hear of any distressing story—finds all this world of fear, from which he has been so rigidly excluded *ab extra,* in his own "thick-coming fancies;" and from his little midnight pillow, this nurse-child of optimism will start at shapes, unborrowed of tradition, in sweats to which the reveries of the cell-damned murderer are tranquillity. (p. 68)

Modernity's failure to preserve T. H. from such terrors exposes both the inadequacy of a civilization based upon exclusion and the illusoriness of progress. Society as a whole is still unable to subdue superstition with the forms of civilization.

The reason for this failure, according to Lamb, is that T. H., like all men, carries within himself the seeds of unreasonable fear. Stories and pictures provide a set of appearances which the mind associates with the terrors, but the origin of the problem is deeper than the world of sense perceptions: "Gorgons, and Hydras, and Chimaeras—dire stories of Celaeno and the Harpies —may reproduce themselves in the brain of superstition—but they were there before. They are transcripts, types—the archetypes are in us, and eternal" (p. 68). Not only does such fear not arise from sense perception; it is also not derived from the possibility of bodily injury. Thus it seems to have a spiritual source, which the orthodox might identify with moral guilt. But this identification is refuted by the tendency of the fears to occur especially in childhood. Neither the materialist nor the Christian explanation suffices: "That the kind of fear here treated of is purely spiritual—that it is strong in proportion as it is objectless upon earth—that it predominates in the period of sinless infancy—are difficulties, the solution of which might afford some probable insight into our antemundane condition, and a peep at least into the shadow-land of pre-existence" (p. 68). In searching for a hypothesis which will account for the difficulties that conventional systems cannot solve, Lamb moves beyond the theory of innate ideas to the theory that the "archetypes" are copies of external realities already experienced in an earlier existence. This conception—a dark variant of the realm of pre-existence intimated by Wordsworth—implies the impossibility of any effective action by society to prevent contact with the invisible world. (The passage is suggestive, also, in relation to Lamb's views on the discontinuity of duration. The unrest of childhood hints that the invisible world is disturbing, and this implication reinforces man's fears of reentering that country after death.)

Since society, by its very nature, is powerless to subjugate demons and to regiment the imaginations of men, we seem to be led to the conclusion that here at least is one area where progress not only has not happened, but cannot happen. Yet Lamb includes in his essay a second movement in which man grows in his power to reduce superstition to manageable proportions. The first suggestion of this potentiality occurs in Elia's narration of how he was saved as a child from Stackhouse's book. It is significant that he is rescued from "such unfit sustenance" (pp. 66–67) only by his own clumsiness in driving his fingers through a picture of an elephant and camel on Noah's ark. The book was promptly put out of his reach. The nature of the incident and the physicality of Elia's description indicate that the heavy prosaic side of his character has saved him. This comic deliverance foreshadows Elia's salvation from night fears later in the essay. After making the comments, quoted above, on the "shadow-land of pre-existence," Elia suddenly steps forward with a *fait accompli:* "My night-fancies have long ceased to be afflictive" (p. 68). He has developed a comic detachment that arms him against the worst that the invisible world can send: "Fiendish faces, with the extinguished taper, will come and look at me; but I know them for mockeries, even while I cannot elude their presence, and I fight and grapple with them" (pp. 68–69). In adulthood his dreams are filled with symbols of civilization, especially cities, with "their churches, palaces, squares, market-places, shops, suburbs, ruins" (p. 69). By progressing from child to adult Elia has achieved what societies cannot accomplish—he has tamed the demons. His accomplishment, however, is not only an increment in strength; it is also a loss of imagination. He now claims that the evil spirits are only "mockeries" (p. 69), but only a few lines earlier he had suggested that the horrifying "archetypes" in all of us correspond to the realities which we encountered before birth. Has the adult bought peace at the price of imperceptiveness? In the finely expressive sentence quoted earlier, Lamb embodies both the positive and negative aspects of Elia's adult dreams:

Methought I was upon the ocean billows at some sea nuptials, riding and mounted high, with the customary train sounding their conchs before me, (I myself, you may be sure, the *leading god,*) and jollily we went careering

over the main, till just where Ino Leucothea should have greeted
it was Ino) with a white embrace, the billows gradually subsidin
a sea-roughness to a sea-calm, and thence to a river-motion, and that i.
(as happens in the familiarization of dreams) was no other than the gentle
Thames, which landed me, in the wafture of a placid wave or two, alone,
safe and inglorious, somewhere at the foot of Lambeth palace. (p. 69)

Elia is both ridiculous and good-natured, weak and endowed with humor.
Without plan and without effort he reaches civilization, much as he stumbled
into a deliverance from his childhood anxieties. Since he thus solves, at least
for himself, the problem recurrent in this essay, of subduing superstitious
fears, his achievement has positive value. But the possibility is raised—though
also mocked—that overcoming the gross security of adulthood in order to
look upon the invisible world would be a more profound achievement. It is,
after all, what Wordsworth and Coleridge do, and their poetry is quoted and
alluded to several times in this essay. Elia's prosaic dreams condemn him to
prose, but in prose he embodies the possibility of progress more completely
than the laws of parliament or the latest educational theories. Yet even his
progress is not unequivocal.

In neither "Modern Gallantry" nor "Witches, and Other Night-Fears" has
society achieved what impresses Lamb as genuine progress. Individuals seem
to do better, but perhaps not much better. Joseph Paice is a paragon because
he is an exception. Elia is just an ordinary fellow, and he achieves something,
but one can never be sure that he would not have been more significant if he
had moved in a contrary direction. In short, the application to individual
and social history of the concept of a progress from the unformed to the
formed yields no satisfactory proof that time has a coherent shape. Perhaps
the alternative theory—that history is a progress from repressive to liberating
forms—will prove more rewarding. Lamb considers this possibility in relation
to the individual in "The Superannuated Man" and in relation to society in
"A Dissertation upon Roast Pig," thus taking part, like the Romantic poets,
in a transference of categories linked with the French Revolution to other,
less overtly political, contexts.[9]

Elia progresses in "The Superannuated Man" from taskwork to retirement,
but the upward movement of this transition may seem to be canceled by the
imminence of death. The objection is anticipated in the essay; the threat of
death is often mentioned. Elia wishes that his benevolent employers might
continue perpetually, as though mutability may pose them problems (p. 195).
In the final sentence a day-night image is invoked, with its hint of inevitable
darkness: "I have worked task work, and have the rest of the day to myself"

(p. 199). Most explicit is the statement which Elia, after speaking of his years to come, puts into the mouth of the reader: " 'Years,' you will say! 'what is this superannuated simpleton calculating upon? He has already told us, he is past fifty' " (p. 196). Elia's clever reply is that a man's time is that which he has to himself. Retirement gives him three years at least in every three hundred sixty-five days since he now has triple the time to himself that he had formerly. One may admire Elia's mental gymnastics, but one is tempted to find his answer disappointingly trivial. Does the essay as a whole provide a framework within which Elia's reply may take on greater resonance?

The essay is on one level a burst of enthusiasm upon Elia's having been let loose. Lamb organizes the basic autobiographical data, however, with two systems of analogy, one of which is the transition from life to afterlife. Elia's vitality in his post has been following a downward curve of late. "My health and my good spirits flagged," he remarks (p. 194). At this point he is unexpectedly summoned before figures of authority, and the meeting is described in terms that suggest a more than commercial last judgment: "I received an awful summons to attend the presence of the whole assembled firm in the formidable back parlour. I thought, now my time is surely come . . ." (p. 195). The last phrase carries into its context some of its idiomatic link with fears of death. The firm's judgment is based upon Elia's "very meritorious conduct during the whole of the time" of his employ (p. 195). He receives the ultimate reward, far more than he expected, of an immediate retirement on a pension good enough to minimize, in the financial respect, the discontinuity between employment and superannuation. Once severed from the working life of the other employees, however, he has the strange sensation "that a vast tract of time had intervened since I quitted the Counting House" (p. 196). A similar feeling was mentioned in "Dream-Children"; there Elia felt, even though his brother had died only an hour before, that a great while had elapsed since John lived. The feeling is explicitly associated with death in "The Superannuated Man" when Elia explains that the partners and clerks "seemed as dead to me" (p. 196) and when he quotes Sir Robert Howard on death's trick of making a moment seem a thousand years.

Although at first Elia concluded that he lived and his former coworkers had died, he realizes when he visits them that they remain at their old labors, while he has been transplanted to a new existence. It is, therefore, more fitting to speak of them as alive and himself as dead. They are "my co-brethren of the quill—that I had left below in the state militant" (p. 196). When he goes among them now, however, he notes a lack of "that pleasant familiarity, which I had heretofore enjoyed among them" (p. 197); he has become an outsider. But he wishes them well, and jokingly approves, with a suitable choice of verb, that his function passes to others: "My mantle I bequeath among ye" (p. 197). After he has reconciled himself entirely to his new existence, he openly affirms this analogy and makes his new satisfaction parallel the traditional notion of eternity: "It was no hyperbole when I ventured to compare the change in my condition to a passing into another world. Time stands still in a manner to me" (p. 198). Elia's mundane experience of work, confrontation with his employers, and retirement is repeatedly compared to the sequence of life, judgment, and afterlife.

One way of interpreting the essay would be to conclude that Elia can cheerfully affirm his progress from drudgery to superannuation because he is confident that upward movement will continue even beyond death. From this point of view, the function of the analogy just considered would be to introduce the religious premises which enable Elia to relish his earthly felicity. But Lamb has taken the trouble to puncture this interpretation by his negative treatment of otherworldliness early in the essay. After mentioning his dissatisfaction with work, Elia recalls his only periods of rest over the last thirty-six years. The first of these was Sunday, which, though it brought freedom from toil, was disappointing since it released Elia into a city where the swirl of life had been arrested. "In particular," he announces, "there is a gloom for me attendant upon a city Sunday, a weight in the air" (p. 193). In place of the pleasing weekday "buzz and stirring murmur of the streets," Sunday's distinctive sound is the chime of church bells, which are not to Elia's taste: "Those eternal bells depress me" (p. 193). Similarly, London's visual impact on Sunday is one of negation, especially by contrast with the color and variety of the rest of the week: "closed shops repel me," "shut out," "No book-stalls," "No busy faces," "Nothing to be seen but unhappy countenances—or half-happy at best" (pp. 193–194). The condition of the city when it observes a religious holiday becomes associated with the religious consolation of an eternity outside of the shifting multiplicity of temporal life. Elia is as uneasy with this consolation as he is with his drudgery.

This interpretation is reinforced by the unfavorable connotation invariably attached to the words "eternal" or "eternity" in this essay. "Those eternal bells depress me" (p. 193) has already been cited. Later, when Elia is commenting upon the psychological difficulties of suddenly abandoning work, he speaks of his new existence as one of eternity: "It was like passing out of Time into Eternity—for it is a sort of Eternity for a man to have his Time all to himself" (p. 195). The third and last use of one of these words occurs after Elia has become adjusted to his retirement. Until this point he has associated work with time, retirement with eternity. But now he reverses the situation: "It is Lucretian pleasure to behold the poor drudges, whom I have left behind in the world, carking and caring; like horses in a mill, drudging on in the same eternal round—and what is it all for?" (p. 198). Eternity, in each of these passages, is an endless series of monotonously similar moments. It is an immense emptiness rather than the ultimate possession of the fullness of being. It cannot be the goal which endows history with meaning.

The function of the analogy between the story of Elia's retirement and the story of a soul passing to heaven is to introduce the most obvious traditional solution to the problem of history and to expose its inadequacy, at least for Elia. Further, this analogy becomes a norm against which Elia's solution to the problem of history can be tested. On one hand, he must affirm some possibility that is more than a negation. On the other hand, he must attempt to meet the difficulty, so well solved by traditional religion, that everything temporal is vulnerable to destruction. Elia's second system of analogy is his attempt to deal with these difficulties.

In this second framework, the narrative of Elia's experiences is organized around three stages, which may be called the Old Order, the Anxieties of Liberation, and the New Equilibrium. A prior stage is briefly alluded to— the "abundant play-time" (p. 193) from which Elia fell (in the essay's one brief concession to the concept of the fall) upon taking employment. The first of the three principal stages was a period when Elia's life was so structured that he had little, if any, time of his own. Time did not serve him; he served time. During working hours he did nothing which expressed his own interests or which struck him as worthwhile. At night, during his later years, he could not rest for fear that he was not competent enough at his dreary job. Sundays were disappointing, and so were summer vacations. The latter were mainly an opiate which kept him efficient for fifty-one repressive weeks by offering him the prospect of one week in the country. When the annual recess finally came, it was no real vacation from time's dominion; instead, Elia's principal feeling during the week was that the slippage of time was inexorably bringing him closer to a return to the office. The "servitude" (p. 194) of the years of labor is emphasized by the recurrence of imagery of rigidity and captivity:

I was fifty years of age, and no prospect of emancipation presented itself. I had grown to my desk, as it were; and the wood had entered into my soul. (p. 194)
. . . and thou, thou dreary pile, fit mansion for a Gresham or a Whittington of old, stately House of Merchants; with thy labyrinthine passages, and light-

excluding, pent-up offices, where candles for one half the year supplied the
place of the sun's light; unhealthy contributor to my weal, stern fosterer of
my living, farewell! (p. 197)
I gradually became content—doggedly contented, as wild animals in cages.
(p. 193)
I was in the condition of a prisoner in the old Bastile, suddenly let loose
after a forty years' confinement. (p. 195)

Desk, counting house, cage, and prison—each blends into the others, and all
severely restrict the centrifugal movement of their inhabitants. Elia's liberation is accomplished by the kindness of his employers, rather than by revolutionary efforts. The essay implies no animosity toward any class. Nevertheless, the structure of Elia's working life is viewed as a life-negating form
and his retirement overthrows that form for himself as surely as revolution-
aries liberated the Bastile.

Liberation is not a complete solution, however, to Elia's difficulties. It
removes restrictive external circumstances, and it eliminates the conditions
which encouraged Elia to continue in his old personality pattern. But his
personality has been so molded by his servitude that he finds himself disturbed at his new opportunities. "It seemed to me," he recalls, "that I had
more time on my hands than I could ever manage" (p. 195). At first, Elia
conceives time as an object which imposes responsibilities of management.
It can be responded to only by doing. A man's time, from this point of view,
is the sum of all his openings for action. Such a relation to time permits no
peace of mind and therefore perpetuates the old servitude in a subtler form.
But Elia carries within himself sufficient "resources" (p. 196) to establish a
new identity: "I am no longer ******, clerk to the Firm of &c. I am Retired Leisure" (p. 198). With this new inner equilibrium comes a new way
of defining time: "For *that* is the only true Time, which a man can properly
call his own, that which he has all to himself; the rest, though in some sense
he may be said to live it, is other people's time, not his" (p. 196). Having
time all to oneself implies, as Elia discovers, relating to time through contemplation rather than action. The whole panorama of London life ministers to Elia's consciousness once he is able to abandon "settled purpose"
(p. 198) in favor of meditative ambling. Time becomes man's element only
when he disengages himself from doing: "Man, I verily believe, is out of his
element as long as he is operative. I am altogether for the life contemplative"
(p. 198). Elia is no longer the servant or prisoner of time; he is a gentleman
with large temporal holdings.

The new structure which Elia achieves enables him to accept Sunday not on its own unique terms, but as just one item in life's cornucopia: it "is melted down into a week day" (p. 198). The reduction of the Sabbath to one item in a series dramatizes the difference between Elia's new equilibrium and the otherworldly consolation which religion offers. Through superannuation and contemplation, Elia has, in the terms of the essay, encompassed the richness of existence more fully than would have been possible in an afterlife. On the other hand, he recognizes that his retirement will end when "the rest of the day" (p. 199) is over. But this circumstance fails to reduce him wholly to servitude. Previously, when death was further in the future and he had no time to himself, he was time's slave. Now, by employing his time on his own terms, he is served by it. Elia succeeds not in escaping from but in gaining possession of time. Such progress is limited, as Lamb clearly indicates by his stress on the inevitability of death; but within those limits it is real. Elia's personal history takes on, though only for a while, some coherent shape as he emerges with difficulties from a repressive form into an inclusive one.

Although the structure of "The Superannuated Man" parallels, in some respects, the logic of revolution, Lamb does not within this essay draw any social corollaries from the pattern of Elia's personal history. In fact, his personal progress from servant to gentleman of leisure is a form of upward mobility which depends for its success upon the continued activity of those who make up London's weekday spectacle. But "A Dissertation upon Roast Pig" applies a similar three-stage narrative pattern to the development of a society. In the story which begins the essay, Lamb includes, in addition to the basic incident on how roast pig was first tasted, a comic portrait of the transformation of a society. Early in the narrative the citizens of China placed a religious taboo on cooking, or, as they phrase it, "improving upon the good meat which God had sent them" (p. 122). Children are expected to obey the rules, and parents are expected to chastise the children when their obedience falters. The symbol of the disciplined old order is the houses of the empire. Through Bo-bo's carelessness, one of the houses—his father's—is burnt to ashes. The conflagration initiates a departure from the society's strictures, for one result of the fire is that Bo-bo gets his first taste of crackling. In the second stage of the story disorder increasingly replaces the traditional discipline. A parent, instead of following his role of enforcer of taboos, abandons the idea of executing his son for eating cooked pig and sits down with him to finish the litter. A jury, instead of finding the father and son guilty in accordance with the law and the facts, acquits them because the meat tastes so exquisite. A judge, instead of speaking out in defense of the law, "winked at the manifest iniquity of the decision" (p. 123) and rounded up all the pigs that he could buy. The society as a whole follows suit, and the demand for pigs outruns the supply all over the country. As disrespect for the traditional taboo spreads, houses are everywhere set afire. The emblem of order is in such trouble that the insurance business collapses. It appears that "the very science of architecture," representative of man's ability to endow his life with form, is in danger of being "lost to the world" (p. 123). Just as superannuation replaced repressiveness with a period of anxieties in the life of Elia, so rigidity gives away to disorder in the history of China. At this point a new equilibrium is established when "in the process of time . . . a sage arose" (p. 123) who discovered that houses need not be set afire for pigs to be cooked. It is possible, in short, to combine form with an openness to new possibilities. Insurance companies can cease worrying, architecture can flourish, law can be preserved, and at the same time the citizens of China may enjoy their pork sizzling. The movement of the Chinese from a repressive order to an inclusive one reveals that time can be meaningful for a society as the dimension through which progress takes place.

The essay also supports the theory of progress through its use of fire imagery. Fire in this essay functions as more than a feature in the natural environment by which man is made comfortable or uncomfortable depending upon his capacities for handling it wisely. It is, more importantly, a means by which man alters the given world in order to make it more pleasing to himself. At first, when Bo-bo accidentally burns down the house, fire is an object external to man and not fully a manifestation of his desires. But after Bo-bo and his father and the other members of society obtain an appetite for roast pork, fire is an external sign of their internal energy. They direct it against two environmental elements which conflict with, or fall short of, their desires. The good meat which God has given them must be improved upon in order to satisfy them fully; so they cook it. The social order prohibits their new appetite; so they burn down houses until someone discovers a way to reintegrate their desires with the social order. In the terms of the old system, this alteration of the given marks a man as "an unnatural young monster" (p. 122). But Elia's more open sensibility not only notes that "nature" (p. 122) prompted people to lick their burnt fingers; he also makes the sequence of happenings in China seem a normal expression of human nature. In the context of this essay, man has the power and the right to transform his environment to suit his desires, and this license makes possible a progress based upon an increasing humanization of the object world.

The applicability of the idea of progress to human history is reinforced by the urbanity with which Elia views the activities of those who inhabit times and places distant from that pinnacle of civilization from which the *London Magazine* emanates. Consider, for instance, the opening sentence: "Mankind, says a Chinese manuscript, which my friend M. was obliging enough to read and explain to me, for the first seventy thousand ages ate their meat raw, clawing or biting it from the living animal, just as they do in Abyssinia to this day" (p. 120). The vividness of the participles brings alive a genial savagery which contrasts with the genial antiquarianism and reasonable tone of the detached speaker. We read on to learn that in China it was accounted a small loss when a house was incinerated: "Together with the cottage (a sorry antediluvian make-shift of a building, you may think it), what was of much more importance, a fine litter of new-farrowed pigs, no less than nine in number, perished" (p. 121). The reader is invited to smile from the vantage point of knowing superiority, as he is again later when Hoti "cursed his son, and he cursed himself that ever he should beget a son that should eat burnt pig" (p. 122). One function of the ironic distance which Elia preserves toward the narrative is to support the reader's conviction that the story relates to a level of progress far lower than that which nineteenth-century London has attained.

There are other progressive elements in this essay—for instance, Elia's remarks (pp. 120 and 123) that the ancients merely discovered the broiling or seething of pig, while moderns know the superior technique of roasting; or the reference to our ancestors' shocking custom in the departed "age of discipline" (p. 125) of whipping pigs to death. But "A Dissertation upon Roast Pig" also makes some use of the notion of a fall. The essay's opening paragraph alludes briefly to classical and Chinese counterparts to Eden: "This period is not obscurely hinted at by their great Confucius in the second chapter of his Mundane Mutations, where he designates a kind of golden age by the term Cho-fang, literally the Cooks' holiday" (p. 120). Likewise, in the second half of the essay, Elia several times suggests that time brings to a "young and tender suckling" (p. 123) nothing but decline, and he makes the point once with an open allusion to *Genesis:* "with no original speck of the *amor immunditiae,* the hereditary failing of the first parent, yet manifest . . ." (p. 123). "A Dissertation upon Roast Pig" is the completest Elian treatment of the shape of history insofar as it presents the two competing conceptual models with considerable fullness.

But the main justification for speaking in the present context of the completeness of this celebrated essay is that nowhere else has Elia so thoroughly exposed man's theories of history to his dissolving laughter. The effect of identifying the golden age with that period when men "ate their meat raw, clawing or biting it from the living animal" (p. 120) is to insert beneath a solemn pedantic surface a mocking view of the whole idea of a fall from paradise. Similarly, the distance between pork and paradise (or, in the essay's last sentence, between a pig and what he is said to be—a "flower") points up the absurdity by which roast pork and falls from innocence can be considered part of the same world. The idea of progress, though more elaborately incorporated into the structure of the opening narrative, fares no better in the essay as a whole. Man is portrayed throughout the main narrative as a fool who accidentally stumbles upon a discovery and who is able to preserve it only because his appetites are stronger than his consistency. As the reader smiles upon the naiveté of the Chinese, he responds not only to an earlier stage of evolution, but also to a mirror in which he discovers the folly of himself and his contemporaries. The dialogue between Bo-bo and his father is recognizably drawn from universal experience of the relation between the generations:

"O father, the pig, the pig, do come and taste how nice the burnt pig eats."
    The ears of Ho-ti tingled with horror. He cursed his son, and he cursed himself that ever he should beget a son that should eat burnt pig. (p. 122)

Ho-ti's quick conversion, the sudden reversal of the jury, and the judge's shrewdness all derive their laughable quality from the application of the quirks of common humanity to the outlandishly elementary problems of the Chinese empire. The parallel between the absurd preoccupations of China and things European is made explicit when Elia comes to speak of man's capacity for seminal thought: "Thus this custom of firing houses continued, till in process of time, says my manuscript, a sage arose, like our Locke, who made a discovery, that the flesh of swine, or indeed of any other animal, might be cooked (*burnt*, as they called it) without the necessity of consuming a whole house to dress it" (p. 123). Upon such achievements is man's greatness based, and Lamb reduces the grandiose to the miniscule under the spell of his laughter. In the second half of the essay Lamb's irony is directed not merely at the rigidity of the orthodox, but also at Elia's feverish libertarianism. When a writer embellishes his infatuation for pork with the flourishes of Latin and the depths of theological speculation, his argument inevitably appears hilariously obsessive. Moreover, the casuistry by which he moves toward resuscitating, for purely gastronomical reasons, the old practice of whipping pigs is humorously similar to the halting mental steps by which the ancients approached the satisfaction of their appetites. That he had to repeat in his childhood the progress of the ancient Chinese casts doubt on whether the centuries have, in fact, added to the wisdom of homo sapiens. No one can fail to see that "A Dissertation upon Roast Pig" is a humorous essay, but the intellectual content of the humor may not be so obvious. One aspect of this content (another will be explored later) is a tension between a multiplicity of reductive ironies and an elaborate utilization of theories of history. Lamb's humor, while it assimilates man's appetites and his illogicality, punctures his more imposing formulations.

"A Dissertation upon Roast Pig" is unique among Lamb's work in the complexity of its treatment of progress and in its sustained criticism of both the fall and progress as adequate models of history. But like all the works considered in this chapter, it subjects the simple constructions of man's mind to the examination of an intelligence which is resistant to oversimplification. Although Lamb did not in his mature work find an adequate paradigm of history, it would be a mistake to conclude that his position on the meaning of time was mindless. He tried out each possibility and found that it corresponded in certain partial ways to his sense of life. He failed to discover coherent shape in the totality of events that constitute the temporal process, but he shaped his own exploratory, skeptical, and ambivalent responses to the problem into a series of meaningful works of art.

NOTES

1. *Essays,* trans. Florio, III, 23.
2. This theme figures prominently in James Scoggins, "Images of Eden in the Essays of Elia," *JEGP,* 71 (1972), 198–210, and in my earlier "The Strategies of Finitude: An Interpretation of Lamb's Elia Essays" (Ph.D. diss., Yale, 1968), chap. 2. Scoggins's view differs from mine in taking the Elia essays, or at least the best of them, as consistently and unequivocally preferring past to present.
3. *Works,* I, 174, 284.
4. Pp. 144–145.
5. The postscript was part of the version published in the *London Magazine,* as well as in the first edition of *Elia.* It is even included in the holograph MS. of this essay now in the Berg Collection. It, therefore, has a clear textual claim to be considered an intrinsic part of the essay.
6. See Lucas's notes in Lamb's *Works,* II, 365, 367.
7. MS. Br.

8. *Works,* I, 158–160. Cf. the corresponding passage in "My First Play," *Works,* II, 99. My account of the significance of the changes which Lamb made in the 1813 version for "My First Play" would be unaffected, however, even if someone else had written the early piece.
9. See M. H. Abrams, *Natural Supernaturalism,* pp. 325–372, part of which overlaps with Abrams's earlier essay, "English Romanticism: The Spirit of the Age," *Romanticism Reconsidered,* ed. Northrop Frye (New York: Columbia Univ. Press, 1963), pp. 26–72.

Chapter Four

THE SPACE OF CONSCIOUSNESS

Familiar essayists had been mulling over their sense of space since Montaigne extolled expansion in the area of our knowledge, but contraction in that of our desires and needs. The same essayist who celebrated travel to distant places in "Of Vanitie" and sympathetic comprehension of geographically remote cultures in "Of the Caniballes" had this to say about our desires: "The cariere of our desires must be circumscribed, and tied to strict bounds of neerest and contiguous commodities. Moreover, their course should be managed, not in a straight line, having another end, but round, whose two points hold together, and end in our selves with a short compasse." Bacon's "Of Travel" and "Of Plantations" (or colonies) discussed the usefulness of each to ambitious individuals and governments, and his "Of the True Greatness of Kingdoms and Estates" showed how "it is in the power of princes or estates to add amplitude and greatness to their kingdoms." In his essay "Of Greatness" Abraham Cowley, whom Elia mentions approvingly (pp. 154, 200), undermined the Baconian ideal of "greatness" not only by confessing a personal preference for "Littleness almost in all things," but also by arguing that "every thing is Little, and every thing is Great, according as it is diversly compared": "Our Country is called *Great Britany*, in regard onely of a Lesser of the same Name; it would be but a ridiculous Epithete for it, when we consider it together with the Kingdom of *China*. That too, is but a pitifull Rood of ground in comparison of the whole Earth besides: and this whole Globe of Earth, which we account so immense a Body, is but one Point or Atome in relation to those numberless Worlds that are scattered up and down in the Infinite Space of the Skie which we behold."[1] Geographical diversity connects easily with intellectual relativism for Cowley, as for many essayists; the combination has natural affinities with a genre that resists the schematic and the doctrinaire. Sir William Temple's "Of Heroic Virtue" ventured beyond the territory of the four monarchies of Mediterranean and western European civilization to consider the merits of less familiar cultures from China to Peru. In a series of *Tatler* papers (Nos. 155, 160, 178, 232) Addison, later to be joined by Steele, mocked the upholsterer who thinks of foreign affairs rather than of his business, and in *The Spectator* Steele exposed the deficiencies of the colonizer's sensibility in his tale of Inkle and Yarico (No. 11), while Addison used the perspective of four visiting Indian kings to satirize his own countrymen (No. 50). Johnson wrote skeptical disquisitions on the pleasures of travel (such as *Rambler*, Nos. 6, 135, 165; *Idler*, No. 58). But it was left to Goldsmith among the major British essayists to supplant the traditional essayist's central perspective of chronological depth—the speaker as long experienced and steeped in ancient learning—with the perspective of spatial amplitude or, in Goldsmith's word, "dissipation" (Letter XLIV). In the *Citizen of the World* essay series an Irishman invented a Chinese traveller to look upon English customs and institutions. Although Lamb's Elia seldom displays an interest in faraway places, a spatial model enters and holds together many of his essays. His treatment of space exemplifies common essayistic and Romantic concerns, but it bears his mark too.

Elia confronts the limits of the human condition under the aspect not only of time, but also of space. In the latter experience he conceives two areas of awareness, one within the other. He is conscious of himself, his sensations, feelings, and thoughts, as well as his immediate vicinity, and he contrasts this familiar ground with a world which extends beyond the area occupied or dominated by himself. The relation between the temporal and spatial aspects of Elia's problems is suggested in "Distant Correspondents," especially in the following passage, where Elia is remembering a period before his friend B. F. (in real life Barron Field) migrated to New South Wales:

I am insensibly chatting to you as familiarly as when we used to exchange good-morrows out of our old contiguous windows, in pump-famed Harecourt in the Temple. Why did you ever leave that quiet corner?—Why did I?—with its complement of four poor elms, from whose smoke-dyed barks, the theme of jesting ruralists, I picked my first lady-birds! My heart is as dry as that spring sometimes proves in a thirsty August, when I revert to the space that is between us; a length of passage enough to render obsolete the phrases of our English letters before they can reach you. (p. 108)

The passage exemplifies the familiar contrast between the unfallen world of the past—not in this instance specifically related to childhood—and the fallen world of the present. Both Elia and B. F.—not just the latter—have left "that quiet corner." In the earlier world, Elia and B. F. occupied "contiguous windows"; in the present they are on opposite sides of the planet. Their former contiguity is reflected by the remembered landscape, with its four elms marking off a small space and the "smoke-dyed barks" of the trees reminding us of the closeness between man and nature, a relation that parallels that between one person and another. In the past Elia did not have to contend with alien territory in maintaining his relationship with B. F.; in the present, he is aware of a little world which he can control and a great world which is intractable and strange. Instead of finding the universe in the microcosm which he inhabits, he is disturbed by the abyss which separates microcosm and macrocosm.

Such an abyss is one version of that pervasive Romantic problem, the subject-object split, and the effort to bridge it is often rendered by the Romantic poets in terms of journeying. The voyage which seeks to assimilate the stuff of the non-self is already a weak presence in Wordsworth's "An Evening Walk," becomes manifest in the early versions of "Descriptive Sketches," *The Borderers*, "Guilt and Sorrow," "Peter Bell," and Book I of *The Excursion*, and reaches its profoundest Wordsworthian expression in the books of *The Prelude* which culminate in the crossing of the Alps (Books II-VI). *The Rime of the Ancient Mariner*, as well as the voluminous reading in travel books which lies behind it, attests to Coleridge's preoccupation with a similar expansive quest. "Now if there is, with Coleridge," writes Georges Poulet in *The Metamorphoses of the Circle*, "one trait which manifests itself more precociously and frequently than any other, it is that of diffusion."[2] Poulet's remarkable study of the image of the circle from the Renaissance to modernity argues convincingly that the Romantics associate the center with the self and the distant circumference with the non-self, and that they move from this premise to a fuller appreciation of subjectivity and to a variety of efforts to span the gulf by means of self-generated energy.

The relevance of such Romantic quests to Lamb's imaginative world becomes apparent in "Distant Correspondents" as Elia treats some strategies by which the self attempts to push out into the great world and extend its dominion. A friend is living in New South Wales. He wants to hear from home, and Elia wants to communicate with him. If communication consisted merely in the sequence of letter-writing, letter-carrying, and letter-reading, Elia and his friend could easily be obliged. The essay insists, however, on a more rigorous understanding of what real communication requires. A means of communication (such as a letter) is conceived as an extension of the self, which, in order to maintain its subordination to the self, must have, when it reaches its reader, the meaning and effect which the writer intended and continues to intend. If facts were told which, by the time the letter arrives, have become untrue, or if lies were told which have turned into the truth, or if an emotion sought in the reader would now be inappropriate to the writer's situation, communication is foiled. If a "brisk sentiment" metamorphoses into "a feature of silly pride or tawdry senseless affectation" (p. 106) or if puns or other verbal levities lose their verve, the essence of communication gets lost. Elia argues that, thanks to a speedy postal system, news and sentiments can be successfully communicated within England, while puns are so "extremely circumscribed in their sphere of action" that "they will scarce endure to be transported by hand from this room to the next" (pp. 106-107). But none of the three usual epistolary topics—news, sentiment, or puns—can survive a journey to New South Wales without losing their rapport with the letter-writer's situation and intentions. The self's expansive energy cannot in these ways fill up the gulf between center and circumference.

Part of this failure is attributable to the direct impact of spatial vastness: Lord C.'s corpse becomes absurd in its troublesome voyage to a nook in Switzerland which he had picked for a grave, and a pun needs proximity if it is to tickle. But the self's incapacity to spread adequately into space is largely caused by the power exercised by time over the area which the self invades. The alteration in facts after the sending of news, the passage of time in the sentiment's (and the body's) journey "till at length it arrives" (p. 106), and the lapse of more than a "moment's interval" (p. 107) in the transmission of a pun foil the ego's plans. The threat of time grows more ominous in the essay's last paragraph: "Come back, before I am grown into a very old man, so as you shall hardly know me. . . . Folks, whom you knew, die off every year. Formerly, I thought that death was wearing out,—I stood ramparted about with so many healthy friends. The departure of J. W., two springs back corrected my delusion. Since then the old divorcer has been busy" (p. 108). The essay's excursion into space has brought Elia into increased contact with the problem of time. Time and space blur together, as in the allusion to "Lycidas" (11. 153 ff.) just before the last paragraph: "But while I talk, I think you hear me,—thoughts dallying with vain surmise—

> Aye me! while thee the seas and sounding shores
> Hold far away." (p. 108)

The last line begins with the word "Wash" in Milton's poem—and in the volume of his poems bearing Lamb's handwritten annotations, now in the British Museum. Lamb's essay alters Milton's verb "wash" to "hold," thus transforming a separation caused in Milton primarily by death and only secondarily by distance into a separation maintained solely by the constraining action of space. Yet this spatial disjunction carries over from "Lycidas" the recollection —and foreshadowing—of the less easily remediable type of disunion. Elia has left behind the sheltered world of being "ramparted," and now he faces the emptiness of a world of separation dominated, aptly enough, by "the old divorcer."

Although in its division of epistolary matter into three sub-categories and in its coherent linkage of time and space "Distant Correspondents" has something of the appearance of a systematic argument, humor is so apparent in much of the essay that we may be tempted to relegate the content of the argument to the status of a put-on. But in this essay the humor reinforces, rather than subverts, the argument. Much of Elia's laughter springs from the incongruity between the trivial circumstances of human life and the enormity of ambition implied in the desire to communicate around the globe. "The weary world of waters between us oppresses the imagination," he remarks in the opening paragraph. "It is difficult to conceive how a scrawl of mine should ever stretch across it. It is a sort of presumption to expect that one's thoughts should live so far." The energetic and colloquial prosaicism of "scrawl" has numerous echoes in the rest of the essay: Elia's wish to make his friend "lick your lips" with envy at his own access to the London theater; his treatment of the etiquette of conversing upon "jacks, and spits, and mops" (pp. 104–105), and then Will Weatherall's action of really marrying a servant-maid; and especially the parodic international journey, putting a sentiment into practice, of Lord C.'s corpse to the "pretty green spot" in Switzerland which he had picked for a grave—"Conceive the sentiment boarded up, freighted, entered at the Custom House (startling the tide-waiters with the novelty), hoisted into a ship. Conceive it pawed about and handled between the rude jests of tarpaulin ruffians—a thing of its delicate texture—the salt bilge wetting it till it became as vapid as a damaged lustring" (p. 106). Another kind of humor fills a paragraph near the end: an exaggerated demonstration that caricatures supplant understanding in a Londoner's conception of so distant a place as the penal colony in Australia. Elia imposes the stereotype of "thief," as well as a few scraps of information, upon the inhabitants of New South Wales, with the result that the pouches of kangaroos become "a lesson framed by nature to the pickpocket" and locksmiths are "your great capitalists" (pp. 107–108). "We hear the most improbable tales at this distance," he confesses. The Elian voice divides in this paragraph into one facet which assents to the improbabilities with simple-minded credulity and a more skeptical facet which joins the reader in laughing at the inevitable fatuousness of an attempt to comprehend so alien a place.

The difficulty of dwelling in a microcosm which is only a point within an alien, enveloping macrocosm leads Elia at the essay's conclusion to appeal to B. F. to return home. Since such a return will not make time pass more slowly, Elia's entreaty, however understandable in human terms, may at first seem less than thematically central, in spite of the emphasis which it receives as the essay's final sentence: "If you do not make haste to return, there will be little left to greet you, of me, or mine" (p. 108). Elia is seeking here to adopt a strategy different from the sending of letters, but similar in that it is conceived in spatial terms. If there is a gulf between the little world of the self and the great world, one can either attempt to expand the self until it fills all conceivable space or one can contract the great world, as Wordsworth did in "Home at Grasmere" and "Nuns Fret Not at Their Convent's Narrow Room," until it is no larger than the microcosm. If the circumference on which B. F. lives shrinks sufficiently, it will eventually become equivalent to the point which is its center. "Distant Correspondents" devotes most of its attention to various forms of the strategy of expansion—proving their futility and yet, as a letter to B. F., continuing to try them. But the essay closes emphatically upon a preference for contraction.

Lamb explored the potentialities of contraction more thoroughly elsewhere, perhaps most explicitly in "The Convalescent." That essay begins with the perspective of common sense according to which a man's inability to think of anything but himself is a limitation upon his awareness: "A pretty severe fit of indisposition which, under the name of a nervous fever, has made a prisoner of me for some weeks past, and is but slowly leaving me, has reduced me to an incapacity of reflecting upon any topic foreign to itself" (p. 183). The note of constriction in "prisoner" is also implicit in the enclosures of house, sick-room, and sick-bed. But the perspective partly shifts by the second paragraph to that of "sick men's dreams," and from this viewpoint, the blotting out of the great world is not without its advantages. When one succeeds in "shutting out the sun" and inducing "total oblivion of all the works which are going on under it" (p. 183), one does not feel constricted by the narrow bounds of one's consciousness. On the contrary, as the circumference of awareness contracts to the dimensions of the self, or that part of the world dominated by the self, a person no longer feels the relative minuteness of his existence. The paradoxical effect of contraction is to supply oneself with a sense of magnitude.

The awareness of limitation which prompts one to adopt the strategy of contraction derives from a perception and a feeling. One perceives oneself as only a unit in a series, one man out of many, and one's self-interest is held in check by feelings of responsibility or sympathy toward other persons. The sick man, however, is not just another citizen; he has the powers of a monarch: "If there be a regal solitude, it is a sick bed. How the patient lords it there! what caprices he acts without controul! how king-like he sways his pillow . . . " (p. 184). He is waited on with all the solicitude ordinarily reserved for a king, and his apparent progression from illness to convalescence is actually "a fall from dignity, amounting to a deposition" (p. 185). A king is a person who dominates the great world, or at least a significant part of it, and Elia's succeeding to the title, even if only in an image pattern, is a sign of his growth from control of the center toward control of the circumference of his awareness. Similarly, the sick Elia never sees himself as one of the physician's many charges: "even in the lines of that busy face he reads no multiplicity of patients, but solely conceives of himself as *the sick man*" (p. 185), the only member of his species. Rather than meditate upon the numerous substances or people which exist outside in the great world, Elia finds diversity within himself: "He makes the most of himself; dividing himself, by an allowable fiction, into as many distinct individuals, as he hath sore and sorrowing members" (p. 184). He thus retains his ability to perceive multiplicity and at the same time he extricates himself from the thought that he is only a unit in a series. In addition, his self-interest is no longer restricted by the commands of responsibility or the impulses of sympathy: "Supreme selfishness is inculcated upon him as his only duty" (p. 184); ". . . he keeps his sympathy, like some curious vintage, under trusty lock and key, for his own use only" (p. 184). He has not had to root out his feelings of responsibility or sympathy, but merely to redirect them from such objects as the friend who may have been ruined in a lawsuit yesterday to the contracted circumference of his new awareness: "How sickness enlarges the dimensions of a man's self to himself! he is his own exclusive object" (p. 184). Although to be an "exclusive object" demands an act of exclusion, the sick man experiences an enlarging of his dimensions.

The essay is written, however, not by a sick man, but by a convalescent. Therefore, it begins by warning us of the limitations of "sick men's dreams" (p. 183), and it ends with a return to the littleness of ordinary experience. The last section moves from the "oceanic surface" of the sick-bed during the illness to "this flat swamp of convalescence, left by the ebb of sickness, yet far enough from the terra firma of established health . . ." (p. 186). Elia journeys, as he had in "Witches, and Other Night-Fears," from ocean toward land, and he changes from the giant of sickness to the person of modest proportions to whom the reader is accustomed: "The hypochondriac flatus is subsiding; the acres, which in imagination I had spread over—for the sick man swells in the sole contemplation of his single sufferings, till he becomes a Tityus to himself—are wasting to a span; and for the giant of self-importance, which I was so lately, you have me once again in my natural pretensions—the lean and meagre figure of your insignificant Essayist" (pp. 186–187). The present of the essay is the fallen world which the mature Elia commonly inhabits, but the present is understood largely by an ambivalent contrast with the past, in this case, the experience of sickness. The sympathy which the sick Elia lavished upon himself receives partly ironic treatment; yet the identity achieved in sickness between microcosm and macrocosm, center and circumference, self and world, arouses an unmistakable yearning ("a magnificent dream for a man to lie a-bed") (p. 183). Because convalescence is a condition midway between healthy realism and "sick men's dreams," it perfectly fits the Elian tension between fact and value.

The essay which refutes the popular fallacy "That a sulky temper is a misfortune" complements the strategy employed in "The Convalescent." In the latter everyone is extremely solicitous toward the speaker; in the former everyone seems to be betraying him. In "The Convalescent" he contracts his sense of what *is*, while in the popular fallacy essay he contracts his sense of what is good. At first Elia, having decided on the basis of equivocal evidence that a friend has slighted him, widens his suspicions by considering other actions by the same person and then stretching even further to another friend and to the abstract idea of friendship: "Enlarge your speculations, and take in the rest of your friends, as a spark kindles more sparks. Was there one among them, who has not to you proved hollow, false, slippery as water? Begin to think that the relation itself is inconsistent with mortality" (p. 274). Suspicions have not yet reached their farthest limit: "Adverting to the world in general, (as these circles in the mind will spread to infinity) reflect with what strange injustice you have been treated in quarters where, (setting gratitude and the expectation of friendly returns aside as chimeras,) you pretended no claim beyond justice, the naked due of all men" (p. 274). The effect of this bloating of suspicions is to diminish the area of worth in the external world so that the self can expand into the sole repository of friendship and justice:

Think the very idea of right and fit fled from the earth, or your breast the solitary receptacle of it, till you have swelled yourself into at least one hemisphere; the other being the vast Arabia Stony of your friends and the world aforesaid. To grow bigger every moment in your own conceit, and the world to lessen: to deify yourself at the expense of your species; to judge the world—this is the acme and supreme point of your mystery—these the true PLEASURES OF SULKINESS. (p. 274)

By the time Elia sets down his ruminations, a visit by his friend has routed his suspicions. As in "The Convalescent," he speaks of an atypical, temporary —and, to some degree, frivolous—psychic state from the point of view of a more commonplace, realistic attitude which succeeds it. More than in "The Convalescent," Elia's tone here is that of an anatomist of human folly, especially his own; but sulkiness remains a seductive folly, because it appeals to man's desire to lessen the dichotomy between the vastness of the world and the smallness of the self.

"Distant Correspondents," "The Convalescent," and "That a Sulky Temper is a Misfortune" have in common a spatial model by which Elia understands his own position in relation to the world and seeks to improve that position by some variety of expansion or contraction. This pattern takes on added interest when it is viewed in relation to more representative traits of the Elia essays. For example, the strategy of contracting the circumference, as in "The Convalescent," finds general applicability in Elia's indifference toward foreign people or places. The natives of New South Wales and China appear in his pages, but they exist there only as butts for humor. This existence is enough, however, to enable them to remind us of the great world from which, for the most part, Elia has chosen to avert his glance. Lamb did not find matter for literary treatment on his trip to Paris in 1822—his only recorded absence from Britain—even though the Elia essays were then appearing in the *London Magazine*. Writing to Southey about the latter's *Madoc* on May 6, 1815, Lamb commented upon his own preference for the familiar:

I have a timid imagination I am afraid. I do not willingly admit of strange beliefs or out of the way creeds or places. I never read books of travels, at least not farther than Paris, or Rome. I can just endure Moors because of their connection as foes with Xians, but Abyssinians, Ethiops, Esquimaux, Dervises & all that tribe I hate. I believe I fear them in some manner. A Mahometan turban on the stage, tho' enveloping some well known face (Mr. Cooke or Mr. Maddox whom I see another day good Christ*n* & English waiters, innkeepers &c.) does not give me pleasure unalloyed. I am a Christian, Englishman, Londoner, *Templar*—God help me when I come to put off these snug relations & to get abroad into the world to come—[3]

Lamb protects himself, in the process of self-revelation, by the humorous precision of the enumerated outlandish names. In his linkage of "creeds" and "places" he reveals a tendency to import a spatial model into his view of ideas, and in the last sentence he associates the enclosed space of the familiar with a defense not only against vastness, but also against time.

The corollary of excluding the geographical expanse of the great world is concentration upon what is near at hand, the area of "snug relations." "Everything," he had once written, "in heaven and earth, in man and in story, in books and in fancy, acts by Confederacy, by juxtaposition, by circumstance & place." In his essays Lamb relishes the perceptions of London life —the smell of Saloop, the cry of *"fired chimney"* (p. 110), the sight of blind beggars with their dogs by the wall of Lincoln's Inn Garden, the gestures of favorite actors—though he avoids the crowdedness of detail which we find, for instance, in Gay's *Trivia.* If London were given too much circumstantiality, it might overwhelm Elia, and it is essential to Lamb's strategy that Elia dominate the scene. Lamb penetrates, at greater length, into the associations of certain places which he has known well, including the South-Sea House, Christ's Hospital, Mackery End, the Inner Temple, and Blakesmoor, each of which lends its name to the title of an Elian essay. "He felt the genius of places," Pater observed, "and I sometimes think he resembles the places he knew and liked best, and where his lot fell . . . ." While Addison and Steele ·tied their essays to the public world of their varied readers by mentioning a cross-section of London places and classes (including but deemphasizing the poor), Elia lingers over places and people that matter in his own world, which is personal but communicable. As early as 1801 Lamb had expressed a similar viewpoint in replying to Wordsworth's invitation to Cumberland:

My attachments are all local, purely local—I have no passion (or have had none since I was in love, and then it was the spurious engendering of poetry & books) to groves and vallies.—The rooms where I was born, the furniture which has been before my eyes all my life, a book case which has followed me about (like a faithful dog, only exceeding him in knowledge) wherever I have moved—old chairs, old tables, streets, squares, where I have sunned myself, my old school,—these are my mistresses—have I not enough, without your mountains?

The next summer Lamb visited Coleridge at Keswick, and after returning home, he admits in letters to Coleridge and Manning that he was much impressed by the mountain country. But upon getting back to the East India House, he finds that the happiness of the experience gives way to a curious

reaction: ". . . you cannot conceive the degradation I felt at first, from being accustommed to wander free as air among mountains, & bathe in rivers
without being controuled by any one, to come home & *work:* I felt very
little. I had been dreaming I was a very great man."[4] The more keenly he
is aware of the spatial amplitude of the great world the less he is able to accept the limits of his ordinary station. The contraction of the geographical
circumference practiced in the Elia essays is one response to the dichotomy
between center and circumference, and its roots reach deeply into Lamb's
mind.

The geographical insularity of the essay has its thematic counterpart in
certain kinds of Elian selectivity. In his emphatic thisworldliness he excludes
with rare exceptions the "invisible world" (pp. 65, 212, 271), that home of
bloodless and alien spirits which Lamb associates with the idea of an afterlife. Conceived by Elia as a place, it is several times mentioned, but except
for the untypical "That We should Rise with the Lark," it is kept at considerably more than arm's length away. "Witches, and Other Night-Fears" is,
among other things, a celebration of his success in putting that region out
of mind. To say that Elia contracted his vision from the invisible world is
not equivalent to saying, as Mulcahy does, that *religion* is virtually excluded
by Elia because it is one of the "facts and emotions which make too many
independent demands" and thus are "too big for his minor-key art."[5] More
likely, Lamb minimized religion in his essays because he no longer believed
in it.

Since the problems of death and afterlife and of the gap between imper-
fection and perfection may be considered intrinsically religious, one cannot
accurately say that Elia omitted religious problems from his consciousness.
His solutions, however, or at least his ways of meeting failure, are non-
religious although they display the residue of attitudes which had been linked
in Lamb's mind with the piety that once had assisted him. At the time of his
mother's death, he had requested and then cherished Coleridge's religious
consolations. When he censured Coleridge for blasphemy a few weeks later,
his premises were still religious, and the seeds of the Elian manner are detect-
able in such a passage as this:

Man, full of imperfections, at best, and subject to wants which momentarily
remind him of dependence; man, a weak and ignorant being, "servile" from
his birth "to all the skiey influences," with eyes sometimes open to discern
the right path, but a head generally too dizzy to pursue it; man, in the pride
of speculation, forgetting his nature, and hailing in himself the future God,
must make the angels laugh.

Lamb's responsibilities at this period give his tone a sobriety which was later replaced by an ability to see, with the angels, a laughable side to human pretensions. About three years after the family crisis, Lamb, still avoiding levity, published a poem entitled "Living without God in the World," in which he contrasted the puniness of man with God's "mighty arm" that guides events. By August 14, 1801, however, he wrote to Walter Wilson explaining that "some slight and light expressions which I may have made use of in a moment of levity in your presence" should not be taken as proof "that I am an inveterate enemy of all religion," but conceding that the importance of religion in his mind had recently receded: "I have had a time of seriousness, and I have known the importance and reality of a religious belief. Latterly, I acknowledge, much of my seriousness has gone off, whether from new company or some other new associations; but I still retain at bottom a conviction of the truth, and a certainty of the usefulness of religion." In late September or early October of the same year, Lamb was even more frank to Thomas Manning: "But seriously what do you think of this Life of ours? Can you make head or tail on't? How we came here (that I have some tolerable bawdy hint of) what we came here for (that I know no more than [an] Ideot.)" When a Protestant friend married a Catholic, the couple agreed to raise their boys in one religion and their girls in the other, and this compromise prompted a tongue-in-cheek resolution by Lamb, expressed in a letter of 1817 or 1818: "I am determined my children shall be brought up in their father's religion, if they can find out what it is." After the *London Magazine* printed "Olen" 's versified "Epistle to Elia," which replied to the pessimism of "New Year's Eve" by offering the solutions of Christian faith, Lamb, writing to his publisher, explained where he now stood:

Poor Elia (call him *Ellia*) does not pretend to so very clear revelations of a future state of being as Olen seems gifted with. He stumbles among dark mountains at best. But he knows at least how to be thankful for this life; and is too thankful indeed for certain relationships lent him here, not to tremble for a possible resumption of the gift. He is too apt to express himself lightly—and cannot be sorry for the present occasion, as it has called forth a reproof so Christian-like. His *animus* at least (whatever become of it in the female termination) hath always been *cum Christianis.*

After Southey declared in the *Quarterly Review* (January 1823) that *Elia* "wants only a sounder religious feeling, to be as delightful as it is original," Lamb at first regretted in a letter to Bernard Barton that the sales of his book would be damaged, then published in the *London Magazine* his "Letter of Elia to Robert Southey," which equivocated on Lamb's religious position while censuring Southey's bigotry.[6] In the Elia essays Lamb's early emphasis upon the weakness of man is retained in his portrayal of Elia, but confidence in God's guidance now tends to be associated rather with an older generation, like the aunt of "My Relations" or the grandmother of "Dream-Children," than with Elia's response to the difficulties involved in being human. Assisted by a humor understandably lacking in some of Lamb's early pronouncements, Elia contends with the perils of a world of limits armed only with the powers —the unmistakably finite powers—of his own mind.

Unlike Spenser's knights and Bunyan's pilgrim, however, he does not have to contend with moral evil. The main temptation which he records is Barbara S——'s hesitation in childhood over whether or not to return the overpayment which she received from her employer. She had "no instinct to evil, but then she might be said to have no fixed principle" (p. 205). Neither principle nor self-restraint saved her, but rather "a strength not her own," "a reason above reasoning," which "transported" her back to Ravenscroft with her refund (p. 206). One cannot derive from this incident a belief in man's natural goodness since Barbara felt that she triumphed through the force of "a strength not her own" and since, in any case, she is hardly an ordinary person. Elia is interested in the incident largely for its illumination of the actress's later greatness in serious roles, rather than for its participation in a cosmic struggle between good and evil. If she had pocketed the money, no great harm would have been done, except, perhaps, to her acting ability. As for Elia, he occasionally uses the Biblical language of prohibitions and sins in treating his behavior in the garden of childhood and his later exclusion from that landscape, but he never concludes that his sinfulness caused his present plight. In adulthood he lives in a universe which condemns him to finitude, and he struggles against his shackles, but he does not have to fight the lure of wickedness.

Villainy, as well as temptation, is characteristically absent from his experience. Matravis, the melodramatic evil-doer of Lamb's early novelette *Rosamund Gray*, has no counterpart in the Elia essays. Insensitivity is, ordinarily, the nearest thing to sin in Elia's world. It is exemplified variously by Ravenscroft in "Barbara S——," the administrators in "Oxford in the Vacation," and the establishment in "The Tombs in the Abbey" and "A Complaint of the Decay of Beggars in the Metropolis." The one exception to this pattern is "Christ's Hospital Five and Thirty Years Ago," which in its early pages recalls the petty tyrants of boyhood. This section, based more on Coleridge's experience than on Lamb's, is unique among the Elia essays for its sense of malice, as a sentence on one of the older students illustrates: "This petty Nero actually branded a boy, who had offended him, with a red hot iron; and nearly starved forty of us, with exacting contributions, to the one half of our bread, to pamper a young ass, which, incredible as it may seem, with the connivance of the nurse's daughter (a young flame of his) he had contrived to smuggle in, and keep upon the leads of the *ward,* as they called our dormitories" (p. 14). For a moment a depraved corner of the human psyche is revealed, but generally Elia gives human cruelty no attention. Part of the explanation is that his imaginative world has largely pulled back from the reality of moral evil, but part too is that he is preoccupied with evil of another sort. His central encounters with the problem of evil concern the suffering which results when a man with more than finite desires is caught in a finite situation with only limited powers.

Among the conspicuous exclusions of the Elia essays are direct treatments of the great public events that had occurred during Lamb's lifetime. One would look in vain for discussions of the French Revolution, the Napoleonic wars, or political conflicts in England. Elia's antiquarian interests do not extend to national or international non-literary incidents of the past. Not only public events, but also public questions, what Pater calls "ideas of practice— religious, moral, political . . .", were not of concern to Elia, except to the extent that they touched directly upon his private experience, as in the issues of whether to eliminate the sight of beggars from London, charge a fee for a visit to Westminster Abbey, or say grace before dispatching a feast. "I am not the man to decide the limits of civil and ecclesiastical authority," he confesses, "I am plain Elia—no Selden, nor Archbishop Usher . . ." (p. 8). We do not go to Elia for political history, moral exhortation, or ideological affirmation, and these omissions from the essays and from Lamb's personal interests leave him open to the scorn of anyone who, like Carlyle, sets a high value upon earnestness in life and art.[7] To concede Lamb's lack of earnestness, however, it is not necessary to deny his artistic seriousness. From the point of view of content, the seriousness of the essays consists in the portrayal of a number of parallel mental processes by which Elia seeks to transcend the limitations of human life. That these processes generally fail and that they do not issue in affirmations of ideas does not prevent their portrayal from evoking and illuminating the human condition in some of its aspiration, some of its folly, and much of its pathos. One of these processes is the effort, by means of expansion or contraction, to eliminate the gulf between the little world of the self and the great world, which includes, among other things, wars, political parties, and ideological disputes. We sense dimly the existence of such matters in the hints of revolution in "The Superannuated Man" and

"A Dissertation upon Roast Pig," in the laconic recollection of "our first boyish heats kindled by the French Revolution" (p. 225) in "Newspapers Thirty-Five Years Ago," and in the allusions to the decrees of authority in "A Complaint of the Decay of Beggars in the Metropolis" and "The Tombs in the Abbey." These intimations help to build into the structure of the Elia essays the notion of a recoil from a large world outside of Elia's principal subjects, a circumference which has been shrunk into an area which Elia can hope to dominate.

To convert this hope into fact the essays engage in a complementary strategy, an attempt to expand the self so that it will occupy more and more of the space between center and circumference. The primary Elian method for advancing this ambition is the reconciliation-of-opposites, a mental habit that has been recognized as central to Coleridge's thinking especially since Alice D. Snyder's pioneer study, *The Critical Principle of the Reconciliation of Opposites as Employed by Coleridge* (1918). M. H. Abrams has recently summarized the importance of such a procedure in Coleridge's writings, particularly the *Biographia Literaria:*

This is the root-principle throughout Coleridge's thought: all self-compelled motion, progress, and productivity, hence all emergent novelty or "creativity," is a generative conflict-in-attraction of polar forces, which part to be reunited on a higher level of being, and thus evolve, or "grow," from simple unity into a "multeity in unity" which is an organized whole. It is in this way that Coleridge conceives, for example, the process of cosmogony ("the eternal act of creation in the infinite I Am," or "absolute self"), of epistemology (the "repetition" of this creation in "the primary Imagination," or act of perceiving in each individual mind), and of the poetic creation effected by "the secondary Imagination" (an "echo" of the primary imagination which, like that faculty, is a "synthetic . . . power" that "reveals itself in the balance or reconciliation of opposite or discordant qualities").

It is possible to distinguish sharply between logical and spatial opposition: in the former, the terms of the opposition have conflicting meanings (for instance, the One and the Many), while in the latter, bundles of matter, similar or indistinguishable in content, jostle, separate, or stay apart. But as Alice Snyder shows, Coleridge often blends the two kinds of antithesis.[8] In the Elia essays Lamb does likewise: he frequently embodies a logical opposition in such spatially distinct entities as separate places, people, or physical objects. Consequently, the reconciliation of logical opposites can participate in the spatial configuration that we have been examining.

In a letter of 1819 to Dorothy Wordsworth, Lamb humorously alludes to the concept of reconciling opposites as it occurred in a passage concerning "Resolution and Independence" in her brother's Preface to *Poems* (1815). The poet's nine-year-old son William was visiting Lamb's home in London, and his stay occasioned this passage on his precociousness:

William's genius I take it, leans a little to the figurative, for being at play at Tricktrack (a kind of minor Billiard-table which we keep for smaller wights, & sometimes refresh our own mature fatigues with taking a hand at) not being able to hit a ball he had iterate aimed at, he cried out, "I cannot hit that beast"—now the balls are usually called men, but he felicitously hit upon a middle term, a term of approximation & imaginative reconciliation, a something where the two ends, of the brute matter (ivory) & their human & rather violent personification into *Men,* might meet, as I take it, illustrative of that Excellent remark in a certain Preface about Imagination, explaining "like a sea-beast that had crawled forth to sun himself."[9]

But Lamb's laughter did not prevent him from using the concept himself in the Elia essays.

"My Relations," which provides a useful introduction to this topic, exists on one level as a pairing of character sketches, but the thematic interest of the essay arises largely from Elia's stance in relation to the explicit subjects, his aunt and his cousin James. His viewpoint is distinguished from theirs partly by his ability to perceive their limitations. Of his aunt's feeling that the child Elia was the sole object of her love, he remarks: "A partiality quite so exclusive my reason cannot altogether approve" (p. 70). James has a rather different limitation: "With great love for *you,* J. E. hath but a limited sympathy with what you feel or do. He lives in a world of his own, and makes slender guesses at what passes in your mind. He never pierces the marrow of your habits" (p. 74). The narrowness of each character is exposed, but the aunt is narrow in her "exclusive" love for one person, while James is narrow in his incapacity to escape the confines of his own sensibility. There is already a kind of inclusiveness in the complementarity of the defects which they exemplify. Elia's norm of inclusiveness, however, is incarnated more specifically in other aspects of their personalities. His aunt, whom "single blessedness had soured to the world," found satisfaction in an illogical blend of Roman Catholicism and Unitarianism, devotional literature and the *Adventures of an Unfortunate Young Nobleman,* faith and French beans (pp. 70–71). Similarly, James encompasses opposite traits: "James is an inexplicable cousin. Nature hath her unities, which not every critic can penetrate; or, if we feel, we cannot explain them. The pen of Yorick, and of none since his, could have drawn J. E. entire—those fine Shandian lights and shades, which make up his story. I must limp after in my poor antithetical manner, as the fates have given me grace and talent. J. E. then—to the eye of a common observer at least—seemeth made up of contradictory principles" (p. 71). Elia views his aunt and his cousin from a perspective sufficiently distinct from their own to let their contradictions show. Yet his purpose is not to stand in judgment over them: "Do I mention these seeming inconsistencies to smile at, or upbraid, my unique cousin? Marry, heaven, and all good manners, and the understanding that should be between kinsfolk, forbid!—With all the strangenesses of this *strangest of the Elias*—I would not have him in one jot or tittle other than he is . . ." (pp. 74–75).

Neither does Elia's portrait of James Elia function, like Goldsmith's very similar Man in Black in *The Citizen of the World,* to criticize society. Both the Man in Black and James Elia are aptly described by Elia's phrases on his cousin—"The genuine child of impulse, the frigid philosopher of prudence" (p. 71). But the Man in Black is largely the creature of social circumstance: it forced him, against his good-natured inclinations (themselves the product of his naively idealistic clergyman-father's rearing), to adopt the mask of a skinflint merely to stay solvent (Letter XXVII), and then as we and Lien Chi Altangi watch, it momentarily tears off the mask by thrusting impoverished, deserving people in the path of this preacher of selfishness (Letter XXVI). The duality of James Elia's personality, by contrast, is not accounted for by reference to environmental pressures. This "wild kinsman" (p. 75) is as "fiery, glowing, tempestuous" (p. 73) in middle age as in youth; nothing has tamed, compromised, or disillusioned him. Why Elia, though not seeking to censure his aunt, James Elia, or society should underline the contradictoriness of his relatives becomes evident in the essay's treatment of temporality.

In the opening paragraph, Elia laments the passing of time, which buries friends and relatives finally in oblivion, and he reintroduces this topic in the middle of his portrayal of James: "I hate people who meet Time half-way. I am for no compromise with that inevitable spoiler. While he lives, J. E. will take his swing" (p. 73). The last phrase suggests not only the aggressiveness, but also the pendulum-like movement between contradictions which is central to James's success. In the present a person enlarges his allotment of time by spilling over the bounds of logic to encompass more possibilities than seem permitted by the rules of reason. Contradictoriness is a form of expansiveness. In the cases of James and Elia's aunt the same strategy also has an effect upon the future. When Elia shifts at the end of his first paragraph from the domain of Oblivion to the recollection of his aunt, he is himself battling "that inevitable spoiler" by rescuing a particular person from Oblivion to be remembered in a work of literature. This stratagem can succeed only if the person lives again on the printed page, and Elia's cousin and aunt successfully elude the pallor of conceptualization through the energy generated by their contradictoriness. Whatever ability James and the maiden aunt have to escape the lifelessness of consistency in the present and the oblivion of the merely dead in the future depends upon their attainment of the reconciliation of opposites.

Elia shares in the benefits of such a feat. Not only does he juxtapose sacred and secular, past and present, feminine and masculine in the two character sketches respectively, but he is also responsible for identifying the significance of the combining of contradictions. His separateness from his subjects extends to a difference between his image of them and their self-images. James's intellect is dominated by ideas of prudence, moderation, practicality, and convention, though his personality violates all these standards, and the aunt presumably sees herself as simply a devoted Christian. But Elia presents each of them in terms which illuminate more of their personalities than was available to their conscious understanding. Insofar as the reconciliation of opposites is a strategy of consciousness, it is Elia's mind, more than that of either of his relations, which attains it. Finally, Elia avoids the limitations which he observed in his subjects. Unlike his aunt, he does not exemplify a love which is either exclusive or indiscriminate; he distributes his affection between very different personalities, and he preserves his selfhood by distinguishing his perspective from theirs. Unlike his cousin, he is able to pierce the marrow of another person's habits; he penetrates more deeply into James's character than James could himself. Elia thus achieves a consciousness of the presence and importance of unifying opposites and a balance of critical intelligence and sympathy.

Elia calls "antithetical" the style which he adopts to portray his cousin, and Mulcahy has shown convincingly that this method of character-sketching "differs only in degree from Lamb's approach to art and life in general": "It is clear that Elia's chosen ground is the twilight borderland from which he can see the affirmative and the negative, the real and the imaginary, without the necessity of taking his stand in one or the other exclusively—and this not from mere reluctance to make a difficult decision, but from a firm conviction that to commit oneself to a partial truth is to deny the just claims of another truth." Mulcahy's account of the Elian dialectic between imagination and reality is among the few indispensable critical treatments of Lamb's essays. Its thesis resembles in one respect the sketch of Lamb in Stuart Tave's *The Amiable Humorist.* Tave, in his analytic history of English comic theory and practice in the eighteenth and early nineteenth centuries, dwells upon the frequency with which writers from the 1820s to the 1840s celebrated Lamb's blending of smiles and tears. This commingling, as Tave demonstrates, shares in the historical process of developing consciousness of a laughter that affirms, instead of negating, its object. Both Mulcahy's and Tave's treatments of Lamb may be viewed, in the present context, as pointing to varieties of the reconciliation of opposites. In the next pages I propose to examine a few Elia essays from a point of view which emphasizes the spectrum of Elian reconciling modes from the definition of the self to the increasingly expansive. "Personality," wrote Coleridge, "is a circumference continually expanding through sympathy and understanding, rather than an exclusive center of self-feeling."[10] Sometimes Elia's unification stresses the linking of apparently contradictory features of himself within himself, and sometimes it stresses the combining of his own sensibility with that of someone else through a sympathy which tends toward, but never reaches, complete empathy.

The purest specimen of linked internal contradictions is "Oxford in the Vacation." Its first paragraph states at once the reader's inquiry and the essay's theme: *"Who is Elia?"* (p. 7).[11] In the rest of the essay Elia identifies himself partly by what he is, partly by what he is not. He begins by facing the classification which he presumes the reader wishes to impose upon him: a clerk. Elia's response is to admit the fact ("Well, I do agnize something of the sort") (p. 7) but repudiate the implication. He admits that he is employed as a clerk, but he denies that he *is* a clerk. The first section of the essay seeks to establish those aspects of his being which the category "clerk" will not accommodate. His "fancy" alleges that his day's routine facilitates his life as a "man of letters" by providing respite from study, waste paper for scribbling, and even material, such as "indigos, cottons, raw silks, piece-goods, flowered or otherwise" for "contemplation" (p. 7). Moreover, he distances himself from the narrowness of the mere operative by wishing that the multiplicity of saint's days which had been free days at school were recognized by his employers. In both cases, he associates his attitudes with what is intellectual or spiritual and free, as opposed to materialistic and mechanical. He is no "votary of the desk" (p. 7), but instead espouses a more honorable (though hardly less orthodox) creed, according to which one humorously mourns "the defalcation of Iscariot" (p. 8) at least partly for depriving the world of one more saint's day, with its liberty.

In the next section he begins to establish his relationship with Oxford and the types of persons who usually dwell there. Oxford is a place which objectifies Elia's values more completely than his place of work or even an antique counting-house like that of the complementary "The South-Sea House," which precedes this essay. Circumstances deprived him of a university education, but he can imaginatively identify with the students and scholars who ordinarily wander about the walks and buildings; he can breathe the atmosphere of "antiquity" and old books. The wholesomeness of Oxford is embodied in the essay's allusions to food, especially in the contrast with the unnaturalness suggested by an earlier reference. A clerk, we were told, is "one that sucks his sustenance, as certain sick people are said to do, through a quill" (p. 7). Even though Elia "has been defrauded in his young years of the sweet food of academic institution" (p. 9), he can still find a plentifulness at Oxford that no clerk's quill can provide: "Then, to take a peep in by the way at the butteries, and sculleries, redolent of antique hospitality: the immense caves of kitchens, kitchen fire-places, cordial recesses; ovens whose first pies were baked four centuries ago; and spits which have cooked for Chaucer! Not the meanest minister among the dishes but is hallowed to me through his imagination, and the Cook goes forth a Manciple" (p. 9). It appears that Elia's spirit discovers at the university an objective embodiment of the values which, back at the clerk's desk, existed only in his mind.

But the third part significantly modifies the essay's endorsement of Oxford and its inhabitants. The section begins when Elia dissociates himself from certain scholarly labors in terms that suggest a threat to his spirituality and to his digestion: "Those *variae lectiones,* so tempting to the more erudite palates, do but disturb and unsettle my faith" (p. 10). Again extending the pattern of references to food, he grows still more critical toward certain administrators who are indifferent to G. D.'s investigations of the two universities' origins: "Your caputs, and heads of colleges, care less than any body else about these questions.—Contented to suck the milky fountains of their Alma Maters, without inquiring into the venerable gentlewomen's years, they rather hold such curiosities to be impertinent—unreverend" (pp. 10-11). It is becoming evident that Oxford fails to provide a completely satisfactory objectification of Elia's values, just as the actual conditions of the past are not an adequate ground for our idolatry of antiquity (p. 9). But the most interesting modification of the essay's import is implicit in the character sketch of G. D. (based on Lamb's friend George Dyer).

Like Elia, G. D. comes to Oxford from more utilitarian surroundings; his usual residence is Clifford's Inn. Also like Elia, G. D. never perverts the university, as do the administrators, into a merely useful source of remuneration. Instead, both have a reverence for the ancient traditions of the place, manifested in the former's researches into its history and in the latter's apostrophe to antiquity. G. D. is kind and courteous, much as Elia sees himself to be.

In some respects, therefore, G. D. is Elia's double. Yet Elia is careful to dissociate himself from G. D.'s sensibility by making evident the latter's absentmindedness: "D. is the most absent of men" (p. 11). The anecdote in which G. D. calls on a friend, finds him to be away for a few days, signs his name in the guest-register, and then forgetfully returns two or three hours later to repeat the process makes G. D. into a figure of humorous narrowness, lacking the flexibility of the perspective from which Elia benevolently smiles upon him. G. D. is reduced from alert consciousness almost to the status of an object, a suggestion planted in our minds when Elia first introduces his friend: "With long poring, he is grown almost into a book. He stood as passive as one by the side of the old shelves. I longed to new-coat him in Russia, and assign him his place" (p. 10). When G. D. stares upon the register which he had signed a few hours before, "his first name (scarce dry) looks out upon him like another Sosia, or as if a man should suddenly encounter his own duplicate" (p. 11). G. D.'s double, his earlier signature, shows him his own diminished status, his deviation from human freedom into a mechanical process of repetition or duplication. But when Elia contemplates *his* double, G. D., the effect is to reveal his own superiority, his possession of a largeness which is not exhausted in G. D.'s duplication of many aspects of himself. Elia has a common sense with which he can measure G. D.'s absentmindedness, but he does not use it as a norm by which to reject him. On the contrary, he relishes him just as he is, and G. D. continues to embody a major portion of himself.[12]

Who, then, is Elia? He is a clerk and a man of letters, but without the narrowness of either. The freedom which he espoused in his discussion of holidays has a significance which transcends his liking for vacations. He uses both the hard-headedness of the clerk and the speculativeness of the author to criticize each other. In his blending of linguistic patterns concerned with food and religion, he reinforces his image of freely moving through an area larger than counting house or university, clerkship or antiquarianism, physicality or spirituality. In the apparently random sequence of his thoughts (an appearance that belies the inner structure of the essay), as well as in the implication that no externality adequately embodies his values, his freedom seems more spacious than even the distance between these polarities. His identity is nothing less than a reconciliation of opposites, though it may be something more.

In "The Wedding" the phrase *"concordia discors"* describes Admiral B.'s household:

I do not know a visiting place where every guest is so perfectly at his ease;

nowhere, where harmony is so strangely the result of confusion. Every body is at cross purposes, yet the effect is so much better than uniformity. Contradictory orders; servants pulling one way; master and mistress driving some other, yet both diverse; visitors huddled up in corners; chairs unsymmetrised: candles disposed by chance; meals at odd hours, tea and supper at once, or the latter preceding the former; the host and the guest conferring, yet each upon a different topic, each understanding himself, neither trying to understand or hear the other; draughts and politics, chess and political economy, cards and conversation on nautical matters, going on at once, without the hope, or indeed the wish, of distinguishing them, make it altogether the most perfect *concordia discors* you shall meet with. (p. 243)

The principal result of the contradictoriness is to create an energy and a sense of crowdedness which enable even a place from which a young daughter has recently departed to remain full of vitality. The basis for valuing the unification of opposites is given more elaboration by the essay as a whole, including the references to passing time. Admiral B.'s "growing infirmities" made an early wedding for his daughter desirable so that her father would be alive when she married (p. 240), and the aftermath of her departure is to bring home an awareness of aging: "It is wonderful how one young maiden freshens up, and keeps green, the paternal roof. . . . The youthfulness of the house is flown. Emily is married" (p. 243). "I take it unkindly to be left out," quips Elia, "even when a funeral is going on in the house of a dear friend" (p. 239). The formidable eye of the parson replaces Elia's levity with "the tristful severities of a funeral" (p. 241). In a world ruled by time, the people of this essay seek to fill every moment, and so to expand it, with maximum contents. When a moment is unfilled, its tightness gets under a man's skin. The young people are in a hurry to get married, but Admiral B. tries to keep his daughter from going off and leaving behind an empty space. More explicit is the explanation of Elia's function after the bride and groom have hastened away on their honeymoon: "I rattled off some of my most excellent absurdities. All were willing to be relieved, at any expense of reason, from the pressure of the intolerable vacuum which had succeeded to the morning bustle" (pp. 242–243). Into that vacuum rushes Elia's levity to create an impression of fullness, and this is the impression that the *concordia discors* in the admiral's house maintains, though imperfectly, some time later despite the fact that "The youthfulness of the house is flown" (p. 243).

Unseriousness at a wedding had twice been remarked upon by Richard Steele in *The Tatler* (Nos. 79, 184), once in explicit relation to the notion of emptiness. Steele wished to encourage respectful approbation toward matrimony, and he viewed as an enemy the "wag" who inappropriately thrusts his "insipid mirth" onto occasions such as that major event in *The Tatler,* the wedding of Isaac Bickerstaff's half-sister, Jenny Distaff. "A wag," Steele wrote sternly, "is the last order even of pretenders to wit and good humour. He has generally his mind prepared to receive some occasion of merriment, but is of himself too empty to draw any out of his own set of thoughts, and therefore laughs at the next thing he meets, not because it is ridiculous, but because he is under a necessity of laughing." The combination in Lamb's essay of Elia's conduct at a wedding and the reference to a "vacuum" points to *The Tatler* as a probable source, but the use to which Lamb puts these elements has no precedent in the earlier essay series. "The Wedding" is governed by the concerns and valuations of the Elian imaginative world.

Elia's suitability for filling the "intolerable vacuum" at Admiral B.'s stems from his position as an opposite to the other characters in the essay. They are all members of a family, the admiral's or Mr. Forester's or the new family established by the day's events. Elia, however, is an outsider, and he feels the limitation of his perspective: "Being without a family, I am flattered with these temporary adoptions into a friend's family; I feel a sort of cousinhood, or uncleship, for the season; I am inducted into degrees of affinity; and, in the participated socialities of the little community, I lay down for a brief while my solitary bachelorship" (p. 239). At the wedding no one behaves unconventionally except Elia, who has a habit of reacting with levity to solemn ceremonies. On this occasion he has to suppress an "incipient jest" (p. 241) after the parson glowers upon him. His black clothing strikes some people as unsuitable, and it contrasts with the more conventional white and green of the bride and attendants. His detached perspective seems so far to be devoid of utility, but it soon proves its worth in dispelling the gloom which succeeds the departure of the young couple. The attitudes of detachment and involvement each have their uses, but regrettably each tends to exclude the other. Just as a young lady has to choose either her father or her husband—the Misses Forester select one alternative, the bride another—in an imperfect world a person ordinarily excludes some good things by the act of opting for others.

Elia, however, manages in part to elude this limitation. Instead of existing merely as one pole in the opposition between detachment and involvement, he is able through sympathy to incorporate within himself an involved perspective. In contrast to "romance writers," who like to dilate upon the "hardheartedness of fathers" (p. 240), Elia is able to appreciate the point of view of the man who opposes his daughter's marriage. Elia sees his severity as deriving from his love for the girl and his reluctance to be separated from her. "I do not understand these matters experimentally," Elia explains, "but I can make a shrewd guess at the wounded pride of a parent upon these occasions" (p. 240). The climax of his portrayal of the worth of sympathy occurs when he accounts for the readiness of mothers to accept their daughters' marriages: a husband supplants a father much more than a mother; and a mother has a keen sense of "the inconveniences (impossible to be conceived in the same degree by the other parent) of a life of forlorn celibacy" (p. 240). Elia penetrates far enough into the feelings of both parents to show that his mind is not confined to the detachment for which his own bachelorhood has prepared him. His sympathy is not simply a surge of fellow-feeling; it is also a way of knowing what goes on in heads other than his own. "Sympathy," wrote Lamb in 1834, "is a young lady's word, rife in modern novels, & is almost always wrongly applied. To sympathise is to feel *with* not simply *for* another."[13] Elia is confined neither by marital status nor by sex in his capacity for such penetration, and he underlines the validity of the resulting knowledge by declaring in "The Wedding" that the mother, whose "trembling foresight" is itself a form of sympathy, provides a "surer guide" to the best interests of the daughter than the unsympathizing father. On the other hand, Elia stops short of empathy by retaining his own selfhood. By showing that a father's judgment has its limits, and noting in the next few sentences "the unbeseeming artifices, by which some wives push on the matrimonial projects of their daughters" (p. 240), he indicates, however gently, where his own attitudes diverge from those of the people with whom he can sympathize. He expands his own awareness by including other sensibilities, but he avoids abandoning his own center, and thereby losing himself in a world without coordinates or coherence. But the impressiveness of his accomplishment is modified by the feeling of incompleteness which he mentions in his first paragraph and by the reminder at the end that any success, even the bustle at the Admiral B.'s, is modest in a world doomed by time.

The value which Lamb attaches to preserving one's selfhood distinguishes his practice from that absence of identity which Keats (expanding upon his own earlier definition of "Negative Capability") attributes to the "poetical Character itself" as contrasted with "the wordsworthian or egotistical sublime."[14] Lamb's artistic world is a median between negative capability and what might descriptively be called the egotistical prosaic. His Elia volumes reveal this union of opposites in the recurrent dialectic of individuality or eccentricity and sympathy. The "Imperfect Sympathies" of the essay by that name and the grouchiness of "A Bachelor's Complaint of the Behaviour

of Married People" act as a counterweight to the innumerable sympathetic
character sketches elsewhere. Elia "was in many respects a singular character" (p. 152), the preface to the *Last Essays* reminds us. His idiosyncrasy is
his guarantee that he has held on to his identity despite his diminutiveness
in an immense cosmos and despite the centrifugal tendencies of his sympathy.
Likewise, memory serves in part as a principle of selection: only those details with the greatest human interest from Elia's perspective return to occupy
him now. His present may sometimes be cluttered with clerkly tasks or unassimilable data, but retrospection operates only upon what, on his terms, is
significant. Discrimination comes, too, with the mutual criticism implied in
juxtaposing opposites; the limitations of each pole of a contrast are present
to Elia's mind. His inclusiveness, then, is not just a matter of embracing all;
there is a kind of measure in his affirmations.

But if individuality, even eccentricity, is preserved, it is not permitted to
imprison. In Elia's refutation of the popular fallacy "That home is home
though it is never so homely," he precedes his grumbling display of his own
visitor-infested residence with a sympathetic portrayal of the poor man's wish
to escape the familial misery of his squalid "home." "Poor Relations" begins
by satirizing the servile, impecunious relatives who drop in to mar one's present appearance of gentility. They are a domesticized version of the double,
and they are treated without compassion, especially in the extraordinary first
sentence, where they are reduced to the status of innumerable objects. But
the tone becomes serious with the story of the Oxford student whose father,
a "little, busy, cringing tradesman" (p. 160), so embarrassed him that he enlisted in the army and soon perished. Still, the poor relation, the parent, is
not treated sympathetically. The seriousness, despite some distancing humor,
continues in the last section, which introduces a poor man who used to visit
Elia's father, and who one day took offense at being told "you do not get
pudding every day" (p. 162). We are made to share the old gentleman's feelings sufficiently to appreciate his hurt pride, and the incident brings the essay
from a merely external view of poor relations to an entrance into their minds.
The essay as a whole combines the self-regarding and sympathetic perspectives,
though its sequence of episodes hints that the latter is the more profound.

The use of sympathy as a means for comprehending the attitudes of the
poor held a potential for social criticism upon which Elia occasionally capi-
talized. To this extent he sought to strike out from his private world to influence the public world, and this endeavor adds to the reconciliation of
opposites a related expansive element. In "That Home is Home though it is
never so Homely" there is a warmth of feeling which includes anger at the

genteel popular fallacy's myopia toward the wretchedness of the impoverished. "A Complaint of the Decay of Beggars in the Metropolis," which is impaired by the weakening of the dialectic's sympathetic pole, rests mainly upon the aesthetic advantages of our having beggars around to look at,[15] but one passage treats sympathetically a legless mendicant's loss of "free air and exercise" in exchange for the "restraints of a poor-house" (p. 119). "The Tombs in the Abbey" protests, on the basis of two acts of sympathy, against the policy of charging admission to Westminster Abbey. Elia, who immediately makes clear that he is not a Church of England man, is sufficiently able to project himself into the viewpoint of a Robert Southey (to whom the essay-letter is addressed) to include the "venerableness of your ecclesiastical establishment" (p. 207) among the interests that would be served by opening the gates. Moving in the opposite direction, Elia appreciates, unlike the authorities, the importance which a child or a poor person would attach to even the two-shilling entrance fee, and he tries to arouse a like sympathy within Southey. But the most memorable Elian essay relating to social criticism is undoubtedly "The Praise of Chimney-Sweepers."

It becomes quickly apparent that here again we have a treatment of opposites. At dawn, we are told, two sorts of people are abroad: "when (as extremes meet) the rake, reeling home from his midnight cups, and the hard-handed artisan leaving his bed to resume the premature labours of the day, jostle, not unfrequently to the manifest disconcerting of the former, for the honours of the pavement" (p. 110). The attraction which chimney-sweepers feel toward Saloop is explained, in part, by a theory of opposites: "or whether Nature, sensible that she had mingled too much of bitter wood in the lot of these raw victims, caused to grow out of the earth her sassafras for a sweet lenitive . . ." (p. 110). The essay as a whole presents Elia as a specimen of a genteel class which contrasts with the chimney-sweepers. He has never been able to overcome his fastidiousness sufficiently to taste Saloop— "a cautious premonition to the olfactories constantly whispering to me, that my stomach must infallibly, with all due courtesy, decline it" (p. 109). He ordinarily likes to stroll undisturbed by the rabble: "I am by nature extremely susceptible of street affronts; the jeers and taunts of the populace; the low-bred triumph they display over the casual trip, or splashed stocking, of a gentleman" (pp. 110-111). Elia brings much that differentiates him from the dirty, uneducated, hard-working chimney-sweepers to the contemplation of that very species.

The result is a challenge to his sympathy which he easily meets. He portrays chimney-sweepers in five epiphanies which capture his imagination and obtain his rapport. He was once a child too, and when a child he identified with a sweep who was performing his duties:

. . . to see a chit no bigger than one's-self enter, one knew not by what process, into what seemed the *fauces Averni*—to pursue him in imagination, as he went sounding on through so many dark stifling caverns, horrid shades! —to shudder with the idea that "now, surely, he must be lost for ever!"—to revive at hearing his feeble shout of discovered day-light—and then (O fulness of delight) running out of doors, to come just in time to see the sable phenomenon emerge in safety, the brandished weapon of his art victorious like some flag waved over a conquered citadel! (p. 109)

In the act of doing his indecorous job the sweep becomes a representative of man's most exemplary efforts to overcome difficulty. Like an epic hero, but lacking his aristocratic status, he enters the underworld,[16] reemerges into daylight, and accomplishes a glorious conquest. We admire him, and to some degree we are him. The second epiphany is pathetic, rather than heroic. Unable to afford a drink of Saloop, the sweep tries to get some enjoyment out of the beverage by merely smelling it: "Being penniless, they will yet hang their black heads over the ascending steam, to gratify one sense if possible, seemingly no less pleased than those domestic animals—cats—when they purr over a new-found sprig of valerian" (p. 110). The pathos is reinforced by the comparison, not with something higher than a chimney sweep (as in the first epiphany), but with something that is lower and yet indigenous to a genteel household—a cat. The third epiphany takes the chimney-sweeper for what he is in himself, a member of a class quite separate from Elia's who reveals in his own way a vitality which his misery has not quashed. Elia, dashing along Cheapside, had just slipped to the ground, "when the roguish grin of one of these young wits encountered me" (p. 111). Elia's response reveals his sympathy to be stronger than his fastidiousness: "There he stood, pointing me out with his dusky finger to the mob, and to a poor woman (I suppose his mother) in particular, till the tears for the exquisiteness of the fun (so he thought it) worked themselves out at the corners of his poor red eyes, red from many a previous weeping, and soot-inflamed, yet twinkling through all with such a joy, snatched out of desolation . . ." (p. 111). At first Elia reacts with the disapproval of a gentleman, as the coolness of "wits" and "mob" suggests. But the introduction of the sweep's mother and his tears alters the balance, and in the end Elia confesses "that I could have been content, if the honour of a gentleman might endure it, to have remained his butt and his mockery till midnight" (p. 111). The fourth epiphany is the incident, not actually witnessed by Elia, in which the chimney-sweeper crept into a luxurious bed in Arundel Castle. Elia utilizes sympathy in his attempt to understand what was in the boy's mind, and he concludes that the sweep had originally been a nobleman's son. The boy mustered the temerity to invade the "magnificent chamber" (p. 112) by simply remembering that such a place was once part of his ordinary experience. Finally, the pleasure of the sweeps at the annual banquet which Jem White used to give for them is the last epiphany by which their nature is disclosed and Elia shows his sympathy for them.

The structure of the essay is intelligible on one level as a series of encounters between opposites, by which the genteel speaker, without surrendering his gentility, expands his awareness by appreciating to some extent the perspective of the chimney-sweeper. The latter's sufferings, however, tempt us to ask what Elia wants to *do* about so deplorable a situation. The answer provided by the surface of the essay is "not very much." Give the poor fellow a penny or two for some Saloop and bread, Elia exhorts us; and his relation of his own experiences indicates that one ought not to get angry if a sweep enjoys our sprawling on the ground. Jem White, Elia, and Bigod went a step further by supplying an annual feast and entertainment for the boys, and the ending contains regret that the custom has ceased. But none of this adds up to a significant alteration of the chimney-sweeper's plight, and Elia's comment that the sweeps, toiling away on a chill December morning, "preach a lesson of patience to mankind" (p. 109), invites us to classify Lamb's response to this instance of human deprivation as reaction spiced with charity and aestheticism.

To accept this invitation, however, would be to overlook the essay's treatment of the relation between nature and social form. The sweeps enter in the act of "blooming" (this is the first verb or verbal applied to them), and they quickly blend with the signs of life by which nature starts a new day. At dawn or earlier their professional cry (Blake rendered it as "weep, weep") sounds "like the *peep peep* of a young sparrow" (p. 108), and the visual impression which they make upon us is similar to the auditory: "liker to the matin lark should I pronounce them, in their aerial ascents not seldom anticipating the sun-rise?" (p. 108). They have a yen for Saloop, the drink which Nature bestows "for a sweet lenitive" (p. 110). Mr. Read, who boasts that he operates "the *only Salopian house*," sells indoors what is actually dispensed to "humbler customers" at numerous outdoor stands (p. 110), and his house with its claim to exclusiveness parallels in its artifice Elia's mannered style. Both contrast with the natural values associated with the boys. Yet the sweeps are compelled to do a certain job, to occupy a certain social niche, to work not only indoors but in chimneys, even if kidnapping is a necessary preliminary: "The premature apprenticements of these tender victims give but too much encouragement, I fear, to clandestine, and almost infantile abductions..." (p. 111). This forcible separation from an earlier life implies an interference with nature by the imposition of an arbitrary and inhumane set of social forms.

That the social forms are arbitrary is underlined in the incident concerning the sweep who crept into an aristocrat's bed in Arundel Castle (another building which signifies social artifice, like the houses in which the boys labor). The puzzle posed by the anecdote is how an urchin could dare to act like a nobleman's son, and the difficulty rests on the premise, derived from society's forms, that an urchin is very different from a nobleman's son. This premise is dismissed by Elia's emphasis on the prevalence of "fairy-spiriting" (p. 111) a child from a genteel home, not to the land of the Erlking but to the grime of London's chimneys. He refers to such children as "poor changelings" (p. 112) although he says nothing of substituting another child for the stolen one. The allusion to changelings has the effect of indicating that class distinctions have no necessary reference to the characters, personalities, or abilities of the persons who are thus classified.[17] The "pre-existent state" (p. 112) which the unintimidated visitant recalls (though "not ... to full consciousness") is, in one sense, that period when he had free access to his own family's baronial bedchambers, but, in a more general sense, it is the period in everyone's life when he has not yet distinguished himself from his surroundings and his limited, historical experience of existence has still to begin. It is the time when he "was used to be lapt by his mother, or his nurse" (p. 112) in sheets which seemed as fine as those which adorn the sleeping quarters of the Howards. By evoking this broader type of previous grandeur, Elia universalizes his negation of class distinctions and supports his suggestion that what prompted the sweep's adventurousness was nothing less than the "great power of nature" (p. 112).

The last section raises the possibility of substituting an alternative order for the established one. The yearly suppers, held near St. Bartholomew's Fair, are preceded by the issuance of invitation cards to young chimney-sweepers; Jem White jokingly ensures that they get nothing that is "not fit for a gentleman's eating" (p. 113); and his series of humorous toasts is a custom not usual in a sweep's experience. The banquet becomes a whimsical inversion of the social order, with Jem White, a nineteenth-century lord of misrule, as the center of a facetious "inaugural ceremony" (p. 113) in which "old dame Ursula" serves as his queen. The climactic, or as Elia says, "crowning" inversionary sentiment is, "May the Brush supersede the Laurel!" (p. 113). The emblem of the sweep's toil would become a badge of honor. When the mock king busses his queen, the boys are momentarily transformed, in Elia's echo of *Paradise Lost,* into re-creations of a more solemn structured alternative to an established order: "whereat the universal host would set up a shout that tore the concave, while hundreds of grinning teeth startled the night with their brightness" (p. 113). But the essay never views the privileged classes as tyrants, and never suggests that the sweeps possess the anger of the insurrectionary. The boys may grin at the discomfiture of a gentleman, but "the grin of a genuine sweep hath absolutely no malice in it . . ." (p. 111). The essay contains much of the pathetic, but none of the enraged. It presents no programs and endorses no revolutionary actions. Yet it does more than make a joke out of Jem White's dinners. It suggests that their apparently nonsensical overturning of the social order makes at least as much sense as the arbitrary indifferent social order which sweeps experience daily. Why the essay does not issue in political activism, however, only becomes clear in the final lines, when the question of who is on top and who on the bottom is suddenly dwarfed by the specter we all must face:

> Golden lads and lasses must,
> As chimney-sweepers, come to dust— (p. 114)

The trouble with seeing an escape from human problems in the effort to get back to nature by eliminating the tyrannous forms imposed upon us is that Nature itself is in the end our unconquerable antagonist. Elia's death is announced in the preface to *Last Essays of Elia* in carefully chosen words: "This poor gentleman, who for some months past had been in a declining way, hath at length paid his final tribute to nature" (p. 151). "Old chimney-sweepers are by no means attractive," Elia had informed us (p. 108), and although that observation may be read as an indictment of what the system eventually does to a sweep, it is more likely a comment on the power of time. Jem White himself is vulnerable—he is "extinct" (p. 114) now—and the suppers have ceased. The wretchedness of the chimney-sweeper, like the devastation by time, seems, in the context of the essay as a whole, to be one aspect of that inescapable frustration of desire which we call the human condition.

In attempting the expansive strategy of reconciling opposites, Elia unified within himself different aspects of himself; and he moved further outward to include not only his own individuality, but also other people's perspectives as understood through sympathy; and, finally, he used such an inclusive private vantage point as a base from which to make some criticisms of the public world. Nevertheless, the culmination of this process is not transcendence over the finitude of human life, for in the end he finds that time qualifies every success and reduces it, from one point of view at least, to dust. But he does not stop laughing, or comprehending, or writing, and in "Old China" he achieves his fullest expression of how to accept and, in a way, triumph in the face of his spatial strategy's certain defeat.

"Old China" is built upon a contrast between the reminiscent speeches of Bridget and Elia and the pieces of blue china which open and close the essay. Previous critics have noted this pattern, and have emphasized the advantage which the timeless world of the china has over the temporal world of Elia and Bridget.[18] There is an evident note of regret for the passing of youth in Bridget's and Elia's speeches, and the latter culminates his retrospection by saying that he would trade any conceivable wealth to get back his earlier days. There is, then, a strong suggestion that the static aritifice of the china possesses something of value which mortals miss. What has not been sufficiently noted, however, is that the attractiveness of the china is balanced by the greater richness of the human experience evoked by the essay. If the china's preciousness resides mainly in its timelessness, the strength of man's finite experience appears in the essay's treatment of space.

Lamb's ostensible topic in "Old China" was in itself nothing new to the familiar essay. Chinaware had appeared often in Steele and Addison—as the object of a feminine craving which was rationally indefensible but which women would not abandon although it embittered relations between the sexes. Steele (*Tatler*, No. 23) cited the husband whose firm negative finally cured his wife of her habit of fainting to get whatever she wanted. He "fell into an invective against china, protesting, he would never let five pounds more of his money be laid out that way as long as he breathed." *The Tatler* left no doubt that his course was wise. One of Steele's *Spectator* papers (No. 326) contained a letter from a husband who endured the expense of his wife's longings during pregnancy. While she had carried one of their children, for example, "she had fix'd her Mind upon a new Set of Plate, and as much China as would have furnish'd an *India* Shop." An essay by Addison on the ability of women to "Talk whole Hours together upon nothing" (*Spectator*, No. 247) mentioned one who could "chide her Servant for breaking a China Cup in all the Figures of Rhetorick," and Steele responded (*Spectator*, No. 252) with a letter from a man whose wife used not only words but also tears, faintings, and beauty to accomplish her ends: "Every Room in my House is furnished with Trophies of her Eloquence, rich Cabinets, Piles of China, Japan Screens, and costly Jarrs; and if you were to come into my great Parlour you would fancy your self in an *India* Warehouse: Besides this, she keeps a Squirrel, and I am doubly taxed to pay for the China he breaks." Addison included in one of his *Spectator* papers (No. 299) a letter from a self-made man who got rich, then married an indigent noble-woman, and now must bear her femininity and gentility: "She next set her self to reform every Room of my House, having glazed all my Chimney-pieces with Looking-glass, and planted every Corner with such heaps of *China,* that I am obliged to move about my own House with the greatest Caution and Circumspection, for fear of hurting some of our Brittle Furniture." In *The Lover* (No. 10) Addison argued that china was overly expensive, fragile, subject to arbitrary changes of style, and useless. "Did our women take delight in heaping up piles of earthen platters, brown juggs, and the like useful products of our British potteries, there would be some sense in it" because these at least are durable and cheap.[19] Instead, the speaker of this essay has been rejected in love by a woman to whom he confided what Addison wholly approved, a low estimate of china.

When Elia qualifies as "almost feminine" his "partiality for old china," he is evoking the treatment of china by his predecessors at the same time that he overturns precedent. In "Old China" a delight in such an object becomes defensible, and it is a man who defends it, while a woman argues against the wealth that underpins it. A sexual stereotype is brushed aside. But a more fundamental difference between this essay and its precursors is that Steele and Addison arranged disputes between a right side and a wrong side, while Lamb let both his conflicting speakers make major contributions toward reaching what his essay conceives as the truth.

The spatial condition portrayed on the jars, cups, and saucers is essentially the transcendence of that gulf between self and other, center and circumference, which Elia so frequently seeks to overcome. Elia sees chinaware not as that which he can apprehend only by moving across the intervening space but as something internal to himself: "I can call to mind the first play, and the first exhibition, that I was taken to; but I am not conscious of a time when china jars and saucers were introduced into my imagination" (p. 248). He must be "taken to" plays and exhibitions, and his ability to remember himself before he encountered these things suggests that his selfhood is independent of them. But china was "introduced into my imagination"; he did not go out to meet it. At the same time, he cannot think of any moment when, in the absence of previous experience of china, he existed. These jars and saucers, like the old familiar faces of one of Lamb's early poems, are not experienced as other. By adding that "distance cannot diminish" the "old friends" pictured on them, Lamb shifts the object to an external position, but he retains the essential element of transcending the disjunction between little world and great world. The interpolation of additional space does not remove these old friends from Elia's microcosm. Moreover, the figures on the crockery stand in a relation to each other that parallels Elia's relation to them. They are "uncircumscribed by any element." In their experience the distinction between distance and proximity virtually disappears; there is no more near nor far. A "young and courtly Mandarin" hands tea to a lady "from a salver—two miles off," while a lady "is stepping into a little fairy boat, moored on the hither side of this calm garden river, with a dainty mincing foot, which in a right angle of incidence (as angles go in our world) must infallibly land her in the midst of a flowery mead—a furlong off on the other side of the same strange stream!" (p. 248). In the world pictured on the china the possibility of large size—such as Elia coveted in "That a sulky temper is a misfortune"—need arouse no yearning since no creature is compelled to remain little in the face of something big. A cow and a rabbit are "coextensive" (p. 248). Finally, it is easy for the beings on the crockery to combine possibilities which are irreconcilable in human experience: they can stand "up in the air" and at the same time "on *terra firma* still" (p. 248). They are not restricted to the status of points in a vast universe which exists part outside of part.

Bridget's retrospection concerns a human effort to push out from a center to encompass more and more of the external world—a modest aspiration in the direction of that identity of center and circumference achieved on the china. She speaks of various excursions—Elia's repeated visits to the shop in Covent Garden which had a folio Beaumont and Fletcher for sale and, finally, his knocking at ten o'clock on Saturday night to make the purchase; Bridget's and Elia's "pleasant walks to Enfield, and Potter's Bar, and Waltham" (p. 249) for a picnic, and the search for an inn where they could, after buying some ale, eat their own food; and their squeezing out "our shillings a-piece to sit three or four times in a season" (p. 250) in the gallery at a London theater. She speaks also, sometimes in the same anecdotes, of reluctant purchases, another means to assimilate external objects to the self: the folio Beaumont and Fletcher which she helped to repair and collate; "that print after Lionardo" (p. 249); and some strawberries or peas while they were yet rare. She and her cousin got great satisfaction out of these two ways of converting elements in the large world into ingredients of their private world. But by the present, Bridget has discovered that when luxuries—including seats in the pit at the theater and old china—can be easily afforded and when she and her cousin have the means to "*ride* part of the way" to a "fine inn," these conquests of exterior space no longer bring "half the relish" (p. 250) they once brought. Her overt conclusion is that their prosperity is the cause of their diminished enjoyment. But in terms of the inner logic of the essay, her speech has demonstrated that the source of their previous satisfaction resided in something other than the conquest of exterior space. It resided in the tension between their outgoing quest and the external difficulties thrust in their way by topography and economics.

Elia answers her overt conclusion by reminding her that "It is true we were happier when we were poorer, but we were also younger, my cousin" (p. 251). Bridget's diagnosis puts the blame on a change in financial circumstances, an alteration that could be negated by their getting rid of their wealth and thus restoring the earlier external obstacles. Elia, more pessimistically, finds that the cause of their unhappiness lies in an invasion of the self by the alien power of time. The result of the interiorizing of this hostile entity is to weaken the expansive force of the self: "The resisting power—those natural dilations of the youthful spirit, which circumstances cannot straiten —with us are long since passed away" (p. 251). Consequently, their dissatisfaction is irremediable although their awareness of it can be reduced by the comforts which wealth can buy. The darkness of Elia's time-haunted perspective is at once heightened and qualified, however, by the long, magnificent sentence almost at the end:

Yet could those days return—could you and I once more walk our thirty miles a-day—could Bannister and Mrs. Bland again be young, and you and I be young to see them—could the good old one shilling gallery days return— they are dreams, my cousin, now—but could you and I at this moment, instead of this quiet argument, by our well-carpeted fireside, sitting on this luxurious sofa—be once more struggling up those inconvenient stair-cases, pushed about, and squeezed, and elbowed by the poorest rabble of poor gallery scramblers—could I once more hear those anxious shrieks of yours— and the delicious *Thank God, we are safe,* which always followed when the topmost stair, conquered, let in the first light of the whole cheerful theatre down beneath us—I know not the fathom line that ever touched a descent so deep as I would be willing to bury more wealth in than Croesus had, or the great Jew R—is supposed to have, to purchase it. (p. 252)

Here in the extended subordinate clause is the effort, the resistance, the sudden command of new space, the thankfulness that the self has been preserved while new horizons have been conquered, in short, the expansive process which Bridget has described. The pathos springs partly from the grammatical construction in which this process is now expressed—a contrary-to-fact conditional. What was once fact can be fact no more despite the fierce will in the main clause that it again be so. The pathos derives also from the contrast between the upward motion of the subordinate clause and the downward motion of the main clause, a correlative for the contrast between previous success and present failure. But Elia's speech does not succeed in completely refuting Bridget's, although he demolishes her overt conclusion that prosperity is the cause of their trouble. What is left standing is her demonstration that fulfillment resides not in the conquest of exterior space, but in tension. Elia introduces the new categories of depth and height, downward and upward movements, which point to a new tension—that between fact and value. Moreover, his speech exists in a dialectical relation with Bridget's, just as both together exist in relation to the old china. Unlike the two-dimensional "world before perspective" (p. 248) of the old china, where "likeness is identity" (p. 248) and everything becomes feminized (pp. 247–248), the world of Bridget and Elia, the human world, is a place of tension, of drama, and therefore of a depth which is at once in three dimensions and in four. The old china excludes this tension, while the work of art which is the essay comprehends it.[20] This tension is the ultimate source of the power and richness of the essay, as well as a means for the reconciliation of opposites to reenter the Elia collection with an additional rationale. Most importantly, it is a consolation, in no sense escapist, for man's inability to complete the conquest of exterior space or to keep expanding forever.

NOTES

1. Montaigne, *Essays,* trans. Florio, III, 262; *The Works of Francis Bacon,* ed. James Spedding, R. L. Ellis, and D. D. Heath, VI (London: Longmans, 1870), 452; Cowley, *The Essays and Other Prose Writings,* ed. Alfred B. Gough (Oxford: Clarendon Press, 1915), pp. 179, 186–187.
2. Trans. C. Dawson, E. Coleman, and G. Poulet (Baltimore: Johns Hopkins Press, 1966), p. 104. Poulet's chapter on Romanticism (pp. 91–118) has greatly influenced my present chapter, although Poulet never mentions Lamb.

3. *Letters,* II, 164 (MS. Hn.). See Lucas, *The Life of Charles Lamb,* II, 601–605, for an account of the visit to Paris.
4. *Letters,* I, 285 (Br.); 241 (Tx.); 312–317; 316 (Hn.); Alan D. McKillop, "Charles Lamb Sees London," *Rice Institute Pamphlet,* 22 (1935), 124; Pater, *Appreciations,* p. 125.
5. Mulcahy, pp. 539–540.
6. *Letters,* I, 48–49, 39–40; 42, 46 (MS. Hn.); 261, 271; II, 231; 301–302 (MS. Hartz); 392–393; *Works,* V, 17–18; I, 226–236, 476–479.
7. Pater, *Appreciations,* p. 111. For Carlyle's reaction to Lamb see his *Reminiscences,* ed. James Anthony Froude (London: Longmans, Green, 1881), I, 232; II, 165–166.
8. *Natural Supernaturalism,* p. 268; Snyder, op. cit. (Ann Arbor: Univ. of Michigan, 1918), esp. pp. 9–10, 24, 55–56.
9. *Letters,* II, 265–266 (MS. Tx.).
10. Mulcahy, pp. 517–518; Tave, op. cit. (Chicago: Univ. of Chicago Press, 1960), esp. pp. 236–237; Coleridge, MS. *Logic* in Poulet, *Circle,* p. 105.
11. Weber, p. 33, notes the thematic centrality of the reader's supposed inquiry, and on pp. 56–59 he acutely analyzes the imagery of the essay's opening sentences in terms of the achievement through language of the freedom of creative play.
12. For the comic utility of the mechanical and the repetitive I am indebted to Henri Bergson, *Laughter* (1900), rpt. in *Comedy* (Garden City, N.Y.: Doubleday, 1956), pp. 61–190; for Lamb's use of a humor which allies with sympathy and does not reject what it laughs at, I have benefited from Stuart Tave's *The Amiable Humorist.* Neither treats "Oxford in the Vacation." Nabholtz, pp. 696–703, on the other hand, discusses this essay in detail. He sees G. D. as affirming a life of imagination which Elia endorses without qualification and into which Elia leads the reader by progressively liberating him from the restrictions of common sense. But Elia's reaction to G. D. is more equivocal and his valuation of common sense is higher than Nabholtz allows.
13. *Letters,* III, 413–414 (MS. R., Marrs transcription).
14. *The Letters of John Keats,* ed. Hyder E. Rollins (Cambridge, Mass.: Harvard Univ. Press, 1958), I, 193, 386–387. For persuasive evidence that Keats indirectly derived the concept of negative capability from Lamb (through the mediation of Hazlitt), see David Scott Perry, "Hazlitt, Lamb, and the Drama," (Ph.D. diss., Princeton, 1966), pp. 303–319.
15. Lamb's aestheticism here, as well as in "The Praise of Chimney-Sweepers," was noted by Bertram Jessup in "The Mind of Elia," *JHI,* 15 (1954), 257, and reemphasized by R. V. Johnson in "Aesthetic Traits in Charles Lamb," *Southern Review* (Australia) 3, ii (1968), 151–158. In "Beggars" Johnson finds a counterbalancing moral perspective.
16. "Fauces Averni" is from the *Aeneid,* VI, 201, as Lucas notes in *Works,* II, 381.
17. The concept of the changeling, with implications critical of class distinctions, was central to Mary Lamb's third chapter of *Mrs. Leicester's*

School, a book of stories for children by Mary and Charles Lamb published in 1809. Elia's use of the changeling for a different purpose in "New Year's Eve" is discussed in chapter two, p. 22.

18. See Mulcahy, pp. 533–534; Haven, pp. 139–142; and Reiman, pp. 476–478. Mulcahy carefully qualifies his principal emphasis by an important concession ("The lost pleasures of which Bridget speaks may have been more intense and robust" than the pleasures provided by the china, but he does not develop this perception further. Although Reiman writes perceptively on the china's transcendence of ordinary space, he does not show how the spatial theme is treated in the essay as a whole.

19. *The Lover*, ed. J. Nichols (London: J. Nichols, 1789), pp. 73, 69–73. No. 10 appeared originally on March 18, 1714. On the other hand, Addison's *Spectator*, No. 69, the panegyric on the Royal Exchange, cited this specimen of the splendid fruits of commerce: "Our Tables are stored with Spices, and Oils, and Wines: Our Rooms are filled with Pyramids of *China*, and adorned with the Workmanship of Japan . . . ." But *The Tatler* and *The Spectator*, when focusing upon the interests of the individual purchaser and her family, consistently took a dim view of china.

20. Cf. Haven, pp. 140–142, which sees the china and the essay as equivalents.

Chapter Five

EATING AND DRINKING

A writer's imaginative world can be entered by way of his recurrent surfaces or depths, his vehicles or tenors. The past three chapters have emphasized tenors: the temporal and spatial themes that the Elia essays keep pondering. But such an approach by itself is open to the objection that it overintellectualizes Lamb by turning aside from what some critics see as the inconsequential particularities, including the oafish materialities, that bulk large in the Elia essays and finally sink their pretensions to intellectual seriousness. The present chapter and the next look hard at two kinds of Elian trivia, without in the end finding that they are trivial. We have shifted perspective; but the goal of our attention is still the same—the figure in the Elian carpet, the configuration that unites vehicles and tenors in a single impressive design.

Edax utters the following confession in Lamb's essay "Edax on Appetite," which, together with the complementary "Hospita on the Immoderate Indulgence of the Palate," first appeared in 1812, the year before the publication of his "Confessions of a Drunkard": "My sufferings . . . have all arisen from a most inordinate appetite . . . an appetite, in its coarsest and least metaphorical sense,—an appetite for *food.*" Although Lamb is not to be equated with the speakers of these essays, he shares with them an extraordinary verbal preoccupation with food and drink. Beginning in 1800, extended outbursts of what E. V. Lucas calls "gustatory ecstasy" punctuate his letters. One of Lamb's last essays, "Thoughts on Presents of Game, &c.," ardently proclaims in 1833 that Elia now prefers "a hare roasted hard and brown—with gravy and melted butter!"[1] over his old favorite, roast pig.

Within the Elia essays of the 1823 and 1833 collected editions, two pieces
—"A Dissertation upon Roast Pig" and "Grace Before Meat"—deal unmistakably with food, and "Christ's Hospital Five and Thirty Years Ago" gives
a detailed menu of what the schoolboys had eaten in Elia's childhood. Even
if we exclude these essays, however, we find that the specific foods and beverages mentioned in the Elia volumes include muffin, cold mutton, punch,
pies, the juices of meats and fishes, wine, beer, gooseberry, port, woodcocks,
dotterels, cod's heads, French beans, lobster boiled, eels, fatted calf, nectarines, peaches, oranges, grapes, Saloop, sausages, hot meat and vegetables,
butter, turbot, claret, soup, Madeira, pudding, salads, biscuit, broths, cordials,
ale, roast fowl, salt, Cognac, water, beef, turkeys, custard, pancakes, cold
fowl, tongues, hams, botargoes, dried fruits, tea, caudle, cold lamb, hare,
grouse, Canterbury brawn, bread and cheese with an onion, cabbage, potatoes,
a leg of goat, a horse's shoulder, pork, veal, Sherry, Malaga, and honey. The
length of this menu falls short of suggesting the prominence which Elia gives
to ingestion, since nearly all his essays make some use of more generalized
language concerned with nourishing and tasting. The Charles Lamb whom
we see in verbal sketches and visual portraits by his contemporaries shows
no signs of corpulence. Why, then, did he keep writing about eating and
drinking?

Some of the facts, including the autobiographical aspects of the Elia essays
(there are also fictive aspects), point to a psychological tic. Elia talks about
many of his friends, such as B. F., G. D., J. W., M., and N. R., and these have
much, perhaps everything, in common with Lamb's friends, Barron Field,
George Dyer, Jem White, Thomas Manning, and Randal Norris. Elia, as well
as Lamb, has dealings with Coleridge and Southey, and his grandmother, aunt,
father, and cousins correspond to Lamb's grandmother, aunt, father,[2] brother
and sister. But Elia's mother is not endowed with the same level of imaginative presence as any of these people. Elia speaks of the "maternal tenderness"
(p. 28) that watched over him as a child while he was sick, but we are not
certain that his literal mother was the person who displayed it, and in "My
First Play" he recalls how, just before the curtain rose on *Artaxerxes,* "I re-
posed my shut eyes in a sort of resignation upon the maternal lap" (p. 98).
In "A Chapter on Ears," he suggests that if he had been born without physical ears, it would have been "Better my mother had never borne me" (p. 38).
But Mrs. Elia's overt existence never surpasses the adjectival or the proverbial;
she never becomes a character. On the fictive level, there is no reason for this
omission, but on the autobiographical level there is good reason. The circumstances of Mrs. Lamb's death—she was fatally stabbed by her daughter Mary

while the latter was insane—were so painful for her son to recall that he suppressed her memory, and therefore he left an unexplained gap in Elia's reminiscences. But repressed material has a way of surfacing in disguised forms, and three such forms are visible in the Elia essays.

One side of Lamb yearns for the security and vitality of childhood. He prevents the recollection of his mother, but his mind dwells upon the period when the mother-son relationship is least inhibited. In short, Lamb's suppression of his mother's memory fostered his nostalgia. A second feature of the Elia essays is their relative sexlessness. We learn in "Dream-Children" that Elia once experienced romantic love, but his old flame Alice W——n exists in the Elia essays as little more than a shadow. Lamb had proposed marriage in 1819 to the actress Fanny Kelly, and her refusal may have been as responsible for Elia's bachelorhood as it was for Lamb's. But this rejection closed one path toward the resolution of Lamb's problem concerning his mother and therefore reinforced the original problem. The third disguise under which the repressed material came to the surface was his fascination with eating and drinking. Among the many maternal contributions to a child's welfare, the provision of nourishment, unlike most of the others, is directed towards something which even the small child knows he wants. Also, it can involve the greatest physical intimacy. As a result, the association between mother and oral intake can be peculiarly basic to a child's, and perhaps less consciously, an adult's attitudes.

Yet, no matter how probable it is in theory that such an association existed in Lamb's mind, one would like to be guided by more concrete evidence, and at this point a difficulty arises. Nowhere in the largely autobiographical Elia essays does he recall his mother, or speak directly of mothers in general, as supplying nourishment. On the contrary, in his recollections of childhood the role of food-giver is occupied by his aunt. In "A Dissertation upon Roast Pig" she "never parted from me at the end of a holiday without stuffing a sweet-meat, or some nice thing, into my pocket," and in the incident which Elia relates she "had dismissed me one evening with a smoking plum-cake, fresh from the oven" (p. 125). "The only secular employment I remember to have seen her engaged in," he recalls in "My Relations," "was, the splitting of French beans, and dropping them into a China basin of fair water" (p. 71). The old gentleman who used to visit Elia's father in "Poor Relations" was always given a special pudding by Elia's aunt, and it was she who offended the man by saying, "Do take another slice, Mr. Billet, for you do not get pudding every day" (p. 162). The difficulty is not to be erased by arguing that Elia's relative is a fictive personality quite distinct from Lamb's aunt. In the early pages of "Christ's Hospital Five and Thirty Years Ago," the one occasion where Elia unequivocally separates himself from Lamb, he remembers how at school the latter obtained an extra supply of edibles: ". . . he had his hot plate of roast veal, or the more tempting griskin (exotics unknown to our palates), cooked in the paternal kitchen (a great thing), and brought him daily by his maid or aunt! I remember the good old relative (in whom love forbade pride) squatting down upon some odd stone in a by-nook of the cloisters, disclosing the viands . . ." (p. 13). The "maid or aunt" quickly simplifies to "the good old relative," more likely an aunt than a maid. In either case, the retrospection of the Elia essays reveals in the lives of Elia and his creator a feminine source of nutriment who is not the subject's mother.

The displacement of mother by aunt in the food-providing function is intelligible, however, even on the hypothesis that in his heart's core Lamb associated nourishment with maternity. If Lamb were to talk overtly about his mother in relation to food, he would not be repressing her memory. If, on a more generalized level, he were capable of saying directly that he thinks of food as a manifestation of maternity, he would, on the supposition that he wishes to repress the memory of his mother, also repress discussion of food. By overtly connecting the aunt, instead of the mother, with the food-supplying function, he is able to dwell upon the thought of food. But the defensiveness that is essential in retrospection is unnecessary in metaphor, and it is on this level that Lamb blurts out what is in the back of his mind. Recall, for instance, the conduct of the academic administrators in "Oxford in the Vacation": "Contented to suck the milky fountains of their Alma Maters, without inquiring into the venerable gentlewomen's years, they rather hold such curiosities to be impertinent—unreverend" (pp. 10–11). In "Distant Correspondents" the overt subject is puns: "Their nutriment for their brief existence is the intellectual atmosphere of the by-standers: or this last, is the fine slime of Nilus—the *melior lutus,*—whose maternal recipiency is as necessary as the *sol pater* to their equivocal generation" (p. 107). The "intellectual atmosphere of the by-standers" is at once the "nutriment" and the mother of a play on words. A sentence from "Blakesmoor in H—— Shire" is even more to the point: "The solitude of childhood is not so much the mother of thought, as it is the feeder of love, and silence, and admiration" (p. 155). Lamb almost says "not mother, but feeder," and to the extent that the construction tends toward antithesis, it at once denies an equivalence between the two words and at the same time asserts a basis for comparison. But the sentence actually reads "not so much mother . . . as feeder," which claims not merely a basis for comparison but a strong functional similarity. It is an affair of wanting to choose the more exact of two metaphors which apply to the same reality. The sentence keeps both, however, and each word spills some of its meaning into the other. Thus "mother" and "feeder" were linked ideas for Lamb, and if the one notion had to be suppressed, he clung the more tenaciously to the other, though shifting his emphasis to ingesting rather than being fed. Lamb's psychic history provides one way of explaining his extraordinary concern with oral satisfaction.

The trouble with this solution is that, while it accounts for the quantity and perhaps the intensity of the gastronomic references, it says nothing about their variations in usage or meaning within one essay or within the Elia collection. As a result, it can say nothing about the inner logic, if any, governing the variations, and very little about the relationships, if any, between the culinary elements and the thematic development of the essays. Lamb's remarks in "The Sanity of True Genius" are applicable to himself. Defending the non-realism of the allegorical writer who qualifies as one of the "true poets," he commented: ". . . his very monsters are tamed to his hand, even as that wild sea-brood, shepherded by Proteus" (p. 188). Lamb's mind was partly that of a psychic victim, a prey for inward monsters, but it was also the mind of a genuine artist. He had an abnormal preoccupation with ingestion; was he able to make use of it to grasp and illuminate some significant aspect of life? The problem of explanation becomes a matter of determining whether there is a perspective from which the food references in the Elia essays can be ratified by our "waking judgment" (p. 189).

When Montaigne regales us with the details of his dietary habits in "Of Experience," he is pointing—as in his observations on scratching and defecating—to those homely physical processes that escape the commentary of idealistic and rationalistic systematizers but are not beneath the notice of an essayist.[3] Steele and Addison treat eating and drinking among the numerous prosaic areas of social life which need reformation. For instance, Steele inveighs against drunkenness but permits moderate indulgence in alcoholic beverages as an antidote to excessive bashfulness and melancholy (*Tatler*, Nos. 241, 252), and Addison commends a temperate diet as a means to health (*Spectator*, No. 195). Steele would stoop to gastronomic detail in *The Guardian* (No. 34), but Addison did it earlier in *The Tatler*. In an essay censuring the custom among the prosperous of requiring clergymen dinner-guests to leave before the dessert, he includes this piece of gustatory casuistry: "No man of the most rigid virtue gives offence by any excesses in plum-pudding or plum-porridge, and that, because they are the first parts of the dinner. Is there anything that tends to incitation in sweetmeats more than in ordinary dishes? Certainly not. Sugar-plums are a very innocent diet, and conserves of a much colder nature than your common pickles" (*Tatler*, No. 255). In another *Tatler* paper (No. 148) Addison surveys the dietary history of England with a view toward restoring the status of such "simple and natural" food as roast beef while ridiculing the elaborate and disguised dishes, largely of French origin, that caused "many great families" to dwindle away "into a pale, sickly, spindle-legged, generation of valetudinarians." "The common people of this kingdom do still keep up the taste of their ancestors," Addison's Bickerstaff notes with resonant satisfaction; "and it is to this that we in a great measure owe the unparalleled victories that have been gained in this reign: for, I would desire my reader to consider, what work our countrymen would have made at Blenheim and Ramillies, if they had been fed with fricassees and ragouts." Johnson's remarks on ingestion likewise center on the dangers of gustatory excess, but he enters the sphere of asceticism, which Steele and Addison avoid. In Johnson's view, even if avarice and shrewdness keep a man from emptying his coffers to delight his palate, he can unbridle his appetite only by subordinating his other faculties and running the risk of ending, like *The Rambler's* Gulosulus, unable to speak or think of anything but a bill of fare (No. 206). Gulosulus's moral antipodes is the man of superior virtue who abstains even from blameless gratifications in order to strengthen his will to resist temptation. *The Idler* (No. 52) recommends such conduct and relates a vivid instance which connects morality and diet: "When the Roman general, sitting at supper with a plate of turnips before him, was sollicited by large promises to betray his trust, he asked the messengers whether he that could sup on turnips was a man likely to sell his country." Montaigne accepted and even celebrated ingestion, while Steele, Addison, and Johnson guarded against its potential snares, but all four writers found it to be among the many mundane subjects suitable for occasional essayistic treatment.

Among several of the major Romantics, however, eating and drinking held a special interest. The subject of orality has often arisen in psychologically oriented critiques of individual Romantic poets. David Beres's study of *The Rime of the Ancient Mariner* argues that "Coleridge's basic character structure is revealed in . . . recurrent memories of food and hunger, the phantasies of satiation, the unconcealed demands for love and admiration—a man who remained in his relationship to persons a never-satisfied, ever-demanding infant. Coleridge describes himself in terms that delineate with almost clinical accuracy the oral character defined by psycho-analysis." More recently, Norman Fruman has remarked in *Coleridge, The Damaged Archangel:* "The emphasis on food and drink in Coleridge's letters, and at key points in the great triad (for example, 'He on honey-dew hath fed, And drunk the milk of Paradise') is heavy enough to justify speculation as to its unconscious meaning." Lionel Trilling's justly celebrated essay on Keats's letters raises a parallel topic: ". . . with Keats the ingestive imagery is pervasive and extreme. He is possibly unique among poets in the extensiveness of his reference to eating and drinking and to its pleasurable or distasteful sensations." In the same essay Trilling observes that "For Wordsworth . . . virtually the only two sense-faculties of which he takes account are seeing and hearing." However, F. W. Bateson supports his own emphasis on Wordsworth's regressiveness by noting that the poet, beginning in 1798, used "images of eating and drinking" with such frequency that "they must be considered symbolic rather than merely metaphorical."[4]

The unassisted perspective of individual psychology is as inadequate to explain why there is so much orality in Romanticism as it is to explain why there is so much anality in Neoclassicism. Such an approach needs to be supplemented by a recognition of the extent to which the same motifs that in psychology symptomatize neurotic or psychotic disorders may in intellectual and literary history contribute to an epoch's ability to cope with its distinctive problems. Since we cherish artistic greatness for its illumination of the human condition rather than for its "normality," we may even be able to concede, without belittling the literary mind, that one kind of abnormal personality had an intellectual advantage in some respects over stabler types in the early nineteenth century, whereas another kind might have articulated quite different societal needs with peculiar intensity a century earlier. In any case, Lamb's orality participates in a cultural, as well as a personal, configuration, and in his Elia essays he used it to ponder the familiar Romantic ambition of closing the gap between subject and object.

In eating and drinking a progression occurs from the existence of an organism and a distinct object to the existence of an organism which has incorporated the object into its structure. A carrot, for instance, becomes part of a human body. For Coleridge this process, considered as generically organic rather than as specifically human, supplied an analogy which illuminated the imagination. ". . . Coleridge describes the imagination as an 'assimilative power,' and the 'coadunating faculty,' " notes M. H. Abrams in *The Mirror and the Lamp;* "these adjectives are imported from contemporary biology, where 'assimilate' connoted the process by which an organism converts food into its own substance, and 'coadunate' signified 'to grow together into one.' " "But it is the active appreciation of natural beauty that is the real theme of

The Prelude," writes Bateson, "and this intimate cooperation between the human subject and the natural object is expressed in Wordsworth's poems of this period in images of eating and drinking." In Lamb's essays an effort is made to assimilate the conditions of life to that structure of demands and approvals which the ego wills upon itself and its environment. The interaction of a biological system—an organism—and the environment in the ingestion of nutriment gives Lamb a physical model with which he can approach the less palpable relationship between value system and experience. Nevertheless, it is one thing to refer, as Wordsworth does, to drinking the visionary power and feeding upon infinity or, as Coleridge does, to eating honey-dew, imbibing the milk of Paradise, or biting one's arm to suck the blood; but it is another thing to speak, as Lamb does, of a taste for roast pig's crackling or bread and cheese with an onion. "Barry Cornwall tells us," notes E. V. Lucas in his biography of Lamb, "that on being asked how he felt when amongst the lakes and mountains of Cumberland, Lamb replied that he was obliged to think of the Ham and Beef shop near Saint Martin's Lane in order to bring his thoughts from their almost too painful elevation to the sober regions of everyday life." "There came this morning," wrote Lamb to Sarah Hazlitt, "a printed prospectus from S. T. Coleridge, Grasmere, of a weekly paper, to be called The Friend—a flaming prospectus—I have no time to give the heads of it—to commence first Saturday in January. There came also a notice of a Turkey from Mr. Clarkson, which I am more sanguine in expecting the accomplishment of than I am of Coleridge's prophecy."[5] Elia's fare is more particularized and more homely than that employed by Lamb's friends, the poets; and its conspicuousness on the verbal surface of his essays reminds his readers of aspects of human life that sag beneath the visionary, prophetic, or Promethean at the same time that it expresses a typically Romantic attempt to assimilate the world of objects.

The Elia essays reveal this aspiration in treating gentility's resistance to contact with the less-than-respectable classes of society. Lamb seeks to move from aversion to assimilation. In "The Praise of Chimney-Sweepers," for example, the representatives of gentility progress in their gastronomic response from Elia's fastidiously phrased rejection of Saloop—"a cautious premonition to the olfactories constantly whispering to me, that my stomach must infallibly, with all due courtesy, decline it" (p. 109)—to Jem White's ability to assimilate, before an audience of chimney-sweepers, something considerably short of an epicurean's feast: "every now and then stuffing into his mouth (for it did not do to be squeamish on these occasions) indiscriminate pieces of those reeking sausages, which pleased them mightily, and was the savouriest part, you may believe, of the entertainment" (p. 114). At the same time, the intrinsic vitality and worth of the sweeps is more and more insisted upon, until we come to doubt that there is much difference between an aristocrat and a chimney-sweeper. "A Complaint of the Decay of Beggars in the Metropolis" argues against the "modern fastidiousness" (p. 116) which has banished, or seeks to banish, from our sight, not only the blind beggars by Lincoln's Inn Garden, but all bankrupt mendicants. Elia does "not approve of this wholesale going to work, this impertinent crusado, or *bellum ad exterminationem,* proclaimed against a species" (p. 114). Why? "Much good might be sucked from these Beggars" (p. 114), he explains. The nutritional value of beggars is not, as the speaker in Swift's "A Modest Proposal" might argue, that they feed our cannibalism, but that they jolt us out of the habit of mistaking a man's niche in society or his clothes for his humanity: "to be naked is to be so much nearer to the being a man, than to go in livery" (p. 115). As the opposites of a rich man or a king, they should be assimilated into our value system if we are to keep a realistic sense of proportion. We would deprive ourselves if we hid beggars in institutions. In both essays, insofar as he depends upon the model of eating, Lamb comes close to regarding people as objects for our use. For the process of eating makes relatively little provision for mutuality, the I-Thou relation, particularly if we contrast it with the model that marriage might supply. Therefore, Elia complicates it by setting various people masticating at once. He seeks to avoid vampirism by speaking of the gastronomic satisfaction of the sweeps and beggars. Through the good offices of Elia and his friends, the chimney-sweepers progress from smelling Saloop to eating a meal, and beggars, we are told, would be deprived of some kinds of nutriment if they were institutionalized. One legless mendicant "seemed earth-born, an Antaeus, and to suck in fresh vigour from the soil which he neighboured" (p. 118), and "he was enabled to retire at night to enjoy himself at a club of his fellow cripples over a dish of hot meat and vegetables" (p. 119), but now he is confined to "one of those houses (ironically christened) of Correction" (p. 119). Elia manages, without ignoring the wants of chimney-sweepers and beggars, to assimilate their presence to a genteel person's value system, just as food can be assimilated to his biological system.

He makes a similar effort regarding some disreputable traits which exist even in himself and his class. At least "four quarters of the globe" can rightfully say *"Stultus sum"* (p. 42), he declares in "All Fool's Day," but instead of being disturbed at this fact, he jokingly drinks to human folly and to assorted historical and fictional characters who conspicuously displayed it.

"Fill us a cup of that sparkling gooseberry," he exclaims, "we will drink no wise, melancholy, politic port on this day . . ." (p. 42). By endowing the rejected port with the human qualities signified by "wise, melancholy, politic," he implies that the "sparkling gooseberry" that he quaffs somehow possesses the opposite characteristics of folly. His tone grows more serious in the last paragraph when he speaks of folly as a positive good: "And take my word for this, reader, and say a fool told it you, if you please, that he who hath not a dram of folly in his mixture, hath pounds of much worse matter in his composition. It is observed, that 'the foolisher the fowl or fish,—woodcocks, —dotterels,—cod's-heads, &c. the finer the flesh thereof,' and what are commonly the world's received fools, but such whereof the world is not worthy?" (p. 44). The biological assimilation of gooseberry and the enumerated meats is equated with the assimilation of human foolishness to Elia's value system.

In "A Dissertation upon Roast Pig" Lamb portrays a movement from rigidity to a new openness on two levels of time—the antiquity of China and the modernity of Elia and his readers. There is unusual economy in the anecdote about China's conversion from taboo to delectation since the biological assimilation of roast pig is not only an analogy for the assimilation of the meat into the Chinese value system but is also the cause. Once a man tastes crackling his scruples crumble. The second half of the essay, concerned with the present age, is taken up with apparently rambling panegyrics to pork, interrupted once for an anecdote from Elia's childhood. Underlying this section is the notion that China's progress out of moral inflexibility has to be repeated anew by individuals and societies. In the context of Elia's society a too fervid attachment to crackling may be thought to violate not a taboo against cooking but the self-restraint and self-sacrifice which suit an inhabitant of a fallen world. Consequently Elia repeatedly associates young pigs with an unfallen condition, a nearer approximation to the ideal than we are accustomed to meet:

. . . guiltless as yet of the sty—with no original speck of the *amor immunditiae*, the hereditary failing of the first parent, yet manifest . . . . (p. 123)
. . . the tender blossoming of fat—fat cropped in the bud—taken in the shoot—in the first innocence . . . . (p. 124)
Unlike to mankind's mixed characters, a bundle of virtues and vices, inexplicably intertwisted, and not to be unravelled without hazard, he is—good throughout. (p. 124)

While roast pig is praised for the intensity of pleasure which it affords, Elia dissociates it from those pleasures which arouse a sense of guilt. Pineapple, we are told, is "a delight, if not sinful, yet so like to sinning, that really a

tender-conscienced person would do well to pause . . ." (p. 124). But on
the other hand, "Pig—let me speak his praise—is no less provocative of the
appetite, than he is satisfactory to the criticalness of the censorious palate"
(p. 124). Just as China learned to integrate the cooking of pig with social
order, Elia is advocating incorporation of a new hedonism into traditional
morality.[6]

His apparent digression, late in the essay, on an incident from his boyhood reinforces this criticism of conventional rigidity. Self-sacrifice is as
much a part of the official code as self-restraint, and it can be equally debili-
tating. In his childhood Elia had given a plum-cake, just cooked for him by
his aunt, to a "grey-headed old beggar" (p. 125) by London Bridge. His motive was "the vanity of self-denial, and the very coxcombry of charity" (p.
125). After such benevolence, he felt a few moments of "self-satisfaction,"
but "before I had got to the end of the bridge, my better feelings returned,
and I burst into tears, thinking how ungrateful I had been to my good aunt . . ."
(p. 125). The youthful Elia's movement across the Thames marks his initia-
tion into a less dogmatic value system than he owned previously. His progress
parallels that of the Chinese society, and it manipulates the reader's sympathies in order to align them with self-indulgence rather than self-restraint or
self-sacrifice. In the essay as a whole roast pig functions as both a satisfying
object for human appetites and as an externalization of animality. Bo-bo
had crammed pork "down his throat in his beastly fashion" (p. 121), and
appetites are a function of animality. The delightful pig which Elia wishes
to assimilate is inside man even before he eats the pork on the table.

But the principal object of Lamb's assimilative efforts is neither pig nor
appetite, but the incongruous hodge-podge of flesh, triviality, illogic, and intellectual constructions which together make up the furniture of the human
mind. The Chinese discovery, after much conflagration, that pigs can be
cooked "without the necessity of consuming a whole house to dress it" is
the achievement of "a sage . . . like our Locke" (p. 123). The advantage of
roasting a pig while he is still young is announced in words inexactly borrowed, as Lamb's editor notes, from Coleridge's "Epitaph on an Infant":

> Ere sin could blight, or sorrow fade,
> Death came with timely care— (p. 124)

Elia remembers the subject of learned debate at St. Omer's: "Whether, supposing that the flavour of a pig who obtained his death by whipping (*per
flagellationem extremam*) superadded a pleasure upon the palate of a man

more intense than any possible suffering we can conceive in the animal, is man justified in using that method of putting the animal to death?" (p. 126). The Latin phrases, the theological speculation, and the bookish vocabulary ("A Dissertation upon Roast Pig") which clothe Elia's hymn to pork participate in a similar incongruous pattern. Also, in structuring his homely narrative on China he makes use of intellectually serious conceptions of history—there are elements of progress in man's gastronomic practices, and there is a three-stage narrative pattern (the rigid old order, the chaotic period of liberation, and finally, thanks to the Chinese Locke, a new equilibrium). Such juxtapositions make the human race as laughable as Ho-ti, but Lamb's essay, staying distinct from satire, exposes and embraces at once.

Within the Elia essays the taboo on some kinds of eating in "A Dissertation upon Roast Pig" is one among many instances where oral intake is conceived as an impeded process. In the garden of childhood recalled in "Dream-Children," the hindrance took the form of a prohibition on eating the nectarines and peaches which hung invitingly about (p. 102). School days brought graver obstacles to the satisfaction of one's palate. Whether we take the first pages of "Christ's Hospital Five and Thirty Years Ago" as portraying Elia's personal experience (as the pages themselves claim to be doing) or a friend's experience under Elia's name (as the preface to *Last Essays* claims they are doing),[7] they evoke the suffering caused by inadequate food. The speaker, like most of the boys at Christ's Hospital, had to put up with a scanty and repugnant diet, older students or nurses sometimes snatched much of one's allotment, and holidays, for those whose families did not live nearby, were spent famished (pp. 12–15). Chimney-sweepers are worse off, and part of their grief is that they cannot afford the Saloop which they covet. Adult life, also, is no picnic. The poor man's home is dominated by "the absorbing consideration of food to be obtained for the family," and for him "At home there is no larder" (p. 263). The best meal Captain Jackson can offer a guest is a "bare scrag—cold savings from the foregone meal—remnant hardly sufficient to send a mendicant from the door contented" (p. 190).

The prohibition on some kinds of eating in "Dream-Children" is one of Elia's first encounters with the separation between self and world. At the time he evaded the restriction by occasional pilfering—"now and then" (p. 102)—and by imaginatively identifying with the living things in the garden. One response was directed toward external change, while the second altered only something internal, his way of seeing. The other obstructions to eating elicit variations of these two types of response. With the exception of the prohibition in "Dream-Children" and the disappearing taboo in "A Dissertation upon Roast Pig," the references to literal deprivation of food concern special segments of society, and an occasional note of social criticism—potentially external in its effects—responds to the problem. In "The Praise of Chimney-Sweepers" the dinner which Jem White gives for the sweeps reminds us that society has done nothing to fill their stomachs. The speaker in "Christ's Hospital" lashes out at the school's authorities for granting L. "some invidious distinction" (p. 12), and he enumerates the differences between L.'s pleasurable menu and his own miserable fare. He recalls persons—especially some older students and nurses—who abused their power within the microcosmic society of the school by extorting or merely grabbing the food that was due the ordinary boys. But Lamb does not sustain a reaction of social criticism, probably because he is not convinced that the authorities are evil men (Do not the governors of Christ's Hospital vote "a present relief" [p. 16] to the family of the boy who smuggled out scraps to keep his parents from starving?) and because he has not learned to formulate a concrete criticism of the structure of society. Moreover, Elia, though an outsider or a minor figure in relation to the institutions of society, has, as "The Superannuated Man" and "Old China" make clear, a sufficient income and, therefore, an ample table. The deprivation which he experiences as an adult is not, in fact, primarily society's doing.

The physically hungry can react internally, as well as practically, to their condition. Take, for instance, the mental activity of the poor man who migrates from his "home" to a comfortable tavern for the evening: "Here there is at least a show of plenty; and while he cooks his lean scrap of butcher's meat before the common bars, or munches his humbler cold viands, his relishing bread and cheese with an onion, in a corner, where no one reflects upon his poverty, he has sight of the substantial joint providing for the landlord and his family. He takes an interest in the dressing of it; and while he assists in removing the trivet from the fire, he feels that there is such a thing as beef and cabbage, which he was beginning to forget at home" (p. 263). The chimney-sweepers, likewise, get pleasure out of sniffing the fumes of the hot beverage which they cannot drink, and Captain Jackson's imagination transforms the modest offerings of his table into "whole beeves . . . spread before you—hecatombs—no end appeared to the profusion" (p. 190). Yet the assimilatory mental trick by which the sight or smell of food substitutes for its taste, or a scrap appears to be a banquet, is not a strategy which Elia himself employs. He sympathizes with those for whom it is necessary, but he never abdicates an awareness that it is an illusion.

"Christ's Hospital Five and Thirty Years Ago" suggests a different internal response to the thwarting of gastronomic satisfaction: "L. has recorded the repugnance of the school to *gags,* or the fat of fresh beef boiled; and sets it down to some superstition" (p. 15), Elia solemnly informs us. L. is Charles Lamb, who in 1813, partly in order to fight a proposed restriction of the student body to the lowest classes of society, had published "Recollections of Christ's Hospital," which, in contrast to the Elian essay on the same subject, is an unrelieved panegyric. In describing the "religious character" of the Christ's Hospital student, Lamb had stressed the boy's tender conscience:

Those who were contemporaries with me at that School thirty years ago, will remember with what more than Judaic rigour the eating of the fat of certain boiled meats ["Under the denomination of *gags,"* Lamb's footnote explains] was interdicted. A boy would have blushed, as at the exposure of some heinous immorality, to have been detected eating that forbidden portion of his allowance of animal food, the whole of which, while he was in health, was little more than sufficient to allay his hunger. The same, or even greater, refinement was shewn in the rejection of certain kinds of sweet-cake. What gave rise to these supererogatory penances, these self-denying ordinances, I could never learn; they certainly argue no defect of the conscientious principle.[8]

Though confessing some puzzlement over the rejection of gags, Lamb renders the boys' behavior intelligible in terms of obedience to an arbitrary moral code. He makes clear in a footnote that gags are edible and nutritional: a more recent steward has succeeded in conquering the boys' prejudice "and thereby restored to one-half of the animal nutrition of the school those honors which painful superstition and blind zeal had so long conspired to withhold from it" (p. 142). Elia, on the other hand, offers a different account: "... these unctuous morsels are never grateful to young palates (children are universally fat-haters) and in strong, coarse, boiled meats, *unsalted,* are detestable. A *gag-eater* in our time was equivalent to a *goul,* and held in equal detestation" (p. 15). Yet even within the Elia essay we learn about a boy's hoarding of gags in order to smuggle them out to his destitute parents, who apparently were glad to get them. The facts, according to the Elia essay, were these: the boys were hungry, gags were edible and nutritional, but the students, pleading the discrimination of their palates, not only rejected them but also rejected anyone who ate them. The hoarder was universally interdicted, until, of course, the nobility of his true motives came to light. The mystery surrounding this set of circumstances may be cleared up if we view the impoverished parents as reacting practically to their hunger (they eat what they can get), while the students react imaginatively to theirs. The Christ's Hospital

boys, confronted by an insufficient gastronomic environment, make it subject to their egos by deliberately rejecting something which it offers. They
become young connoisseurs, and if there is insecurity in their achievement,
they can still band together and excommunicate persons who fail to conform
to their tastes. They show their symptoms of adolescence in their tribal response to nonconformity, but they demonstrate that fastidiousness has a use
for other people, as well as their peers. By shifting his explanation from morality in the first essay to taste in the second, Lamb is able to overleap a
hindrance to oral satisfaction while maintaining the terms of his gustatory
model. Discriminating taste buds, paradoxically, are a means of assimilating
an insufficient gastronomic environment to one's own value system.

The adult Elia has enough to eat, but, despite all the edibles which he
manages to name, his mouth is very unlike the postal service in "Valentine's
Day," that "all-swallowing indiscriminate orifice" (p. 57). James Elia, who
himself shrinks from the spectacle of a "lobster boiled, or eels skinned *alive*"
(p. 74), urges him to keep mum about the peculiarities of his taste: "On my
once letting slip at table, that I was not fond of a certain popular dish, he
begged me at any rate not to *say* so—for the world would think me mad"
(p. 71). Elia takes the risk and, in another essay, announces that his method
extends to much besides food: "Whatever is, is to me a matter of taste or
distaste; or when once it becomes indifferent, it begins to be disrelishing"
(p. 58). At times Elia's tastes seem to be governed by universal standards.
If a clerk is "one that sucks his sustenance, as certain sick people are said to
do, through a quill' (p. 7), clerkship is not fully adequate to human needs.
When, in speaking of Stackhouse's *History of the Bible*, he refers to "such
unfit sustenance as these husks afforded" (pp. 66–67), we understand that
he rejects the book on substantive grounds. Similarly, he praises the sonnets
of Sir Philip Sidney by contrasting them with much modern verse: "But
they are not rich in words only, in vague and unlocalized feelings—the failing
too much of some poetry of the present day—they are full, material, and cir-
cumstantiated. Time and place appropriates every one of them. It is not a
fever of passion wasting itself upon a thin diet of dainty words . . ." (p. 218).
The gastronomic language points up a substantive superiority of Sidney over
some modern poets. On the other hand, Elia's tastes often have no such un-
derpinning of universal norms. His literary preferences differ from his cousin
Bridget's, but he does not imply that one is more correct than the other:
"We agree pretty well in our tastes and habits—yet so, as 'with a difference.' . . .
While I am hanging over (for the thousandth time) some passage in old Burton,
or one of his strange contemporaries, she is abstracted in some modern tale,

or adventure, whereof our common reading-table is daily fed with assiduously fresh supplies" (p. 75). Elia's dislikes are also introduced without being offered as objectively true judgments. In "Imperfect Sympathies," often in gastronomic language, he confesses an irrational antipathy for Scotchmen, Jews, Negroes, and Quakers. The Hebrew, he declares, "is least distasteful on 'Change—for the mercantile spirit levels all distinctions, as all are beauties in the dark. I boldly confess that I do not relish the approximation of Jew and Christian, which has become so fashionable" (p. 62). A dinner is at once a social occasion and an act of biological assimilation, and hence a test for the compatibility of people is whether they can dine satisfactorily together. Of Jews he remarks: "If they can sit with us at table, why do they keck at our cookery?" (p. 62). "But I should not like," he declares concerning Negroes, "to associate with them, to share my meals and my good-nights with them—because they are black" (p. 62). Despite a love for "Quaker ways, and Quaker worship," as well as a veneration for "Quaker principles," Elia admits: "I should starve at their primitive banquet. My appetites are too high for the salads which (according to Evelyn) Eve dressed for the angel, my gusto too excited 'To sit a guest with Daniel at his pulse' " (pp. 62–63). By insisting upon the finickiness and idiosyncrasy of his tastes, Elia transforms an environment which is not wholly a mirror of himself, and is often alien to himself, into something subject to himself. He can affirm even an alien world insofar as it is a field for his connoisseurship.

The success of this strategy depends upon his ability to avoid what he dislikes, to take it or leave it. But every moment brings Elia closer to that fearful confrontation which he cannot elude, the encounter which "New Year's Eve" anticipates. Children discern in New Year's merely the easily digestible "cake and orange" (p. 27) of a holiday, but the adult Elia, with all his capacities for relishing "the delicious juices of meats and fishes, and society, and the cheerful glass" (p. 29), cannot readily assimilate to the eating model what for him the occasion calls to mind, his eventual meeting with Death. He almost screams: "In no way can I be brought to digest thee, thou thin, melancholy *Privation*, or more frightful and confounding *Positive!*" (p. 30). But then in the concluding sentences he adopts a desperate gaiety, calls for "another cup of wine" (p. 31), recites Cotton's poem ending with the appeal to "line ourselves with sack," and compares these verses to a consolatory beverage: "Do they not fortify like a cordial; enlarging the heart, and productive of sweet blood, and generous spirits, in the concoction? Where be those puling fears of death, just now expressed or affected—Passed like a cloud—absorbed in the purging sunlight of clear poetry—clean washed away by a wave of genuine Helicon, your only Spa for these hypochondries—And now another cup of the generous! and a merry New Year, and many of them, to you all, my masters!" (p. 32). Elia is talking once again about oral satisfaction, and he announces that this model has triumphed over the indigestibility of death. But the triumph is factitious in its literal sense and its tone, for instead of assimilating death to his value system, he has expelled it from his awareness, and his shrillness betrays the fragility of his accomplishment.[9]

Elia juxtaposes the food model with the invisible world again in "Grace Before Meat," an essay that touches upon a question which had attracted earlier familiar essayists: whether a clergyman's spiritual function is consistent with his eating more and better than he requires in order to stay healthy. In *The Tatler* (No. 255) Addison, by ridiculing the custom of expecting a priestly dinner-guest to leave before dessert, ridiculed also the host's perception of an incongruity between the guest's clerical vocation and his staying for the last course of a meal. When Addison referred to a situation close to the subject of Lamb's essay, he implied that, from his own point of view, there was no conflict between prayer and a full stomach: "I would fain ask these stiff-necked patrons, whether they would not take it ill of a chaplain that, in his grace after meat, should return thanks for the whole entertainment, with an exception to the dessert?" Goldsmith's *Citizen of the World* (Letter LVIII) used a gastronomic occasion to dramatize the distance between the spiritual duties and the actual behavior of clergymen. At one time the "principal priests" of England had visited parishes to evaluate the performance of their clergy, but partly because such journeys exposed them to unpalatable food and wine, they substituted the custom of the Visitation Dinner. Now once a year the parish priests came as a group to dine with their superior, a practice which entirely subverted the pastoral function of visitation but ensured a good meal to everybody concerned. When Goldsmith's Chinese philosopher attended one of these affairs, he expected to profit from learned and wise conversation, but instead he discovered that the meal itself was the principal topic, and inarticulateness, together with overeating, prevailed. After a while he imagined a beggar reprimanding the assemblage with blunt words: *"Prithee pluck those napkins from your chins; after nature is satisfied all that you eat extraordinary is my property, and I claim it as mine. It was given you in order to relieve me, and not to oppress yourselves."* Like Lamb, Goldsmith based his essay on a perception of incongruity between gastronomy and piety, but unlike Lamb, he built on this perception a satiric indictment of the clergy's dereliction of duty. Lamb is satirizing no one; his essay is another of his experiments in assimilation.

In "Grace Before Meat" Elia observes that, while thanking God may be appropriate before partaking of simple sustenance, it seems out of place before consuming an elaborate banquet: "The very excess of the provision beyond the needs, takes away all sense of proportion between the end and means. The giver is veiled by his gifts" (p. 92). If Elia's purpose were to remove this veil, presumably he would propose a curbing of appetites. Instead, he not only stresses the intensity of his own gustatory delight—"Those unctuous morsels of deer's flesh were not made to be received with dispassionate services" (p. 95)—but he also suggests that delectation extends to such activities as walking, meeting a friend, solving a problem, or reading (p. 91). If one kind of delectation veils the invisible world, other kinds spread the veil through a large part of human existence. Elia's gustatory interests function, like his drinks at the end of "New Year's Eve," partly as a means to direct his attention away from the discomfiting thought of what lies behind the veil. But in the present essay he makes no claim to having assimilated death or the invisible world to his value system. Instead, he directs the assimilatory possibilities of the eating model at the human illogic which combines the incongruous elements of appetite and spirituality. A sense of awkwardness, of embarrassment, characterizes the clergymen and other authority figures who are called upon to say grace in Elia's experience, and their difficulty parallels the attitude displayed by "some pious benefactor" who, "commiserating the decencies" of Christ's Hospital boys, had some of the institution's funds used for "trowsers instead of mutton" (p. 96). In both cases, the premises of piety interfere with the assimilation of human appetite. Elia can cheerfully accept the sensualism and illogic which disturb the orthodox, but this successful assimilation in the forefront of the essay does not wholly conceal his inability to assimilate the invisible world behind the veil. As in "New Year's Eve," though with no significant lapses in tonal control, a show of victory coexists with a more basic defeat of the gastronomic model.

Among the phenomena of earthly experience, the one which for Elia comes nearest to the invisible world in its radical otherness is the sea. In "Witches, and Other Night-Fears" he had observed: ". . . when once the invisible world was supposed to be opened, and the lawless agency of bad spirits assumed, what measures of probability, of decency, of fitness, or proportion—of that which distinguishes the likely from the palpable absurd—could they ["our ancestors"] have to guide them in the rejection or admission of any particular testimony?" (p. 65). A similar point is made in "The Old Margate Hoy" about the effect of the sea upon some travelers' response to a virtuoso liar: "Had the confident fellow told us half the legends on land, which he favoured us with on the other element, I flatter myself the good sense of most of us would have revolted. But we were in a new world, with everything unfamiliar about us, and the time and place disposed us to the reception of any prodigious marvel whatsoever" (p. 179). For the human imagination, as Elia declares a few paragraphs later, the sea is "THE COM-MENSURATE ANTAGONIST OF THE EARTH" (p. 180). Elia ponders its digestibility.

The first time he saw the sea he traveled in the old Margate hoy of the title, and this venerable boat created the illusion that the place was nourish-ing. One of its crew-members, whom Elia addresses, was a "comfortable ambassador between sea and land!—whose sailor-trowsers did not more con-vincingly assure thee to be an adopted denizen of the former, than thy white cap, and whiter apron over them, with thy neat-fingered practice in thy culi-nary vocation, bespoke thee to have been of inland nurture heretofore—a master cook of Eastcheap" (p. 178). A storm drives the passengers below deck, where this sailor-cook was "still catering for our comfort, with cards, and cordials, and thy more cordial conversation" which alleviated "the close-ness and the confinement of thy else (truth to say) not very savoury, nor very inviting, little cabin" (p. 178). Just as this originally inland personage projects onto the watery element an aura of digestibility, so most of the passengers brought from the land "our private stores—our cold meat and our salads" (p. 180) with them to eat when the dinner-bell rang. The human con-tributions, including the personalities of the sailor-cook, the liar, and the scrofulous boy, make Elia's first experience of the sea something which even yet he can "chew upon" (p. 180). But more mature deliberation leads him to conclude that, at least for an inland native like himself, the sea cannot really be assimilated. The shore reveals "dusty innutritious rocks" (p. 181); most "visitants from town" have "no more relish of the sea than a pond perch, or a dace might be supposed to have" (p. 182); the "honest citizen" brings "his wife and daughters, to taste the sea breezes," but they quickly lose interest in the scene (pp. 182–183). Elia's conclusion is inevitable: "I am sure that no town-bred, or inland-born subjects, can feel their true and natural nourishment at these sea-places" (p. 183). By the end it is clear that the eating model cannot successfully be applied to something as alien as the sea, except in an ironic, limiting sense: "The salt foam seems to nourish a spleen" (p. 183).

The otherness of the sea, like that of the invisible world, connects for Lamb with the idea of nihility. Death was perhaps a "thin, melancholy *Privation*" (p. 30), he had noted in "New Year's Eve." "A Chapter on Ears"

associates the discomfiting phenomenon of music with the invisible world
by comparing the audience at an oratorio to the inhabitants of "some cold
Theatre in Hades" (p. 40). The same essay describes the process of listening
to a musical performance in terms of attending to vacuity: "to gaze on empty frames, and be forced to make the pictures for yourself; to read a book,
all stops, and be obliged to supply the verbal matter . . ." (p. 40). Elia is relieved when a musical evening is ended by the entrance of "the friendly
supper-tray" and "a draught of true Lutheran beer" (p. 41). In "The Old
Margate Hoy" human beings first approach the sea in the expectation of en-
countering some kind of fullness—*"all the sea at once"* or a complex of literary, mythological, and historical associations (pp. 180–181). The resulting
disappointment prompts the question, "Is this the mighty ocean?—is this
all?" (p. 181). Likewise, Elia, in objecting to the flimsiness of a seashore
tourist attraction, says the place ought to have kept its original substantiality:
"If it were what it was in its primitive shape, and what it ought to have remained, a fair honest fishing town, and no more, it were something . . ." (p.
182). Elia's world consists of a crowded, individualized, largely urban area
surrounded—so it sometimes seems—by spatial emptiness (the sea) and temporal emptiness (the realms of pre-existence and the afterlife).[10] In the
miniaturist form of the familiar essay he cultivates a dense spot in the midst
of vacuity, and his distinction between nourishing substantiality and lean,
innutritious barrenness has, on occasion, metaphysical implications.

Elia likes to think that the sea is very different from a river. "Witches,
and Other Night-Fears" makes the distinction in the remarkable sentence
(p. 69), quoted earlier, which sums up Elia's movement away from terrifying
dreams of the "invisible world" (p. 65). As Elia is carried from ocean to
river, he moves from doubtfulness about names ("I think it was Ino") to a
certainty about them ("the gentle Thames," "the foot of Lambeth palace").
The Thames and its banks do not constitute a ground for heroism, but they
are at least old and manageable friends. "Old Benchers of the Inner Temple"
notes that in childhood "what was this king of rivers to me but a stream that
watered our pleasant places?" (p. 82). It "washes the garden-foot" of the
Temple "with her yet scarcely trade-polluted waters" (p. 83). Lamb chooses
Lambeth Palace as Elia's landing point in "Witches, and Other Night-Fears"
not because the Archbishop of Canterbury lives there but because the name
of the place, sounding like a pun on Lamb's own name, outdoes all its com-
petitors in familiarity and because the location of Lambeth Palace is further
upstream, that is, further away from the sea, than such other Thames-side
landmarks as the Tower of London or even the Temple.

Almost as familiar to Elia as the Thames was the New River, which he had often explored: "I paced the vales of Amwell to explore your tributary springs, to trace your salutary waters sparkling through green Hertfordshire, and cultured Enfield parks" (p. 211). The shock which begins "Amicus Redivivus" derives not only from the spectacle of a friend's near drowning; nor only from the circumstance that his "unreserved motion towards self-destruction" occurred in "broad open daylight" (p. 209). It derives additionally from the surprise of finding danger lurking even in a familiar inland waterway and from the confrontation unexpectedly provoked with the "invisible world" (p. 212). This essay makes clear that a casual visit to one's cottage by an old friend (G. D.) can quickly metamorphose into an encounter with the capriciousness of the natural—including the human—world and the mystery of the afterlife.

In "Amicus Redivivus" Elia confronts both natural and post-natural otherness and seeks to assimilate them to his value system in accordance with the paradigm of ingestion. Monoculus, the unlicensed physician who restores G. D., shows that the natural phenomena which daze Elia can be assimilated to a cognitive system. His consciousness is symbolized by the "little watch-tower" by the river, from which he can not only "distinguish a plunge at a half furlong distance" but can also "tell, if it be casual or deliberate" (p. 210). Attempted suicides by rope, as well as by water, do not surprise him, and he is capable of taking quickly whatever action the occasion requires. His alertness, his skill, and his kindness enable him to assimilate human vagaries and natural dangers to his structure of thinking and his capacity for acting. Elia cannot compete with him on his own pragmatic level. But Elia, unlike the physician, is seeking to assimilate the visible and invisible realities evoked by the incident, not merely to his understanding or his actions but to his structure of affirmations. The task is simplified by circumstances: G. D. is revivified, and we learn that, though his experience evokes in Elia's mind a procession of *"suicidal faces,"* his near drowning was actually the product of nothing more disturbing than insufficient spectacles and absentmindedness (p. 212).

Of the two passages concerned with ingestion, the first deals with Monoculus's treatment of G. D.:

His remedy—after a sufficient application of warm blankets, friction, &c., is a simple tumbler, or more, of the purest Cognac, with water, made as hot as the convalescent can bear it. Where he findeth, as in the case of my friend, a squeamish subject, he condescendeth to be the taster; and showeth, by his own example, the innocuous nature of the prescription. Nothing can be more kind or encouraging than this procedure. It addeth confidence to the patient, to see his medical adviser go hand in hand with himself in the remedy. When the doctor swalloweth his own draught, what peevish invalid can refuse to pledge him in the potion? (pp. 210–211)

The similarity between drinking and drowning is that both are forms of liquid intake; the difference is that the first ministers to the self, while the latter overwhelms it. In applying his tact and knowledgeability Monoculus converts liquid, including water, from the destructive to the invigorating element. That drinking together is a matter of going "hand in hand . . . in the remedy" makes explicit both the similarity and the transformation between drowning and drinking. The reality that formerly looked murderous is now easily assimilated, at least physically.

However, Elia's value system is not yet reconciled with the watery element. He upbraids the river for turning upon himself, an old acquaintance, but then he begins to reduce its otherness by assigning it motives. Perhaps the river wanted to adopt G. D. as its "tutelary genius"; perhaps, dissatisfied with its present name—the New River—it sought to be renamed the Stream Dyerian (pp. 211–212). But he abandons this line of reasoning, counsels George to watch his step in the future, and avoids applying gastronomic language to his own attitude toward the water.

The second application of the model of ingestion in "Amicus Redivivus" occurs at the end of a discussion of the invisible world. Dreams of watery deaths and rescues have led Elia to consider the perspective of Death, the "grim Feature" himself. More than anywhere else in the Elia essays, here the invisible world is made to seem similar to the world of earthly experience. Just as Elia's cottage and Monoculus's watch-tower each represented a consciousness with a set of expectations, so Death has a "palace" with a door upon which a soul knocks when it approaches (p. 212). But science, we are told, often snatches such a soul back to life, and the disappointed "grim Feature" is as disconcerted as Elia had been at the start of the essay. Similarly, the shades which awaited the arrival of G. D. included ancient writers upon whose works he had labored and modern scholars with whom he would have much in common. The last named is "the mild Askew," who "with longing aspirations, leaned foremost from his venerable Aesculapian chair, to welcome into that happy company the matured virtues of the man, whose tender scions in the boy he himself upon earth had so prophetically fed and watered" (p. 213). The closing words of this passage—they also conclude the essay—insinuate the ingestive model into a section on the invisible world. Their resonance creates an impression of capping a solution to the problems raised by the essay, and such an interpretation seems to be reinforced by the familiarization of the invisible world. But, as in the earlier passage, Elia does not apply the assimilatory language to his own perspective. Furthermore, within G. D.'s experience the feeding and watering occurred in childhood, and it prepared G. D. for his mature life on earth. This feeding and watering was the work of a physician, Askew, a man professionally dedicated, like Monoculus, to combatting death. In no sense does G. D., even within Elia's imagination, manage to digest death; in fact, Elia, before beginning his own reverie, left his friend thanking Providence for rescuing him again from catastrophe. The resonance of the concluding words and their implicit claim of making the afterlife seem familiar reveal that in this essay, as in "Grace Before Meat," Lamb has kept beneath the surface his failure at gastronomic assimilation.

Apart from these encounters with unassimilable materials, the schema of ingestion is limited in its egocentrism, as "Barbara S——" makes clear. The celebrated actress of the title was once a "little starved, meritorious maid" (p. 205), whose theatrical apprenticeship brought in needed money for her family: "Enough to say, that her Saturday's pittance was the only chance of a Sunday's (generally their only) meal of meat" (p. 205). The girl was reduced to tears when a prankster ruined, with a great quantity of salt, some roast fowl which the hungry Barbara had to eat in one of her roles. This background of deprivation inclines her to consider keeping an accidental overpayment made to her by her employer: "And then it was such a bit of money! and then the image of a larger allowance of butcher's meat on their table next day came across her, till her little eyes glistened, and her mouth moistened" (p. 206). But she returned the money, after thinking of her employer's kindnesses and, especially, after having been carried "without her own agency, as it seemed," by "a strength not her own" to give back the surplus (p. 206). Her resistance to the temptation sprang not from self-control but from a submission to realities outside the self, and her conduct exposes the incompleteness of ingestion as a guide to one's life-style. From a psychoanalytic point of view, it is significant that Elia's one indication that orality, whether or not it works, is an insufficient model of how the self relates to the world occurs in an essay based largely upon the life of Fanny Kelly, the actress to whom in 1819 Lamb had proposed marriage.[11]

Elia's use of the gastronomic paradigm brought a combination of successes and failures. He was able to use it to assimilate much that seemed undesirable, but within and beyond our world he met or anticipated realities which were so alien to what he knew as human that he stumbled. In one essay, "Barbara S——," he called into question the worth of using ingestion as a generally applicable model, even if the thing were possible. His efforts, however, including his defeats, did not fail to dramatize and illuminate the relation between value system and experience, which is one aspect of the relation between subject and object. Whatever the origins of Lamb's peculiar fascination with gastronomy, he made it serve his Romantic and skeptical art remarkably well.

NOTES

1. *Works*, I, 119, 343; *Letters*, I, 214–216, 385–386 (MSS. Hn.); II, 211–213 (MS. Peal). Denys Thompson cites Lamb's fascination with food and drink as evidence that his essays are trivial (*Determinations*, pp. 206, 212–213).
2. Lamb's father appears in the Elia essays as Elia's father in "Poor Relations" and, more memorably, as Lovel in "The Old Benchers of the Inner Temple."
3. *Essays*, trans. Florio, III, 364–379, 362, 346–347, 384–385.
4. Beres, "A Dream, A Vision, and a Poem: A Psycho-Analytic Study of the Origins of the Rime of the Ancient Mariner," *International Journal of Psycho-Analysis*, 32 (1951), 102–103; Fruman, op. cit. (New York: George Braziller, 1971), p. 547 (I am indebted to Raimonda Modiano for calling my attention to the footnote in Fruman's book from which this quotation is taken); Trilling, "The Poet as Hero: Keats in His Letters," *The Opposing Self* (1955; rpt. New York: Viking, 1959), pp. 15–25, esp. 15 and 17; Bateson, *Wordsworth: A Re-Interpretation* (1954; rpt. London: Longmans, 1956), pp. 182–183.
5. *The Mirror and the Lamp* (1953; rpt. New York: Norton, 1958), p. 169; Bateson, p. 182; *The Prelude*, Bk. II, l. 311; Bk. XIV, l. 71 (cited in Bateson, p. 182); "Kubla Khan," ll. 53–54, and *Rime of the Ancient Mariner*, ll. 156–160, in S. T. Coleridge, *Poems*, ed. E. H. Coleridge (London: Oxford Univ. Press, 1912), pp. 298, 192; Lucas, *Life*, p. 280; *Letters*, II, 60–61: facsimile of MS. in *The Letters of Charles Lamb* (Boston: The Bibliophile Society, 1905), I.
6. Pineapple is repeatedly associated with sexuality, while pork is given no sexual connotations. Lamb's hedonism is curiously sexless, and although this circumstance may have a rhetorical origin deriving from the prudishness of his audience, it probably owes something to his personal attitudes.
7. Lucas calls the essay "a curious blend of Lamb's own experiences at school with those of Coleridge" (Lamb's *Works*, II, 316), but this commingling of sources does not make necessary the internal inconsistency regarding whether the experience is Elia's.
8. *Works*, I, 142–143.
9. Cf. Mulcahy, p. 540: "the forward flow of time towards decline and death . . . gave Lamb a great deal of trouble when he did presume to treat it (in 'New Year's Eve')."

10. Elia's treatment of a far from consoling realm of pre-existence occurs in "Witches, and Other Night-Fears": "That the kind of fear here treated of is purely spiritual—that it is strong in proportion as it is objectless upon earth—that it predominates in the period of sinless infancy—are difficulties, the solution of which might afford some probable insight into our ante-mundane condition, and a peep at least into the shadow-land of pre-existence" (p. 68).

11. "Barbara S— shadows under that name Miss Kelly's early life, and I had the Anecdote beautifully from her," wrote Lamb in March 1833 (*Letters,* III, 355). Miss Kelly's version of the incident, given in 1875 in a letter to Charles Kent, an editor of Lamb's works, is reprinted in L. E. Holman, *Lamb's 'Barbara S—'; The Life of Frances Maria Kelly, Actress* (London: Methuen, 1935), pp. 74-79.

Chapter Six

PLAYING

Lamb was neither the first familiar essayist nor the first Romantic to be fascinated with playing games or playing roles, but he made playing in both senses more central to his speaker's current existence than Coleridge, Wordsworth, or any major familiar essayist with the possible exception of Montaigne had done previously. "If any say to me, It is a kinde of vilifying the Muses, to use them onely for sport and recreation," asserts Montaigne, "he wots not as I doe, what worth, pleasure, sport and passe-time is of: I had well nigh termed all other ends rediculous." "How One Ought to Governe His Will" uses thespian terms in distinguishing between Montaigne's inner self and his occupancy of such public positions as that of Mayor of Bordeaux: "Wee must play our parts duly, but as the part of a borrowed personage."[1] The eighteenth-century English periodical essayists take note of such adult games as hunting, card-playing, and horse-racing, and partly because their genre began the century by offering itself as an alternative to the allegedly immoral amusements provided by such Restoration comedies as Etherege's *She Would If She Could* and *The Man of Mode* (*Tatler,* No. 136; *Spectator,* Nos. 51, 65), these essayists give play-going and acting a special prominence among the diversions of the Town that they sketch. Addison claims in the potential audience for *The Spectator* "every one that considers the World as a Theatre, and desires to form a right Judgment of those who are the Actors on it" (No. 10), but his persona, like those of his eighteenth-century successors, characteristically watches and judges rather than himself participating in play.

Playing in Wordsworth and Coleridge, unlike its presentation in the earlier essay tradition, is often unstructured and uninhibited by social forms; it is frequently the spontaneous effusion of children and nature. The "Immortality Ode" claims the continued capacity to "see the Children sport upon the shore" (l. 167), and the early books of *The Prelude* include memorable recollections of the ice-skating and boating of the poet's early years. In "Lucy Gray" "You yet may spy the fawn at play" (l. 9), though the girl's presence is more problematic. "And I bethought me of the playful hare," recalls the speaker of "Resolution and Independence" (l. 30). The Albatross of *Rime of the Ancient Mariner* came "every day, for food or play" (l. 73) until the mariner shot him. And Coleridge's "Hymn Before Sun-Rise, in the Vale of Chamouni" addresses:

> Ye wild goats sporting round the eagle's nest!
> Ye eagles, play-mates of the mountain-storm! (ll. 65-66)

An early poem by Coleridge points to that dawn of self-consciousness which makes adult playing sparse in both poets:

> . . . I too could laugh and play
> And gaily sport it on the Muse's lyre,
> Ere Tyrant Pain had chas'd away delight,
> Ere the wild pulse throbb'd anguish thro' the night![2]

The "Immortality Ode" reaches the affirmation,

> We in thought will join your throng,
> Ye that pipe and ye that play,

but the poet's "thought" includes the sadness of "an eye / That hath kept watch o'er man's mortality" and deters the adult speaker from engaging in anything more playful than "primal sympathy" (ll. 172-204). To play as a grown-up, even when possible, is sometimes regarded as frivolous. In Book III of *The Prelude* Wordsworth contrasts his "deeper pleasures" (l. 238) with Cambridge superficialities such as these:

> We sauntered, played, or rioted; we talked
> Unprofitable talk at morning hours;
> Drifted about along the streets and walks,
> Read lazily in trivial books, went forth
> To gallop through the country in blind zeal

Of senseless horsemanship, or on the breast
Of Cam sailed boisterously, and let the stars
Come forth, perhaps without one quiet thought.
(ll. 251–258)

When Coleridge in *Biographia Literaria* opposes the imagination, which "dissolves, diffuses, dissipates, in order to re-create; or . . . struggles" with the fancy, which "has no other counters to *play* with, but fixities and definites," he fosters that denigration of the playful which would issue in Arnold's insistence upon the solemnities of "high seriousness."[3]

The few passages in Wordsworth's poetry that anticipate Lamb's cultivation of play as a strategy of mature existence are untypical. One example is the speaker's resolve in "The Kitten and Falling Leaves" (one of the Poems of the Fancy, in Wordsworth's classification) to join the "Sporting" (l. 4) kitten, "have my careless season" (1.111), and

Spite of care, and spite of grief,
To gambol with Life's falling Leaf. (ll. 127–128)

A second instance is the section of the "Immortality Ode" that describes a child's and, implicitly, a man's life in terms of role-playing:

The little Actor cons another part;
Filling from time to time his "humorous stage"
With all the Persons, down to palsied Age,
That Life brings with her in her equipage;
As if his whole vocation
Were endless imitation. (ll. 103–108)

When, in Coleridge's greatest poem, the Ancient Mariner's fate is decided by a dice game, an adult confronts a vision of life as a game, but the players are Death and Life-in-Death, rather than man. (The Elia essays, as a result more of skepticism than of self-confidence, never make man the sport of other beings.) Finally, although Coleridge made major contributions to dramatic theory and the criticism of Shakespeare's plays, he did not characteristically think of himself as an actor or player.

The human capacity for play, despite Wordsworth's and Coleridge's failure to realize its full potentialities, had much to offer the Romantic sensibility. An intellectual movement which aspired to end the separation between subject and object was inevitably interested in assimilation, and play, like ingestion, can be an assimilatory tactic. Two recent thinkers in the behavioral sciences stress the assimilatory function of play. For Erik Erikson, play "is a function of the ego, an attempt to synchronize the bodily and the social processes with the self." He advances the theory that "the child's play is the infantile form of the human ability to deal with experience by creating model situations and to master reality by experiment and planning." Jean Piaget's formulation focuses less upon futurity and more upon the present structure of playful behavior: "If every act of intelligence is an equilibrium between assimilation and accommodation, while imitation is a continuation of accommodation for its own sake, it may be said conversely that play is essentially assimilation, or the primacy of assimilation over accommodation." That is to say, in play a person can incorporate into his own cognitive structure certain bothersome elements of reality without having to adjust himself to their sharp edges. Such a procedure is a short-cut toward closing the gap between subject and object, though for Piaget it is based upon an illusion, a refusal or failure to accommodate. The value system implied here by Piaget is very different from that of Friedrich Schiller's *On the Aesthetic Education of Man*, which proclaims: ". . . Man plays only when he is in the full sense of the word a man, and *he is only wholly Man when he is playing*." But assimilation is already involved in Schiller's conception of play: "The sense impulse requires variation, requires time to have a content; the form impulse requires the extinction of time, and no variation. Therefore the impulse in which both are combined (allow me to call it provisionally the *play impulse*, until I have justified the term), this play impulse would aim at the extinction of time *in time* and the reconciliation of becoming with absolute being, of variation with identity." Schiller in the 1790s was conceptualizing some of what Elia practiced in the 1820s, but the first English translation of Schiller's book appeared in 1845,[4] and, though the possiblity that Coleridge or Henry Crabb Robinson told Lamb about the Schillerian play impulse cannot be eliminated, there is no evidence that Lamb had heard of Schiller's theory. He of course knew Byron's poetry, where, especially in *Don Juan*, the strategies of game-playing and role-playing are explored. But Lamb's epistolary references to Byron are infrequent and predominantly cool; the Elia essays allude to Coleridge, Wordsworth, Southey, and even Barry Cornwall among contemporary poets, but never to Byron; fourteen of the sixteen cantos of *Don Juan*, as well as "The Vision of Judgment," were published after such Elian treatments of play as "The South-Sea House" and "Mrs. Battle's Opinions on Whist"; and, most decisively, Lamb had established himself as a devotee of theater and a playful character in the literary society of London long before the publication of "Beppo," *Don Juan*, I and II, and the first Elia essays in 1818, 1819, and 1820 respectively. Schillerian or Byronic influence upon Lamb's cultivation of play is therefore improbable, but whether or not it existed, the three writers' interest in the same activity argues for its responsiveness to the Romantic cultural situation.

Although, as an assimilatory procedure, playing is like eating or drinking, in some other respects it is not only different but more promising. The note of necessity clings to the process of eating. Our appetite, even our instinct for self-preservation, demand that we get nourishment, and within Lamb's experience there is a psychic, as well as an appetitive, compulsion at work in the treatment of ingestion. Not only is eating necessitated; it is also solitary. A meal can be a social occasion, but the act of taking in food is an individual response to an inanimate object. Although we can eat alongside other people, we cannot, short of cannibalism, include them in our ingestive process. Perhaps the defeat of the gastronomic model in the Elia essays can be blamed upon these two characteristics. The thought of stepping into the invisible world cannot be assimilated so long as we stay on the level of the necessitated, and the solitary man trembles before the prospect of radical discontinuity. If a strategy could be found which avoids necessity and builds on sociality, the chances of successfully assimilating experience might be improved.

Johan Huizinga's discussion of the nature of play stresses characteristics which contrast sharply with what we have seen to be features of eating. "First and foremost, then," he writes, "all play is a voluntary activity. Play to order is no longer play: it could at best be but a forcible imitation of it. By this quality of freedom alone, play marks itself off from the course of the natural process." He continues: ". . . for the adult and responsible human being play is a function which he could equally well leave alone. Play is superfluous." Secondly, it is characterized by "disinterestedness": "Not being 'ordinary' life it stands outside the immediate satisfaction of wants and appetites, indeed it interrupts the appetitive process. It interpolates itself as a temporary activity satisfying in itself and ending there." There had been a similar thrust in some of Schiller's comments, for instance: "Not content with bringing an aesthetic surplus into the necessary, the freer play impulse finally breaks completely away from the fetters of exigency, and Beauty for her own sake becomes the object of its endeavour. Man *adorns* himself. Free delight takes a place among his wants, and the superfluous is soon the chief part of his pleasures." Finally, according to Huizinga, although not all playing is social, "the higher forms of play" are, and such play "promotes the formation of social groupings which tend to surround themselves with secrecy and to stress their difference from the common world by disguise or other means."[5] Other people can play *in,* not merely *alongside,* one's game, and the playing of actors, we might add, establishes links with other performers and with an audience. As a model for human life, then, playing offers the enticement of skirting the necessitated and the solitary, while matching ingestion's strength, the power to assimilate.

Playing was especially suited to the identity that Lamb forged for himself and turned to literary use in the Elia essays. It fit his position as an urban enthusiast who delighted in celebrating the pleasures of London, where theaters could easily be frequented and theatrical people cultivated. "You have no theatre, I think you told me," Elia reminds his friend in New South Wales, "in your land of d——d realities" (p. 104). It also could be expressive of his hybrid existence as a clerk and a man of letters. Necessity made Lamb spend most of his life toiling routinely in the East India Company—from the likes of which Wordsworth and Coleridge were spared. One side of Lamb prized the financial security and commonsensical outlook that went with this employment. When Bernard Barton considered quitting his job in a bank to try supporting himself as an author, Lamb urged him not to do it, remarking: "[I b]less every star, that Providence, not seeing good to make me independent, has seen it next good to settle me upon the stable foundation of Leadenhall." But another side of Lamb often chafed at the boredom and confinement of his alienated work and regarded play as a precious alternative: "I hope you have some holydays at this period," he wrote Barton in December 1822. "I have one day, Christmas day, alas! too few to commemorate the season. All work & no play dulls me. Company is not play, but many times hard work. To play, is for a man to do what he please, or to do nothing—to go about soothing his particular fancies." An autobiographical sketch penned by Lamb in 1827 similarly conceives the playful as a satisfying antithesis to work and adds the notions that play can be both social and literary: "Has been guilty of obtruding upon the Public a Tale in Prose called Rosamund Gray, a Dramatic Sketch named John Woodvil, A Farewell Ode to Tobacco, with sundry other Poems & light prose matter, collected in Two slight crown Octavos, & pompously Christened his Works, tho' in fact they were his Recreations, & his true Works may be found on the Shelves of Leaden Hall Street, filling some hundred Folios." Finally, playing manifested Lamb's and Elia's tendency to engage in Romantic quests in a manner which underlined the modest resources which he and perhaps man brings to such an undertaking. In a diary entry for March 29, 1811, Henry Crabb Robinson tersely reported a conversation about Lamb in which "Hazlitt imputed his puns to humility." Benjamin R. Haydon's record of the celebrated dinner shared on December 28, 1817, by Wordsworth, Keats, Lamb, and others includes a noteworthy contrast: "Lamb got excessively merry and witty, and his fun in the intervals of Wordsworth's deep & solemn intonations of oratory was the fun & wit of the fool in the intervals of Lear's passion."[6] Playing, for Lamb, was another version—the most successful version to appear in the Elia essays—of the Promethean drive to transcend finitude, while it also called attention to that human foolishness and triviality, that incurable unseriousness, which bards might neglect but familiar essayists remember.

Elia's attachment to play was formed in part where Coleridge learned to think—at school. Christ's Hospital figures in Coleridge's *Biographia Literaria* as the place where "I enjoyed the inestimable advantage of a very sensible, though at the same time a very severe master," the Rev. James Boyer.[7] In the second half of "Christ's Hospital Five and Thirty Years Ago," Elia, though he was never a member of Boyer's class, remembers the Upper Master's severity and his efficacy in producing "many good and sound scholars" (p. 20). But the main function of Boyer's portrait is to contrast with Elia's permissive teacher, the Rev. Matthew Field, who let his charges do what they pleased. Boyer's "pupils cannot speak of him without something of terror allaying their gratitude; the remembrance of Field comes back with all the soothing images of indolence, and summer slumbers, and work like play, and innocent idleness, and Elysian exemptions, and life itself a 'playing holiday' " (p. 19). Life under Boyer was work, but under Field it was play, and the pleasantness of play consisted in its freedom from exacting demands and in its cultivation of a social bond. Elia had remarked earlier that he was "never happier" than when engaging in "exercise and recreation *after* school hours" (p. 18). What Field represents in Elia's retrospection is the breaking down of the separateness of recreation from the rest of life, or, in more positive terms the extension of the model of play to the whole of experience.

The sportiveness of Christ's Hospital boys was free, social, and assimilatory. Their playing was voluntary and undirected; the students made up their own games when the authorities left them alone. On the other hand, the activities of a "petty Nero" who branded a boy and extorted food from forty students to feed an ass which he kept hidden nearby are a "game" (p. 14), and the barbarous ritualistic punishments which the school's authorities meted out to runaways are "solemn pageantries" which were "played off" (p. 17). By registering his disapproval of these games of cruelty, Elia makes clear that he acknowledges the inviolability of other persons and seeks only a freedom which does them no harm. In addition to being free, the playing of Christ's Hospital boys was communal. They swam together in the New River (p. 13) and had "classics of our own, without being beholden to 'insolent Greece or haughty Rome,' that passed current among us—Peter Wilkins—the Adventures of the Hon. Capt. Robert Boyle—the Fortunate Blue Coat Boy—and the like" (p. 18). When one student began hoarding the detested food *"gags,"* he was expelled from the ludic group: "No one would play with him" (p. 15). Although the emphasis upon freedom and the separate society of players may make the world of play seem utterly apart from "real life," autonomous, Elia emphasizes its utility in helping children to cope with the object world: ". . . we cultivated a turn for mechanic or scientific operations; making little sun-dials of paper; or weaving those ingenious parentheses, called *cat-cradles;* or making dry peas to dance upon the end of a tin pipe; or studying the art military over that laudable game 'French and English,' and a hundred other such devices to pass away the time—mixing the useful with the agreeable—as would have made the souls of Rousseau and John Locke chuckle to have seen us" (p. 18). The boys easily assimilate the world of objects to their manipulative capacities, but in this activity they face no terrifying challenges. Their "little sun-dials" are just one more mechanical device; they are not perceived as an attempt to subdue the threatening reality of time.

As Elia looks back upon his youth at Christ's Hospital, he demonstrates his possession of a knowledge which renders difficult the claim that life is equivalent to play. Even as a child he knew hunger, loneliness, and cruelty, but these things did not interfere with his capacity for playful satisfaction. Now, however, he also has a knowledge of history. In the concluding paragraphs he reveals what became of the students after they grew up, and not only laurels come to mind: "Then followed poor S——, ill-fated M——! of these the Muse is silent. 'Finding some of Edward's race/Unhappy, pass their annals by' " (p. 21). Two of Elia's old friends are dead now, and time has not been benevolent even to Coleridge: "Come back into memory, like as thou wert in the day-spring of thy fancies, with hope like a fiery column before thee—the dark pillar not yet turned—Samuel Taylor Coleridge—Logician, Metaphysician, Bard!" (p. 21). Time for schoolboys had no existence, except as a bundle of opportunities. In the absence of required work, playing filled up a superfluity of time. For the adult, however, time is subtractive, as well as additive. It is an open question whether playing is possible for a person once history has inducted him into a sense of history.

Part of what constitutes history is the experience of personal mutability, and a passage in "The Old and the New Schoolmaster" relates this experience to playing. The adult Elia adverts to the youthful playing from which he, like the schoolmasters who spend their lives in the society of young people, are disqualified:

The noises of children, playing their own fancies—as I now hearken to them by fits, sporting on the green before my window, while I am engaged in these grave speculations at my neat suburban retreat at Shacklewell—by distance made more sweet—inexpressibly take from the labour of my task. It is like writing to music. They seem to modulate my periods. They ought at least to do so—for in the voice of that tender age there is a kind of poetry, far unlike the harsh prose-accents of man's conversation.—I should but spoil their sport, and diminish my own sympathy for them, by mingling in their pastime. (p. 53)

A spatial distance is a correlative and a consequence of the temporal distance which separates boy from man. The very medium by which Elia expresses himself—prose, rather than poetry—marks him as one who can neither play with children nor play as they do. Nevertheless, he has a "sympathy for them," which is safeguarded by the distance separating him from them. Perhaps this link will be enough to preserve or resurrect in his adult being something of their playful spirit. In any case, he starts with a keen sense of all that differentiates him from the child or adolescent player.

Besides personal aging, the process of history includes changes in society as a whole, and these too have created obstacles to play. "The Old Benchers of the Inner Temple" laments the passing of the "Four little winged marble boys" who "used to play their virgin fancies, spouting out ever fresh streams from their innocent-wanton lips, in the square of Lincoln's-inn, when I was no bigger than they were figured. They are gone, and the spring choked up. The fashion, they tell me, is gone by, and these things are esteemed childish" (p. 84). Elia offers no economic or social explanation for this change of fashion, but he makes clear that it involves an increased reliance on utilitarian standards. "Newspapers Thirty-Five Years Ago" notes a similar alteration in the tastes of readers: "But, as we said, the fashion of jokes passes away; and it would be difficult to discover in the Biographer of Mrs. Siddons, any traces of that vivacity and fancy which charmed the whole town at the commencement of the present century. Even the prelusive delicacies of the present writer—the curt 'Astraean allusion'—would be thought pedantic, and out of date, in these days" (p. 224). The essay traces Elia's journalistic path many years before, from inventing jokes for Dan Stuart's *Morning Post* to writing "treason" for John Fenwick's *Albion.* Since the latter performance was

fostered by "Recollections of feelings—which were all that now remained
from our first boyish heats kindled by the French Revolution" (p. 225),
there is a hazy suggestion that pressures for political commitment arising
directly or indirectly from the French Revolution are responsible for the
decay of the playful spirit. A longer segment of history is utilized and a more
searching account is offered in a passage concerning the teachers of an earlier
epoch in "The Old and the New Schoolmaster":

Rest to the souls of those fine old Pedagogues; the breed, long since extinct,
of the Lilys, and the Linacres: who believing that all learning was contained
in the languages which they taught, and despising every other acquirement
as superficial and useless, *came to their task as to a sport!* Passing from infancy to age, they dreamed away all their days as in a grammar-school. Revolving in a perpetual cycle of declensions, conjugations, syntaxes, and
prosodies; renewing constantly the occupations which had charmed their
studious childhood; rehearsing continually the part of the past; life must
have slipped from them at last like one day. They were always in their first
garden, reaping harvests of their golden time, among their *Flori* and their
Spici-legia; in Arcadia still, but kings . . . . (p. 51)[8]

The old schoolmasters were in the happy condition of believing that a structure of learning roughly incorporated into their minds in childhood and adolescence contained all of reality. They advanced with time in knowledge of
details, but their adulthood was spent in the unalterable possession of a mental schema within which each fact had its waiting niche. Further, the world
that they saw through belletristic spectacles had a pastoral stability and
beauty. They came to their task as to a sport, not only because their way
of life perpetuated youth, but also because it was so totally and effectively
assimilatory. The world of fact and the world of value were one. For moderns like the new schoolmaster and Elia the old order has been dissolved, and
only bits and pieces are left. Elia's head is filled with "cabinet curiosities"
gleaned from "Odd, out of the way, old English plays, and treatises" (p. 49).
He knows that he knows almost nothing of facts, and therefore he dreads being questioned by a knowledgeable inquisitor. On the other hand, the mind
of the new schoolmaster is a grab-bag of useful facts which have no connection with each other and each of which reduces a reality to a lesson. Life for
the new schoolmaster is an incessant business of submitting to new clutters
of information, as well as to the demands of one's role, while life for Elia is
a matter of defining himself in terms of his own idiosyncratic readings and
values. Fragmentation and the separation between fact and value incapacitate
the moderns for the assimilatory sport of the old schoolmasters. Even to call

their task a sport is to betray the skepticism of the modern, the suspicion that the happiness of the old schoolmasters was nurtured in illusion. The game of those venerable pedagogues could be played only by people who did not know it was a game.

Elia's ludic problem is whether and how playing can be combined with a historical consciousness. The hoaxes which abound in Lamb's letters point toward a solution. Writing to John Mathew Gutch in 1800, Lamb used the first page to suggest that Gutch's business partner had absconded with the firm's money, and the same year he sent to Manning a letter which on its first page announced that Lamb had decided to visit the Lake Country, instead of Manning's residence at Cambridge, as planned. In both cases, the second page confessed that the first was a joke. In the winter of 1807–1808 Lamb participated in circulating the story that Hazlitt had slit his own throat. He wrote to Louisa Martin in 1809 that "Hazlitt's child died of swallowing a bag of white paint, which the poor little innocent thing mistook for sugar candy." On Christmas Day, 1815, he sent off a letter to Manning in Asia claiming that Mary Lamb, Godwin, Coleridge, and Wordsworth had died; the letter's exaggerating tone made the joke clear, but the next day Lamb wrote Manning another letter admitting the hoax. A letter in 1822 to John Lamb's widow contains a detailed story about the death of a Mr. Henshaw; "He is not dead," a marginal note concedes. Lamb jocularly claims in a letter of 1827 that his ward, Emma Isola, "has just died."[9] Sometimes he jests about happy events, but calamities, especially death, enter frequently enough to require explanation. Lamb betrays a wish to subordinate catastrophe to his ego, and within the sphere of the hoax this feat can be managed. Mutability, instead of existing as an exterior threat to play, is incorporated within the playful construct. In fact, it is so thoroughly assimilated that, when encountered in a single letter, it lacks the grisliness or pathos that is apparent when a series of hoaxes on the same subject are isolated.

Within the Elia essays the attempt to achieve a playful assimilation of time exists in a continuing tension with vulnerability to time. In "Mrs. Battle's Opinions on Whist," the most explicit Elian treatment of adult playing,[10] Mrs. Battle assimilates life to her ego by subjecting it to a process of selection and restructuring. Her name, her frequent military terms, and her emphasis upon the necessity of playing for a tangible prize suggest the centrality of struggle in her procedure. The object of her will is not primarily the money for which the game is ostensibly played—if it were, other card games, other activities, would serve as well—but the transformation of life which whist makes possible. She "was a gentlewoman born" (p. 35), and the vulgarity

and messiness which repelled her in life and in cribbage posed no problem
in whist. Cribbage "was an essentially vulgar game, I have heard her say,—
disputing with her uncle, who was very partial to it. She could never heartily
bring her mouth to pronounce 'go'—or 'that's a go.' She called it an ungram-
matical game" (p. 35). As for whist, "A grave simplicity was what she chiefly
admired in her favourite game. There was nothing silly in it, like the nob in
cribbage—nothing superfluous" (p. 34). Similarly, she disliked the pedantry
of the terms in piquet, and believed whist to be innocent of such "affectation" (p. 35). Another disagreeable reality which whist eliminated was isolation. In games of two or three persons, the individual player has only oppo-
nents and shifting partners. Spectators are too detached to make much
difference. But in the four-hand game of whist, "You glory in some surprising
stroke of skill or fortune, not because a cold—or even an interested—by-stander
witnesses it, but because your *partner* sympathises in the contingency. You
win for two. You triumph for two. Two are exalted. Two again are morti-
fied . . ." (p. 36). Vulgarity and isolation are kept outside the boundaries of
a game of whist, but aggression is sublimated rather than excluded: "Two
losing to two are better reconciled, than one to one in that close butchery.
The hostile feeling is weakened by multiplying the channels. War becomes a
civil game" (p. 36). The threat of time is neutralized in a still subtler way.
Mrs. Battle was "old" (pp. 32, 36, 37) as Elia remembers her, and by the time
he writes this essay she is "with God" (p. 32). Her perception of the change
from youth to age is organized by her contrast between quadrille and whist.
The former "was her first love; but whist had engaged her maturer esteem"
(p. 33). Quadrille "was showy and specious, and likely to allure young persons," while "whist was the *solider* game" (p. 33). She ferrets out all that
would be disturbing in the aging process, the pathos of the change disappears,
and what is left is a preference for one game, her mature choice, over another.
In addition, a memorable passage distinguishes the two games partly on the
basis of the kind of duration which each creates:

[Whist] was a long meal; not, like quadrille, a feast of snatches. One or two
rubbers might co-extend in duration with an evening. They gave time to form
rooted friendships, to cultivate steady enmities. She despised the chance-start-
ed, capricious, and ever fluctuating alliances of the other. The skirmishes
of quadrille, she would say, reminded her of the petty ephemeral embroil-
ments of the little Italian states, depicted by Machiavel; perpetually changing
postures and connexions; bitter foes today, sugared darlings to-morrow; kissing and scratching in a breath;—but the wars of whist were comparable to the
long, steady, deep-rooted, rational, antipathies of the great French and English nations. (pp. 33–34)

Mrs. Battle betrays her increasing sense of vulnerability to time by admitting that now she despises discontinuous duration. Instead of preventing her from playing, her awareness of temporality leads her to be attentive to the kind of duration which exists inside the game. Whist, unlike quadrille, creates a structure within which duration is continuous. The circumscribed segment of time occupied by the game is the counterpart of the circumscribed space of the card-table, "that nice verdant carpet (next to nature's), fittest arena for those courtly combatants to play their gallant jousts and turneys in!" (p. 35), as Elia describes it. Within this sphere duration is subject to her desires. A world without sudden hiatuses is "rational" and "great," and it gets her loyalties, but it is in constant danger of evaporating if she admits that life is rather different.

To avoid this admission she adopts three basic defenses, all of which aim at blurring the distinction between life and the game. The first is to detest anyone who looks upon cards as nothing more than a diversion from more important matters. Such persons "do not play at cards, but only play at playing at them" (p. 32). For Mrs. Battle the game "was her business, her duty, the thing she came into the world to do . . ." (p. 33). To subordinate it to other things would be to undermine the efficacy of the game as an assimilatory strategy. The second defense was to consider the selectivity which whist necessitates as an essentializing activity, a means toward the essence of life. She was contemptuous of *"flushes"* (p. 34) because "She despised superficiality, and looked deeper than the colours of things" (p. 34). Her arguments in defense of her favorite game draw upon so extensive a knowledge of human nature that one almost loses sight of the peripheral status of whist within all of human experience. Finally, she admits that cards are only a game, but she quickly turns the concession to her purposes by claiming that all the "serious" activities of life are games also. Cards and these undertakings use "mighty means for disproportioned ends" (p. 37) and are equally "diverting." The difference is that cards are "a great deal more innoxious, than many of those more *serious* games of life, which men play, without esteeming them to be such" (p. 37). Mrs. Battle's achievement has been to approach an equation between cards and life, while using the structure of whist to blunt the prickliness of life. In this way, she can achieve what Piaget calls assimilation without accommodation. At this point, however, the tenuousness of her accomplishment is apparent. If cards alone are "innoxious," they provide only an illusory assimilation.

The characteristic activity of Mrs. Battle had already been introduced into the familiar essay by Lamb's eighteenth-century predecessors. Steele had published Rachel Basto's letter asking the Spectator to "say something upon the Behaviour of some of the Female Gamesters" and noting their weakness for letting an "Ombre Table" turn them into "the veriest Wasps in Nature" (*Spectator,* No. 140). Although *The Spectator* never devoted a whole essay or extended character sketch to the topic, Steele gave us the lady who digresses from cards to pray for an hour, "for which time another holds her Cards, to which she returns with no little Anxiousness till two or three in the Morning" (No. 79), and Addison's Will Honeycomb dreamed of how the women in a besieged English town, when the enemy general let them take away safely whatever each could carry on her back, abandoned their husbands but rescued a sack of China ware, a gallant, "a huge Bale of Cards," and a monkey (No. 499). Card-playing, suggested Addison, is at best a senseless loss of time (No. 93). At last in *The Guardian* appeared an entire essay by Addison on female gamesters, whose conduct, "when it runs to excess," was summed up as "the most shameful, but one, that the female world can fall into."[11] Gaming, we are told, can even lead to dishonor since a woman may be tempted to pay with her person the debts which her pin-money will not cover, but short of that, it will ruin her beauty and keep her thoughts and passions from their proper objects:

Could we look into the mind of a female gamester, we should see it full of nothing but trumps and mattadores. Her slumbers are haunted with kings, queens, and knaves. The day lies heavy upon her until the play-season returns, when for half a dozen hours together all her faculties are employed in shuffling, cutting, dealing, and sorting out a pack of cards, and no ideas to be discovered in a soul which calls itself rational, excepting little square figures of painted and spotted paper. (No. 120)

Johnson took a similar line in *The Rambler,* No. 15, with its unmarried and married female letter-writers, the first a still-resisting victim of pressure to waste her intelligence and beauty on a life of fashionable card-playing, the second a confirmed gamester who neglects her duties as a wife and mother and can think of nothing more satisfying than a hand at cards. In *The Idler,* No. 39, he mingled censure with sadness in noting "a set of ladies who have outlived most animal pleasures, and having nothing rational to put in their place, solace with cards the loss of what time has taken away, and the want of what wisdom, having never been courted, has never given." Goldsmith's Chinese philosopher ostensibly praised English women for never equalling that passion for gaming which leads Chinese ladies to bet and lose their clothing, teeth, and even eyes. But amidst such commendation, he inserted enough ironical qualifiers to indicate that his true subject is what, among English women, gaming becomes at its worst. For instance, "It is true they often stake their fortune, their beauty, health, and reputations at a gaming table," and a few paragraphs later they are wagering their honor (*Citizen of the World,* Letter CII). For the eighteenth-century essayist gambling and card-playing were, or often became, moral aberrations, and the card-playing of women was a recurrent object of satirical condemnation. For Lamb, on the other hand, Mrs. Battle's dedication to whist is the object of sympathetic understanding, though Elia's own stance is clearly distinguished from hers. Like her, he is a player who sets a high value upon play.

The distinction between her perspective and Elia's is most evident in the essay's final paragraph:

That last game I had with my sweet cousin (I capotted her)—(dare I tell thee, how foolish I am?)—I wished it might have lasted for ever, though we gained nothing, and lost nothing, though it was a mere shade of play: I would be content to go on in that idle folly for ever. The pipkin should be ever boiling, that was to prepare the gentle lenitive to my foot, which Bridget was doomed to apply after the game was over: and, as I do not much relish appliances, there it should ever bubble. Bridget and I should be ever playing. (p. 37)

Mrs. Battle requires that a card game be played for a prize not because the prize is her goal but because the prize facilitates her complete concentration on the game. Elia does not need to play for a prize because he maintains a dual consciousness: the game is one thing, time is another, and the latter, instead of being assimilated to the former, will eventually annihilate it. He wishes that the duration of the game could be without limit, but he knows it is not, and he refuses to restrict his temporal awareness to the game's boundaries. The Elian pathos, produced by the inescapable tension between play and the threat of time, contrasts with Mrs. Battle's crispness, caused by her effort to encompass reality within a game of cards. One reason for Elia's interest in play is that it is an especially pleasant part of life, and its portrayal therefore heightens the pathos of transience. But playfulness is also a way of fighting necessity, and this function of play makes intelligible the contrast between Mrs. Battle's and Elia's stylistic preferences. "A grave simplicity was what she chiefly admired in her favourite game" (p. 34), Elia informs us; color, pedantry and vulgarity she abhorred. She wanted "nothing superfluous" (p. 34). Elia, by contrast, emphasizes the value of the useless aspects of cards: "... the pretty antic habits, like heralds in a procession—the gay triumph-assuring scarlets—the contrasting deadly-killing sables—the 'hoary majesty of spades'—Pam in all his glory!" (p. 34). "All these might be dispensed with," he continues, "and, with their naked names upon the drab pasteboard, the game might go on very well, picture-less. But the *beauty* of cards would be extinguished for ever. Stripped of all that is imaginative in them, they must degenerate into mere gambling" (pp. 34-35). Even though visual charm has no necessity within the structure of the game, Elia insists upon it, and he does the same with aural fancifulness. To win a game by holding four cards of the same suit Mrs. Battle thought was "a solecism"—"as pitiful an ambition at cards as alliteration is in authorship" (p. 34). It is no accident that Elia expresses her judgment in an alliterative passage; he has a liking for verbal jugglery. The game which in his illness he plays with Bridget at the end of the essay is piquet, whose "terms" Mrs. Battle had ridiculed as pedantic (p. 35): "At such times, those *terms* which my old friend objected to, come in as something admissible.—I love to get a tierce or a quatorze, though they mean nothing. I am subdued to an inferior interest. Those shadows of winning amuse me" (p. 37). This procedure is inferior to victory, but it is better than defeat. It demonstrates within the bounds of finitude (here specifically sickness) a superfluity of energy, an excess over what the situation demands. Pictorial and verbal embellishment is an expression of freedom which is possible even if the situation cannot be transformed.[12] By this means Elia can simultaneously acknowledge his mutability and avoid surrendering to experience. He is at once incapable of controlling reality and endowed with more powers than reality requires; he is constricted and free, an adult and a player. Like Mrs. Battle, he lives with the reality of time through playing, but in contrast to that lady, he never diminishes his consciousness of imminent doom.

The first essay in the Elia collection indicates the general applicability of this playful method. Near the end of "The South-Sea House," Elia makes an admission: "Reader, what if I have been playing with thee all this while . . ." (p. 7). Play in this context is a response to a situation in which economic and temporal circumstances impinge upon everyone. In the opening sentence the speaker and the reader are viewed as parts of an economic system: "Reader, in thy passage from the Bank—where thou hast been receiving thy half-yearly dividends (supposing thou art a lean annuitant like myself) . . ." (p. 1). The clerks described later in the essay are also dependent upon and circumscribed by the realities of economics: "They were mostly (for the establishment did not admit of superfluous salaries) bachelors" (p. 3). The place, even as it existed when Elia knew it forty years earlier, pointed to the destructive activity of time. Once a prosperous "house of trade," it had been put virtually out of business by the breaking of the South-Sea Bubble. Pictures of dead worthies hung on the walls, the tables were "worm-eaten" (p. 1), and moths were "battening upon its obsolete ledgers and day-books" (p. 2). By the time Elia writes his reminiscence things, he assumes, have probably gotten worse. The clerks whom Elia recalls in the second half of the essay were forty years ago already advanced in age; what mutability has done to them in the interval is not difficult to guess. Even Elia's retrospection is subject to time: "But it is time to close—night's wheels are rattling fast over me —it is proper to have done with this solemn mockery" (p. 7).

The establishment that occupied the place responded to the realities of economics and temporality by trying to control them, that is to say, by work. The management aimed at, and for a while attained, financial success. The pretentiousness of the house made it a temple for Mammon, who is imagined enjoying the sight of the money once heaped in the basement. The building's construction is directed also at subduing time: "The long passages hung with buckets, appended, in idle row, to walls, whose substance might defy any, short of the last, conflagration . . ." (p. 1). But time has brought the concern from prosperity to ruin, and the firm's effort to control the realities of money and mutability has failed. That the temporary success of the company was based upon a hoax, a bubble which was soon punctured, indicates the thin line separating what the marketplace considers greatness from an absence of being.

Elia responds to the realities of commerce and time by "playing" (p. 7). The game consists in the manifestation of superfluous energy, a process that is not necessitated by circumstances. Elia's directing the reader to the "magnificent relic" (p. 2) of the South-Sea House is emblematic of his interest in subjects which do not demand attention. "He prefers *bye-ways* to *highways*," as Hazlitt observed in *The Spirit of the Age*.[13] Elia's retrospection will get neither him nor us anywhere; it is a superfluous activity when judged by the criteria of getting and making, or planning for the future. Within his recollection he is particularly interested in whatever demonstrates an excess of verve. Consider, for instance, his sketches of the clerks of the South-Sea House. Evans liked to expatiate on "old and new London" (p. 3), Thomas Tame had a wife who cheered herself with the thought of her noble blood, and John Tipp played the fiddle after hours but discharged his duties fanatically during them. Elia's fascination with these men centers not upon their competence in business but upon the personal eccentricities which coexist with their commercial function. Earlier in the essay he displays a parallel attitude in an address to the house:

But thy great dead tomes, which scarce three degenerate clerks of the present day could lift from their enshrining shelves—with their old fantastic flourishes, and decorative rubric interlacings—their sums in triple columniations, set down with formal superfluity of cyphers—with pious sentences at the beginning, without which our religious ancestors never ventured to open a book of business, or bill of lading—the costly vellum covers of some of them almost persuading us that we are got into some *better library,*—are very agreeable and edifying spectacles. (p. 2)

There was no economic necessity for all this embellishment, but it is valuable because it demonstrates that even if man is destined to defeat, he has a kind of dominance over his surroundings since not all his energy is used up in meeting the requirements of the situation. He is capable too of finding superfluity even in the evidence of ruin. The moths that flit about the "obsolete ledgers and day-books" of the South-Sea House have long been "making fine fretwork among their single and double entries. Layers of dust have accumulated (a superfoetation of dirt!) upon the old layers . . ." (p. 2). Such elements of the Elian style as archaisms, the use of rare or nonce words, and occasional puns[14] are intelligible, likewise, as playful decoration, which is more than a structural excrescence because within the Elia essays the superfluous energy of playing is, from a thematic viewpoint, anything but superfluous. For Elia it is not a means for escaping into a wholly separate sphere; it is a strategy which enables him to exceed the demands of life while fully aware that he is doomed.

A second type of playing that is available to Elia in his adulthood is the manner of the comic actors. In childhood "I knew not players" (p. 99) he recalls, using a word that links theatricality with games and other forms of playful behavior. He did not know the names of players, and he did not fully realize that the action on stage was only acted. Maturity, as we have seen, brought both an appreciation for acting as acting and a sensitivity to comedy. In the *Tales from Shakespear* (1807), the tragedies were Lamb's preserve while his sister did the comedies and romances, and in his *Specimens of English Dramatic Poets Who Lived About the Time of Shakspeare* (1808) Lamb preferred "not so much passages of wit and humour, though the old plays are rich in such, as scenes of passion, sometimes of the deepest quality, interesting situations, serious descriptions, that which is more nearly allied to poetry than to wit, and to tragic rather than to comic poetry."[15] In 1811 he published an essay "On the Tragedies of Shakspeare, Considered with Reference to their Fitness for Stage Representation." But in the Elia essays his theatrical criticism is confined almost exclusively to comic plays and comic acting. Lamb's choice of theatrical subjects in the essays of the 1820s and early 1830s is intelligible partly as the result of the aging process as he conceives it. The increasing concern with comedy which Elia experienced between childhood and adulthood was paralleled in Lamb's shifting critical interests between his thirties and his later years. But in another sense, the concentration upon comedy in the Elia essays is intelligible as part of the playfulness of the Elian response to life. One exaggerates only slightly to say that when Elia is talking about the comic actors he is talking about himself. Therefore, those Elia essays which explicitly deal with the theater function, on one level, as contributions to dramatic theory and to the practical criticism of such subjects as Restoration comedy, *Twelfth Night*, and *School for Scandal*; but on another level (the theme of the following pages), they function as expressive elements in the work of art which is the Elia essays. The first level has been much discussed by commentators on Lamb, on the history of critical theory, and on English drama, but the second has been neglected in spite of its central relevance to the understanding of Lamb as an imaginative writer.[16]

In the realm of comedy mutability can be assimilated. Elia recalls a performance of *Twelfth Night* and cites the presentation of temporality in Mrs. Jordan's Viola. When she spoke, one idea followed another "as by some growing (and not mechanical) process, thought springing up after thought, I would almost say, as they were watered by her tears" (pp. 132-133). In the part of Sir Andrew Aguecheek the actor Dodd did laughably what Mrs. Jordan accomplished romantically: "In expressing slowness of apprehension this actor surpassed all others. You could see the first dawn of an idea stealing slowly over his countenance, climbing up by little and little, with a painful process, till it cleared up at last to the fulness of a twilight conception—its highest meridian" (p. 136). Within the artificial world of comedy twilight can be the meridian, just as the passing of time can be pleasant. Ben can forget about his brother's death in *Love for Love* (p. 140) because death in the comic sphere is rendered impotent. The actor Elliston transfers the comic perspective into life and by his artificial manner seems to triumph over the downward curve of his fortunes. "What if it is the nature of some men to be highly artificial?" asks Elia in "Ellistoniana." "The fault is least reprehensible in *players*" (p. 169). Elia means comic players, as a piece of dialogue between Elliston and himself makes clear: " 'Have you heard' (his customary exordium)—'have you heard' said he, 'how they treat me? they put me in *comedy*.' Thought I—but his finger on his lips forbade any verbal interruption—'where could they have put you better?' " (p. 170).

Comic artifice eludes not only vulnerability to time, but also the pangs of conscience. "On the Artificial Comedy of the Last Century" links with the threat of death the moralism demanded by the modern audience. When witnessing *The School for Scandal,* the modern spectators, according to Elia, expect in Joseph and Charles Surface "a bad man and a good man as rigidly opposed to each other as the death-beds of those geniuses are contrasted in the prints . . . of the bad and good man at the hour of death; where the ghastly apprehensions of the former,—and truly the grim phantom with his reality of a toasting fork is not to be despised,—so finely contrast with the meek complacent kissing of the rod,—taking it in like honey and butter,—with which the latter submits to the scythe of the gentle bleeder, Time, who wields his lancet with the apprehensive finger of a popular young ladies' surgeon" (p. 145). Since time and death are tamed within the comic world, such a vision of life is rendered irrelevant. Similarly, where no convincing harm can be suffered there is no occasion for moral guilt. Ben can forget his brother's death in *Love for Love,* and we do not feel that he has shown "insensibility": ". . . when you read it in the spirit with which such playful selections and specious combinations rather than strict *metaphrases* of nature should be taken, or when you saw Bannister play it, it neither did, nor does wound the moral sense at all" (p. 140). Insofar as "On the Artificial Comedy of the Last Century" and "Stage Illusion" stress the immoral character-types—profligates, strumpets, misers, and cowards—whom comedy can assimilate into a sphere where morality has no existence, they diverge from a description of Lamb's own practice in the Elia essays. He keeps these types outside his universe while admitting other people's theatrical renditions of them. In this way, he can acknowledge the reality of time and death but maintain an artistic world which, like the artificial comedy, constitutes a holiday from personal conscience. His portrayal of Elia exemplifies this method even more strikingly.

Lamb had long written obsessively about the problem of guilt and forgiveness, or at least shame and acceptance. His novelette *Rosamund Gray,* published in 1798, portrays a title character who more or less unwittingly brings about her own disgrace and the death of herself and her grandmother. Another central character, Elinor Clare, writes letters full of expressions of guilt for not having treated her mother, now dead, more kindly. In 1802 Lamb published a "tragedy," *John Woodvil,* about a protagonist who by his indiscreet talk causes his father's capture and death, while he himself becomes tormented by guilt. *Mr. H——: A Farce in Two Acts* (1806) marks a change in emphasis from guilt to shame. The title character has to conceal his real name, Hogsflesh, in order to maintain his social acceptability. In another farce, *The Pawnbroker's Daughter* (1825), Flint the pawnbroker is ashamed of his trade, and in *The Wife's Trial* (1827), a dramatic poem, the wife has concealed from her husband a previous marriage, while her confidante is guilty of blackmailing her, but the husband forgives both in the end. More extraordinarily, Lamb was fascinated by the thought of having been in the gallows or pillory. "On the Inconveniences Resulting from Being Hanged" (1811), as well as the Jack Pendulous plot in *The Pawnbroker's Daughter*, treats the sense of shame which hounds the man who has been in the gallows only to be rescued before the execution has been finished. "I was never, I thank my stars, in the pillory" (p. 38), announces Elia in "A Chapter on Ears," but Lamb's "The Confessions of H. F. V. H. Delamore, Esq." (1821) and "Reflections in the Pillory" (1825) concern men who were. Lamb's extended preoccupation with people who had a skeleton in the closet probably results from the traumatic circumstances of his mother's death and the concealment of the incident from his sister's and his own reading public during their lifetimes. (The secret was first revealed in the *British Quarterly Review* for May 1848.) But in the character of Elia, Lamb created someone who could be candidly confessional because, unlike Lamb and many of Lamb's creations, he had nothing to hide. Elia's problems stem from limitations inherent in the human condition and never from guilt or shame. He enabled Lamb to release, more than in any of his other writings, the springs of retrospection precisely because Elia had done nothing for which to be judged. Like the comic roles, as Lamb conceives or misconceives them, Elia makes irrelevant the activity of conscience.[17]

In three of the Elia essays on theatrical subjects, Lamb considers the technical means by which the comic actors transmute a "very disagreeable reality" —whether temporal or moral—into "a diverting likeness" (p. 164). "On Some of the Old Actors" introduces a contrast, expanded in "On The Artificial Comedy of the Last Century," between the roles of Iago and Joseph Surface. Of Bensley's performance as the villain of *Othello* Elia remarks: ". . . his Iago was the only endurable one which I remember to have seen. No spectator from his action could divine more of his artifice than Othello was supposed to do.' His confessions in soliloquy alone put you in possession of the mystery. There were no by-intimations to make the audience fancy their own discernment so much greater than that of the Moor . . ." (pp. 133–134). By contrast, he comments in the same essay upon Jack Palmer's performances in comic parts, including that of Joseph Surface:

Jack had two voices,—both plausible, hypocritical, and insinuating; but his secondary or supplemental voice still more decisively histrionic than his common one. It was reserved for the spectator; and the dramatis personae were supposed to know nothing at all about it. The *lies* of young Wilding, and the *sentiments* in Joseph Surface, were thus marked out in a sort of italics to the audience. This secret correspondence with the company before the curtain (which is the bane and death of tragedy) has an extremely happy effect in some kinds of comedy, in the more highly artificial comedy of Congreve or of Sheridan especially, where the absolute sense of reality (so indispensable to scenes of interest) is not required, or would rather interfere to diminish your pleasure. (p. 140)

"On the Artificial Comedy of the Last Century" asserts, concerning Palmer's performance as Joseph Surface: "He was playing to you all the while that he was playing upon Sir Peter and his lady. You had the first intimation of a sentiment before it was on his lips. His altered voice was meant to you, and you were to suppose that his fictitious co-flutterers on the stage perceived nothing at all of it" (p. 145). Joseph Surface's villainy escapes moral censure because it is so clearly artificial. "Stage Illusion" is entirely devoted to the contrast, already briefly indicated in the two earlier essays, between tragic and comic illusion. We cry at a story only if we believe it, but we are willing to laugh at something less than truth. Accordingly, the tragic actor must give "undivided attention to his stage business" and appear "wholly unconscious of the presence of spectators," while the comic actor "keeps up a tacit understanding with them; and makes them, unconsciously to themselves, a party in the scene" (p. 163). Elia's contrast can be transposed into two imperatives for the achievement of comic artificiality: let the actor make clear his lack of identification with his role, and let him form a special link with his audience.

Lamb follows this advice in the Elia essays. At the end of "Dream-Children" he explicitly breaks the illusion that Elia is a real person, and the preface to *The Last Essays of Elia* announces Elia's death in a manner which undermines his "real" status: "To say truth, it is time he were gone. The humour of the thing, if there was ever much in it, was pretty well exhausted; and a two years' and a half existence has been a tolerable duration for a phantom" (p. 151). The nature of his name—it does not sound English, and it lacks the traditional form of first and last names—suggests its fictionality. He makes clear, especially in "Oxford in the Vacation," that he is as detached from the roles of clerk and author as Montaigne was from that of Mayor of Bordeaux. At the same time, he has a habit of addressing his readers directly; the first word of the Elia collection is "Reader." "Reader, what if I have been playing with thee all this while" (p. 7), he asks near the end of "The South-Sea House." Weber has rightly claimed that Lamb lessens the distance between speaker and reader through the use of the apostrophe and the rhetorical question, as well as the use of subjects rooted in personal experience.[18] The familiar essay by its nature allows Elia to interpose himself between his readers and his subject even when—as in "Barbara S——"—his overt subject is not autobiographical. The author's manifest separation from the ostensible speaker and Elia's frequent reference to the audience have an effect not unlike that of Jack Bannister's cowards: "We saw all the common symptoms of the malady upon him; the quivering lip, the cowering knees, the teeth chattering; and could have sworn 'that man was frightened.' But we forgot all the while—or kept it almost a secret to ourselves—that he never once lost his self-possession; that he let out by a thousand droll looks and gestures—meant at *us*, and not at all supposed to be visible to his fellows in the scene, that his confidence in his own resources had never once deserted him" (pp. 163-164). Whatever Elia's vulnerability, he is not wholly a victim, just as Bannister's creation is not wholly a coward, so long as he and his audience form a special society which supplements the society of personages within the play or essay; by existing on two levels, Elia, like Bannister's cowards, is to some extent liberated from the constriction of his role. Elia's relations to his creator and to his audience bring into existence an element of human freedom and therefore complement the presentation of Elia's entrapment in a finite spatio-temporal condition.

The playing of the comic actors, however, does not solve Elia's problems. Although time and death may be made innocuous within a comic play, Elia retains a sense of human vulnerability to time. "On Some of the Old Actors" centers upon a performance of *Twelfth Night* many years before: Mrs. Jordan is too old to play Viola now, and Dodd is dead. Elia observed the latter shortly before his demise, walking along, sunk "in meditations of mortality" (p. 137), and by recalling this incident he shows that neither his own nor Dodd's awareness is restricted to the victories of comic acting. Elia tells of Elliston's grand manner after Elliston has died. The two principal plays which Elia recalls each contain an element that is subversive of successful comic assimilation. In discussing *Twelfth Night* Elia is particularly fascinated by Malvolio, who not only brings a moral sense into Illyria but also meets with—in Lamb's view—a nearly tragic defeat in the end. *The School for Scandal*, rather than an earlier play, is Elia's main example of artificial comedy, and this contains, as Elia notes, foreshadowings of the style which buried artificial comedy beneath the demands of morality: "Not but there are passages,—like that, for instance, where Joseph is made to refuse a pittance to a poor relation,—incongruities which Sheridan was forced upon by the attempt to join the artificial with the sentimental comedy, either of which must destroy the other . . ." (pp. 144–145), but in the performance which Elia recalls the actors still knew how to make an artificial manner triumph over such impurities. Both in the comedies which he recalls, and in his supplementing of comedy by the life and death of the comic actors, Elia is particularly attentive to the tension between assimilation of time and vulnerability to it.

As he expresses his vision of inevitable death, he shifts the meaning of his theatrical model. "The drama has shut in upon us at the fourth act" (p. 270), he declares: "The mighty changes of the world already appear as but the vain stuff out of which dramas are composed. We have asked no more of life than what the mimic images in play-houses present us with" (p. 270). Theater now provides not a way of transcending finitude, but rather a terminology for denigrating life. This use of the theatrical model, though traditional, is uncharacteristic of Elia. He does not revert to it in the final lines of his concluding essay, "That a Sulky Temper is a Misfortune," when he quotes Horace on the Argive gentleman who sat happily in an empty theater applauding what he imagined to be a performance by tragic actors. When cured of his delusion, he upbraided his rescuer for depriving him of great satisfaction. The Elia collection ends with a man's discovery that the comfort of the theater has given way to nothingness, and now he must face what comes.

NOTES

1. *Essays*, trans. Florio, III, 50, 262. "Theatricality and Illusion" are among the baroque elements in Montaigne's style that Imbrie Buffum documents in *Studies in the Baroque from Montaigne to Rotrou* (New Haven: Yale Univ. Press, 1957), pp. 29–40.
2. "Pain," *Poems*, ed. E. H. Coleridge, p. 17.
3. Ed. J. Shawcross (Oxford: Clarendon Press, 1907), I, 202; Matthew Arnold, "The Study of Poetry."
4. Erikson, *Childhood and Society*, 2nd ed. (New York: W. W. Norton & Co., 1963), pp. 211, 222; Piaget, *Play, Dreams and Imitation in Childhood*, trans. C. Gattegno and F. M. Hodgson (New York: W. W. Norton & Co., 1962), p. 87; Schiller, op. cit., trans. Reginald Snell (London: Routledge & Kegan Paul, 1954), pp. 80, 74, 19.
5. Huizinga, *Homo Ludens* (1950; rpt. Boston: Beacon Press, 1955), pp. 7–9, 13; Schiller, p. 136.
6. *Letters*, II, 364, 356 (MSS. BM.); *Works*, I, 320–321 (MS. Br.); *Henry Crabb Robinson on Books and Their Writers*, ed. Edith J. Morley

(London: Dent, 1938), p. 28; Haydon, *Diary*, ed. Willard Bissell Pope (Cambridge, Mass.: Harvard Univ. Press, 1960), II, 173. René Fréchet, "Lamb's 'Artificial Comedy,' " *A Review of English Literature*, 5 (July 1964), 27–41, has stressed Lamb's attachment to play and at the same time his ability to face the serious issues of life. Fréchet sees playing as a reaction against the problems in Lamb's private life and the rising tide of "Evangelical earnestness" in the England of his time. But he does not show in detail how the concept of play illuminates the structure of the Elia essays.

7. I, 4–6.

8. The first italics are mine.

9. *Letters*, I, 195–196 (MS. Peal); 223–224 (MS. Hn.); II, 41–44 (MSS. L., Marrs transcription); 67 (MS. Hn.); 182–184; 184–186 (facsimile of MS. in Boston Bibliophile edition); 326–327 (MS. Bd.: Ms. Montagu d. 5); III, 126.

10. Reiman, pp. 471–474, suggests that the playing of Mrs. Battle and Elia serves as a substitute for religious belief (though, rather confusingly, Mrs. Battle loved her devotions even more than whist). She liked the game for its ethical usefulness, while Elia valued it aesthetically, that is, in the way that he valued life—as a transient pleasure which he relished for its own sake regardless of what followed it.

11. *The British Essayists*, ed. A. Chalmers (London: Nichols, Son, and Bentley, et. al., 1817), XVII, 322–325 ("On Female Gamesters").

12. On superfluity, embellishment, play, and freedom, see Schiller, *Aesthetic Education*, pp. 131–136.

13. *The Complete Works of William Hazlitt*, ed. P. P. Howe, XI (London: Dent, 1932), 178.

14. Some examples of these categories are listed in Tsutomu Fukuda, *A Study of Charles Lamb's Essays of Elia* (Tokyo: Hokuseido Press, 1964), pp. 18–31, 80–82. Horst Weber relates the Elia essays to the notion of art as play and cites as evidence the conclusion of "The South-Sea House," the verbal wit of "Oxford in the Vacation," and the Elian irony and puns, but he does not treat the assimilatory possibilities of play or the relation between juvenile and adult playing. See Weber, pp. 56–62, 101, 109.

15. *Letters*, II, 35 (MS. W.); *Works*, IV, xi (Lamb's preface to *Specimens*).

16. A recent exception to this neglect is the interesting discussion of "On the Artificial Comedy of the Last Century" in Nabholtz, pp. 683–696. Nabholtz argues that this essay lures the reader from the world of understanding through fancy to the imagination as exemplified most completely in the actor Kemble's tragic consciousness, which is evoked in the essay's final paragraph. But Lamb, it should be noted, praises Kemble especially for the "precision" of his "pointed and witty dialogue," while affirming, as he would not in an O altitudo of tragic consciousness, that "His Macbeth has been known to nod" (p. 147).

17. Lamb's "Confessions of a Drunkard," often printed as part of *The Last Essays of Elia*, would be an exception to this pattern if its author had clearly meant it to be included in the Elia collection. But it was not included in the only collected editions published in England during his lifetime—the 1823 and 1833 volumes. Lamb originally published

it in 1813, long before the start of the Elia series, and it was reprinted as an Elia essay in the *London Magazine* of August 1822, when Lamb's trip to Paris interrupted his writing of new contributions.

18.   Weber, pp. 30–34.

Chapter Seven

THE IDENTITY OF ELIA

Lamb's achievement in the Elia essays has seemed small to modern criticism because the critics have been looking only at fragments. In the process, an organ has sometimes been mistaken for an entire organism, and a literary corpus has sometimes been dismembered and then, not surprisingly, pronounced dead. The present study is the first book that has been devoted to using modern critical techniques to consider Lamb's major essay-series as a whole.

Not only the article length but also the explicative mode have set limits on what recent criticism of Elia has been able to accomplish. Close reading of individual essays, as in the valuable articles of Haven, Reiman, and Nabholtz, was needed to demonstrate that individual Elia essays are artistic unities that can stand up under the kind of intensive analysis that the New Critics perfected for dealing with poems. But such a procedure by itself could not unveil the configuration which binds together all the Elia essays, and without this larger framework the meaning of many particular essays was bound to stay elusive. The present study has combined the formalist's concern with the structure and meaning of individual works and the phenomenologist's interest in defining a writer's distinctive imaginative world. We have seen, for instance, that the formal intricacy and perfection of "Dream-Children" bring to fruition a recurrent concern in the Elia essays with the discontinuities of man's temporal experience. "Old China" likewise draws upon a spatial model that Elia often uses, and "A Dissertation upon Roast Pig" seems both funnier and more serious if it is viewed in the context of Elia's ruminations on history. The treatment of play in "Mrs. Battle's Opinions on Whist" gains in significance when we notice its connection with Elia's memories of childhood playing, his recognition of the obstacles to playing as an adult, and his stylistic peculiarities. Playing, further, takes its place as one of Elia's several stratagems for trying to wrench some kind of victory out of a life of finitude.

"The unthinking man in the street," Denys Thompson observed contemptuously, "shares a number of Lamb's tastes and interests—drink, gastronomy and smoking." Such trivia, we are expected to agree, are beneath the regard of intellectuals and readers of *Scrutiny*. Lamb's more sympathetic recent critics have underlined the thematic seriousness of certain Elia essays but kept silent about the sort of earthy detail that so offended Thompson—and so endeared Lamb to the early twentieth-century's "heartier journalists and professors," as Thompson sarcastically described them.[1] Modern criticism, in short, has generally set Lamb before us as an essayist of body or an essayist of mind, but not as an essayist of both at once. Mulcahy countered this trend by exposing a dialectic of imagination and reality in Lamb's essays, and the present book goes a step further by emphasizing Elia's concern with bodily appetites and apparent foolishness while arguing for the persistent seriousness of the Elia volumes. I have sought to make intellectually respectable a fascination with roast pig's crackling, the aroma of Saloop, and the game of causing dry peas to dance on the end of a tin pipe.

Lamb's personal burdens have long attracted the notice of commentators. There is a venerable tradition of admiration for his sense of responsibility and even heroism toward his sister. But the man who suffered and the artist who created have seldom been convincingly portrayed as one—and never from the point of view of detailed literary analysis of the Elia essays. I have attempted to show concretely how neurotic preoccupations have been transformed in these essays into ways of coping sanely and responsibly with the requirements of artistic form and the dominant intellectual problems of the age. Lamb's allusions to his father and reticence about his mother, his ambivalence toward the two great poets who were his friends, his regressiveness, orality, sense of guilt, and delight in hoaxes—all these have been considered from a point of view that stresses his achievement more than his psychic sources, but that reserves a special admiration for such an achievement issuing from such origins.

When Lamb's modern critics have attended at all to his links with literary tradition, each has focused upon a single strand. For the Leavis-ite Thompson, whose judgments are closely paralleled by G. D. Klingopulos, writing in a widely used *Guide to English Literature*,[2] the Elia essays need to be compared with the eighteenth-century periodical essay, the Addisonian vehicle of bracing didacticism, which Thompson charges Lamb with having debased. For the American critics Haven, Nabholtz, and Scoggins, Lamb is a full-fledged Romantic, whose values in the Elia essays are essentially those of Romantic poetry in at least some of its phases. But the former view overlooks the historicity of Lamb's genre, its capacity to remain true to its unchanging essence while adapting to the new circumstances of a new period. The Romantic essay is no less essayistic or meaningful than *The Spectator*, but it presents itself as an alternative to Romantic poetry rather than to Restoration wit. Only by giving due weight to the contemporary literary context into which Elia talks can we come to realize the full range of significance of the Elia series and its particular mode of realizing its genre's potential. On the other hand, to identify Lamb's perspective entirely with that of Romantic poetry is to overlook the reservations which he declares in "Witches, and Other Night-Fears" and the skepticism which he keeps showing whenever he experiments with a Romantic pattern. It is to forget Lamb's conscious participation in a genre which sets a high valuation upon common sense, ironizes claims to extraordinary powers, and minimizes its distance from the life of the ordinary reader. In the Elia essays Lamb writes about the quest to unify past and present, near and far, subject and object, and he never abandons such ideals to churn out a merely cautionary tale. To the continuing pursuit of these Promethean aspirations he owes in large measure his perceptions of what he can do and how valuable, finally, that is. Yet large ingredients in his wisdom are the realistic sense that his aspirations remain frustrated or only equivocally successful and the ability to detect much that is laughable in such a fate. At the same time, he imitates again and again the topics, character types, situations, and even phrasings of earlier familiar essayists, but always with a difference that reveals the spirit of his own age speaking in him. By fusing two disparate traditions at the center of the Elia series, Lamb was enabled to do something other than duplicate or debase his exemplars. He wrote one of the masterpieces of Romantic prose.

NOTES

1. *Determinations*, p. 206.
2. Ed. Boris Ford, 2nd ed. (London: Cassell, 1965), V, 145–148. (Originally published in 1957 as the *Pelican Guide to English Literature*.)

INDEX